Alan Cowell, *The New York Times*

'*Globalization and Its Discontents* is a war story from inside the halls of
the White House and the World Bank, the confession of a powerful
economist with a political conscience and a healthy degree of
common sense' Lenora Todaro, *Village Voice*

'A brilliant critique ... No one has so effectively identified the
fundamental weaknesses in American capitalism since John Kenneth
Galbraith published his original critique of the market economy, *The
Affluent Society*, in 1958' ... is Joseph Stiglitz's remarkable
achievement ...

GLOBALIZATION AND ITS DISCONTENTS

Joseph E. Stiglitz

PENGUIN BOOKS

PENGUIN BOOKS

Published by the Penguin Group
Penguin Books Ltd, 80 Strand, London WC2R 0RL, England
Penguin Putnam Inc., 375 Hudson Street, New York, New York 10014, USA
Penguin Books Australia Ltd, 250 Camberwell Road, Camberwell, Victoria 3124, Australia
Penguin Books Canada Ltd, 10 Alcorn Avenue, Toronto, Ontario, Canada M4V 3B2
Penguin Books India (P) Ltd, 11, Community Centre, Panchsheel Park, New Delhi – 110 017, India
Penguin Books (NZ) Ltd, Cnr Rosedale and Airborne Roads, Albany, Auckland, New Zealand
Penguin Books (South Africa) (Pty) Ltd, 24 Sturdee Avenue, Rosebank 2196, South Africa

Penguin Books Ltd, Registered Offices: 80 Strand, London WC2R 0RL, England

www.penguin.com

First published in the USA by W. W. Norton & Company 2002
First published in Great Britain by Allen Lane The Penguin Press 2002
Published with a new afterword in Penguin Books 2002

6

Copyright © Joseph E. Stiglitz, 2002

Set in Bembo
Printed and bound in Great Britain by Clays Ltd, St Ives plc

ISBN 0–713–99664–1

To my mother and father who taught me to care and reason,
and to Anya who put it all together and more

CONTENTS

PREFACE

I N 1993 I left academia to serve on the Council of Economic
Advisers under President Bill Clinton. After years of research and
teaching this was my first major foray into policy making, and
more to the point, politics. From there I moved to the World Bank in
1997, where I served as chief economist and senior vice president for
almost three years, leaving in January 2000. I couldn't have chosen a
more fascinating time to go into policy making. I was in the White
House as Russia began its transition from communism and I worked
at the Bank during the financial crisis that began in East Asia in 1997
and eventually enveloped the world. I had always been interested in
economic development and what I saw radically changed my views
of both globalization and development. I have written this book
because while I was at the World Bank, I saw firsthand the devastating effect that globalization can have on developing countries, and
especially the poor within those countries. I believe that globalization—the removal of barriers to free trade and the closer integration
of national economies—can be a force for good and that it has the
potential to enrich everyone in the world, particularly the poor. But I
also believe that if this is to be the case, the way globalization has
been managed, including the international trade agreements that
have played such a large role in removing those barriers and the poli-

cies that have been imposed on developing countries in the process of globalization, need to be radically rethought.

As a professor, I spent a lot of time researching and thinking about the economic and social issues I dealt with during my seven years in Washington. I believe it is important to view problems in a dispassionate way, to put aside ideology and to look at the evidence before making a decision about what is the best course of action. Unfortunately, though hardly surprisingly, in my time at the White House as a member and then chairman of the Council of Economic Advisers (a panel of three experts appointed by the president to provide economic advice in the executive branch of the U.S. government), and at the World Bank, I saw that decisions were often made because of ideology and politics. As a result many wrong-headed actions were taken, ones that did not solve the problem at hand but that fit with the interests or beliefs of the people in power. The French intellectual Pierre Bourdieu has written about the need for politicians to behave more like scholars and to engage in scientific debate, based on hard facts and evidence. Regrettably, the opposite happens too often, when academics involved in making policy recommendations become politicized and start to bend the evidence to fit the ideas of those in charge.

If my academic career did not prepare me for all that I encountered in Washington, DC, at least it did prepare me professionally. Before entering the White House, I had divided my time spent on research and writing between abstract mathematical economics (helping to develop a branch of economics that has since come to be called the economics of information), and more applied subjects, including the economics of the public sector, development, and monetary policy. I spent more than twenty-five years writing about subjects such as bankruptcy, corporate governance, and the openness of and access to information (what economists call *transparency*). These were crucial issues when the global financial crisis began in 1997. I had also been involved for nearly twenty years in discussions concerning transitions from Communist to market economies. My experience with how to handle such transitions began in 1980, when I first discussed these issues with leaders in China, as it was beginning its move toward a market economy. I had been a strong advocate of the gradualist policies adopted by the Chinese, policies that have proven their merit over the past two decades; and I have been a strong critic of some of the extreme reform strategies such as "shock therapy" that have failed so miserably in Russia and some of the other countries of the former Soviet Union.

My involvement in issues of development dates back even further—to the time I spent in Kenya on an academic posting (1969–71) shortly after its independence in 1963. Some of my most important theoretical work had been inspired by what I saw there. I knew the challenges facing Kenya were difficult, but I hoped that it might be possible to do something to improve the lives of the billions of people there and in the rest of the world who live in extreme poverty. Economics may seem like a dry, esoteric subject but, in fact, good economic policies have the power to change the lives of these poor people. I believe governments need to—and can—adopt policies that help countries grow but that also ensure that growth is shared more equitably. To take but one issue, I believe in privatization (selling off, say, government monopolies to private companies), but only if it helps companies become more efficient and lowers prices for consumers. This is more likely to happen if markets are competitive, which is one of the reasons I support strong competition policies.

Both at the World Bank and the White House, there was a close link between the policies I advocated and my earlier, largely theoretical work in economics, much of it related to market imperfections— why markets do not work perfectly, in the way that simplistic models which assume perfect competition and perfect information claim they do. I brought to policy making my work on the economics of information, in particular, on *asymmetries of information*—the differences in information between, say, the worker and his employer, the lender and the borrower, the insurance company and the insured. These asymmetries are pervasive in all economies. This work provided the foundations for more realistic theories of labor and financial markets, explaining, for instance, why there is unemployment and why those most in need of credit often cannot get it—there is, to use the economist's jargon, credit-rationing. The standard models that economists had used for generations argued either that markets worked perfectly—some even denied the existence of genuine

unemployment—or that the only reason that unemployment existed
was that wages were too high, suggesting the obvious remedy: lower
wages. Information economics, with its better analyses of labor, capital, and product markets, enabled the construction of macroeconomic
models that provided deeper insights into unemployment, models
that explained the fluctuations, the recessions and depressions, that
had marked capitalism since its beginnings. These theories have
strong policy implications—some of which are obvious to almost
anyone in touch with the real world—such as that if you raise interest rates to exorbitant levels, firms that are highly indebted can be
forced into bankruptcy, and this will be bad for the economy. While I
thought they were obvious, these policy prescriptions ran counter to
those that were frequently insisted upon by the International Monetary Fund (IMF).

The IMF's policies, in part based on the outworn presumption
that markets, by themselves, lead to efficient outcomes, failed to allow
for desirable government interventions in the market, measures
which can guide economic growth and make *everyone* better off.
What was at issue, then, in many of the disputes that I describe in the
following pages is a matter of *ideas*, and conceptions of the role of the
government that derive from those ideas.

Although such ideas have had an important role in shaping policy
prescriptions—in development, in managing crises, and in transition—they are also central to my thinking about reforming the
international institutions that are supposed to drive economic
development, manage crises, and facilitate economic transition. My
research on information made me particularly attentive to the consequences of the lack of information. I was glad to see the emphasis
during the global financial crisis in 1997–98 of the importance of
transparency; but saddened by the hypocrisy that the institutions, the
IMF and the U.S. Treasury, which emphasized it in East Asia, were
among the least transparent that I had encountered in public life. This
is why in the discussion of reform I emphasize the necessity for
increased transparency, improving the information that citizens have
about what these institutions do, allowing those who are affected by
the policies to have a greater say in their formulation. The analysis of

the role of information in *political* institutions evolved quite naturally from my earlier work on the role of information in economics.

One of the exciting aspects of coming to Washington was the opportunity not only to get a better understanding of how government works but also to put forward some of the perspectives to which my research had led. For instance, as chairman of Clinton's Council of Economic Advisers, I tried to forge an economic policy and philosophy that viewed the relationship between government and markets as complementary, both working in partnership, and recognized that while markets were at the center of the economy, there was an important, if limited, role for government to play. I had studied the failures of both markets *and* government, and was not so naive as to think that government could remedy every market failure. Neither was I so foolish as to believe that markets by themselves solved every societal problem. Inequality, unemployment, pollution: these were all issues in which government had to take an important role. I had worked on the initiative for "reinventing government"—making government more efficient and more responsive; I had seen where government was neither; I had seen how difficult reform is; but I had also seen that improvements, modest as they might be, were possible. When I moved to the World Bank, I had hoped to bring this balanced perspective, and the lessons I had learned, to the far more difficult problems facing the developing world.

Inside the Clinton administration, I enjoyed the political debate, winning some battles, losing others. As a member of the president's cabinet, I was well positioned not only to observe the debates and see how they were resolved but, especially in areas that touched upon economics, to participate in them. I knew that ideas mattered but so did politics, and one of my jobs was to persuade others not just that what I advocated was good economics but also that it was good politics. But as I moved to the international arena, I discovered that neither dominated the formulation of policy, especially at the International Monetary Fund. Decisions were made on the basis of what seemed a curious blend of ideology and bad economics, dogma that sometimes seemed to be thinly veiling special interests. When crises hit, the IMF prescribed outmoded, inappropriate, if "standard" solutions, without considering the effects they would have on the people in the countries told to follow these policies. Rarely did I see forecasts about what the policies would do to poverty. Rarely did I see thoughtful discussions and analyses of the consequences of alternative policies. There was a single prescription. Alternative opinions were not sought. Open, frank discussion was discouraged—there was no room for it. Ideology guided policy prescription and countries were expected to follow the IMF guidelines without debate.

These attitudes made me cringe. It was not just that they often produced poor results; they were antidemocratic. In our personal lives we would never follow ideas blindly without seeking alternative advice. Yet countries all over the world were instructed to do just that. The problems facing developing countries are difficult, and the IMF is often called upon in the worst of situations, when the country is facing a crisis. But its remedies failed as often, or even more often than they worked. IMF structural adjustment policies—the policies designed to help a country adjust to crises as well as to more persistent imbalances—led to hunger and riots in many countries; and even when results were not so dire, even when they managed to eke out some growth for a while, often the benefits went disproportionately to the better-off, with those at the bottom sometimes facing even greater poverty. What astounded me, however, was that those policies weren't questioned by many of the people in power in the IMF, by those who were making the critical decisions. They were often questioned by people in the developing countries, but many were so afraid they might lose IMF funding, and with it funding from others, that they articulated their doubts most cautiously, if at all, and then only in private. But while no one was happy about the suffering that often accompanied the IMF programs, inside the IMF it was simply assumed that whatever suffering occurred was a necessary part of the pain countries had to experience on the way to becoming a successful market economy, and that their measures would, in fact, reduce the pain the countries would have to face in the long run.

Undoubtedly, some pain was necessary; but in my judgment, the level of pain in developing countries created in the process of globalization and development as it has been guided by the IMF and the international economic organizations has been far greater than necessary. The backlash against globalization draws its force not only from the perceived damage done to developing countries by policies driven by ideology but also from the inequities in the global trading system. Today, few—apart from those with vested interests who benefit from keeping out the goods produced by the poor countries—defend the hypocrisy of pretending to help developing countries by forcing them to open up their markets to the goods of the advanced industrial countries while keeping their own markets protected, policies that make the rich richer and the poor more impoverished—and increasingly angry.

The barbaric attacks of September 11, 2001, have brought home with great force that we all share a single planet. We are a global community, and like all communities have to follow some rules so that we can live together. These rules must be—and must be seen to be—fair and just, must pay due attention to the poor as well as the powerful, must reflect a basic sense of decency and social justice. In today's world, those rules have to be arrived at through democratic processes; the rules under which the governing bodies and authorities work must ensure that they will heed and respond to the desires and needs of all those affected by policies and decisions made in distant places.

THIS BOOK IS based on my experiences. There aren't nearly as many footnotes and citations as there would be in an academic paper. Instead, I tried to describe the events I witnessed and tell some of the stories that I heard. There are no smoking guns here. You won't find hard evidence of a terrible conspiracy by Wall Street and the IMF to take over the world. I don't believe such a conspiracy exists. The truth is subtler. Often it's a tone of voice, or a meeting behind closed doors, or a memo that determines the outcome of discussions. Many of the people I criticize will say I have gotten it wrong; they may even produce evidence that contradicts my views of what happened. I can only offer my interpretation of what I saw.

When I joined the World Bank, I had intended to spend most of my time on issues of development and the problems of the countries trying to make the transition to a market economy; but the global financial crisis and the debates about reforming the international economic architecture—the system by which the international eco-

nomic and financial system are governed—in order to make globalization more humane, effective, and equitable occupied a large fraction of my time. I visited dozens of countries all over the world and
spoke to thousands of government officials, finance ministers, central
bank governors, academics, development workers, people at nongovernmental organizations (NGOs), bankers, business people, students, political activists, and farmers. I visited Islamic guerrillas in
Mindanao (the Philippine island which has long been in a state of
rebellion), trekked through the Himalayas to see remote schools in
Bhutan or a village irrigation project in Nepal, saw the impact of
rural credit schemes and programs for mobilizing women in Bangla-
desh, and witnessed the impact of programs to reduce poverty in villages in some of the poorest mountainous parts of China. I saw
history being made and I learned a lot. I have tried to distill the
essence of what I saw and learned and present it in this book.

I hope my book will open a debate, a debate that should occur not
just behind the closed doors of government and the international
organizations, or even in the more open atmosphere of universities.
Those whose lives will be affected by the decisions about how globalization is managed have a right to participate in that debate, and
they have a right to know how such decisions have been made in the
past. At the very least, this book should provide more information
about the events of the past decade. More information will surely
lead to better policies and those will lead to better results. If that happens, then I will feel I have made a contribution.

ACKNOWLEDGMENTS

THERE IS AN ENDLESS list of those to whom I am greatly indebted, without whom this book could not be written: President Bill Clinton and World Bank President Jim Wolfensohn, in giving me opportunities to serve my country and the peoples of the developing world, also gave me an opportunity, relatively rare for an academic, to glimpse decision making that affects all of our lives. I am indebted to hundreds of colleagues at the World Bank, not only for the vigorous discussions that we had over the years about all the issues discussed in this book but for sharing with me their years of experience in the field. They also helped arrange the many trips through which I could get unique perspectives on what was happening in the developing countries. I hesitate to single out anyone, lest I slight others, but at the same time I would be remiss if I did not acknowledge at least some of those with whom I worked most closely, including Masood Ahmed, Lucie Albert, Amar Bhattacharya, Francois Bourgignon, Gerard Caprio, Ajay Chhibber, Uri Dadush, Carl Dahlman, Bill Easterly, Giovanni Ferri, Coralie Gevers, Noemi Giszpenc, Maria Ionata, Roumeen Islam, Anupam Khanna, Lawrence MacDonald, Ngozi Ojonjo-Iweala, Guillermo Perry, Boris Pleskovic, Jo Ritzen, Halsey Rogers, Lyn Squire, Vinod

Thomas, Maya Tudor, Mike Walton, Shahid Yusuf, and Hassan Zaman.

Others at the World Bank whom I would like to thank include Martha Ainsworth, Myrna Alexander, Shaida Badiee, Stijn Claessens, Paul Collier, Kemal Dervis, Dennis de Tray, Shanta Devarajan, Ishac Diwan, David Dollar, Mark Dutz, Alan Gelb, Isabel Guerrero, Cheryl Gray, Robert Holzman, Ishrat Husain, Greg Ingram, Manny Jimenez, Mats Karlsson, Danny Kaufman, Ioannis Kessides, Homi Kharas, Aart Kray, Sarwar Lateef, Danny Leipziger, Brian Levy, Johannes Linn, Oey Astra Meesook, Jean-Claude Milleron, Pradeep Mitra, Mustapha Nabli, Gobind Nankani, John Nellis, Akbar Noman, Fayez Omar, John Page, Guy Pfeffermann, Ray Rist, Christof Ruehl, Jessica Seddon, Marcelo Selowski, Jean Michel Severino, Ibrahim Shihata, Sergio Shmuckler, Andres Solimano, Eric Swanson, Marilou Uy, Tara Viswanath, Debbie Wetzel, David Wheeler, and Roberto Zagha.

I am also indebted to the many people in the other international economic organizations with whom I discussed the numerous issues that are reflected upon here—including Rubens Ricupero at UNCTAD (the UN Conference on Trade and Development); Marc Malloch Brown at the UNDP; Enrique Iglesias, Nancy Birdsall, and Ricardo Haussman at the Inter-American Development Bank; Jacques de Larosière, the former head of theEuropean Bank for Reconstruction and Development; and a host of others at the UN regional offices and the Asian and African Development Banks. Next to my colleagues at the World Bank, I perhaps interacted more with those at the IMF, and, while it will be clear from the ensuing pages that I often disagreed with much of what they did and how they went about doing it, I learned much from them and the long discussions we had, not the least of which was a better understanding of *their* mind-sets. I should also be clear: while I am highly critical, I also appreciate the hard work that they put in, the difficult circumstances under which they work, and their willingness at a personal level to have far more open and free discussions than they can at an official level.

I am also grateful to the numerous government officials in the developing countries, from large countries like China and India to small countries like Uganda and Bolivia, from prime ministers and heads of state to finance ministers and central bank governors, to education ministers and other cabinet officials on down, who willingly shared their time to discuss with me their visions for their countries, as well as the problems and frustrations they faced. In our long meetings, they often talked to me in confidence. Many of those, such as Vaclav Klaus, the former prime minister of the Czech Republic, would disagree with much that I have to say, yet I learned a great deal from talking to them. Others, such as Andrei Illarionov, currently Putin's chief economic adviser, and Grzegorz W. Kolodko, former deputy prime minister and finance minister of Poland, Meles Zenawi, prime minister of Ethiopia, or Yoweri Museveni, president of Uganda, would be sympathetic with much, if not most, of what I have to say. Some of those at the international economic organizations who have been helpful have also asked me not to thank them, and I have honored their request.

While much of my time was spent in discussions with government officials, I was also able to meet large numbers of businessmen, who also gave of their time as they described the challenges that they faced and provided their interpretations of what was going on in their countries. While it is difficult to single out any single individual, I should mention Howard Golden, whose detailed descriptions of experiences in a multitude of countries were particularly insightful.

As an academic, I had my own entrée into the countries I visited, so I could see matters from perspectives that were not dictated by "official positions." This book owes a great deal to this global network of academic colleagues—one of the healthier aspects of globalization. I am particularly indebted to my colleagues at Stanford, Larry Lau, at the time head of the Asia Pacific Center, Masa Aoki, currently research director at the Ministry of Economics and International Trade in Japan, and Yingyi Qian, not only for the insights that they provided into Asia but for the many doors they opened. Over the years, academic colleagues and former students such as Jungyoll Yun in Korea, Mrinal Datta Chaudhuri in India, K. S. Jomo in Malaysia, Justin Lin in China, and Amar Siamwalla in Thailand helped me see and understand their countries.

The hectic years at the World Bank and the Council of Economic Advisers have been followed by a more reflective period of research and teaching. I am deeply indebted to the Brookings Institution, Stanford, and Columbia—and my students and colleagues at those institutions—for invaluable discussions on the ideas contained here, and to my associates Ann Florini and Tim Kessler, who worked with me to create the Initiative for Policy Dialogue, originally centered at Stanford University, and the Carnegie Endowment for Peace, now located at Columbia University (www.gsb.edu/ipd), to promote the kind of informed democratic discussion of alternative policies that I call for in this book During this period, financial support has also been provided by the Ford, MacArthur, and Rockefeller Foundations, the UNDP, the Canadian International Development Agency, and the UNDP.

In writing a book like this, while I have relied mostly on my own experiences, those have been amplified not only by my colleagues but by a host of reporters. A theme in this book that I hope has some resonance is the importance of open access to *information*: many of the problems I describe arise because so much goes on behind closed doors. I have always believed that an active and free press is a critical check on these abuses and is necessary for democracy, and many of the reporters with whom I dealt regularly were dedicated to that mission. I learned much from them, as we shared our interpretation of the events that were occurring. Again, at the risk of singling out a couple when so many should be recognized: Chrystia Freeland was a huge help with the Russia chapter, and Paul Blustein and Mark Clifford provided valuable insights on the East Asian experience.

Economics is the science of choice. From the wealth of insights and information, on the subjects as complicated and fascinating as those discussed here, volumes could be written. Unfortunately, that was one of my main challenges in writing this book: the volumes I did write had to be shaped into a far shorter narrative. I had to let go of some of the ideas and skip some of the qualifications, as important as I thought they were. I had grown accustomed to two forms of writing: serious academic tomes and brief popular speeches. This work represents, for me, a new genre. It could not have been published without the tireless efforts of Anya Schiffrin, who spent months working with me on the writing and the revisions, helping me make those hard choices, as painful as they sometimes seemed.

Drake McFeely—my editor for twenty years—encouraged and supported me throughout. Sarah Stewart's edits were terrific, Jim Wade worked tirelessly to pull the final manuscript together, and Eve Lazovitz offered important support at several key stages.

Nadia Roumani has been my right-hand woman for years. Nothing would be possible without her. Sergio Godoy and Monica Fuentes diligently checked the facts and found the statistics I needed. Leah Brooks helped a lot with the earlier drafts. Niny Khor and Ravi Singh, my research assistants at Stanford, worked hard on the penultimate version.

This work rests on a considerable body of academic work, both my own, in conjunction with a large number of coauthors, and that of others, again too numerous to cite. I have also benefited from innumerable discussions with colleagues around the world. I should mention Professor Robert Wade of the London School of Economics, a former World Bank staff member, who has written insightfully not only about the general problems of the international economic institutions but also about several of the specific topics covered here, East Asia and Ethiopia. The transition from Communism to a market economy has been a subject that has engaged the interest of academic economists greatly over the past fifteen years. I have benefited in particular from Janos Kornai's insights. I should also mention four other leading scholars: Peter Murrell, Jan Svejnar, Marshall Goldman, and Gerard Roland. A central theme of this book is the value of open debate, and I have learned much from discussions with and reading those whose interpretations of events I sometimes, perhaps often, disagree with—in particular Richard Layard, Jeff Sachs, Anders Aslund, and Andrei Shleifer. I have also benefited from discussions with a multitude of academicians in the economies in transition, including Oleg Bogomolov and Stanislav Menshikov in Russia.

Steve Lewis, Peter Eigen, and Charles Harvey all provided me with insights into Botswana from their firsthand experiences, and Charles Harvey gave me detailed comments on chapter 2. Over the years, work and discussions with Nick Stern (who succeeded me at the World Bank after serving as chief economist at the EBRD), Partha Dasgupta, Ravi Kanbur (who was responsible for the landmark World Development Report on Poverty of 2001, initiated while I was still chief economist at the World Bank), Avi Braverman (now president of Ben-Gurion University but a longtime researcher at the World Bank), Karla Hoff, Raaj Sah, David Bevan, Mark Gersovitz, David Newbery, Jim Mirrlees, Amartya Sen, and David Ellerman have been particularly influential in shaping my thinking. I am particularly indebted to Andy Weiss for his practical insights into the problems of transition, for his empirical analyses of the consequences of privatization, and for his broader insights into capital market imperfections. My earlier work on East Asia for the World Bank, done with Marilou Uy, in conjunction with, among others, Howard Pack, Nancy Birdsall, Danny Leipziger, and Kevin Murdoch, provided me with insights into the region that put me in good stead in dealing with the crisis when it occurred. I owe an especial debt of gratitude to Jason Furman, who worked with me both at the White House and at the World Bank, for all his work, but especially that on East Asia and the critique of the Washington Consensus. Thanks are due to Hal Varian for suggesting the title. Anyone who reads this book will also see clearly the influence of ideas concerning imperfect information and markets—central, I believe, for understanding how any market economy works, but especially developing ones. Work with Carl Shapiro, Michael Rothschild, Sandy Grossman, Steve Salop, and Richard Arnott helped provide insights into unemployment, capital market imperfections, the limitations of competition, and the importance—and limitations—of institutions. At the end of it all, there is always Bruce Greenwald—my collaborator and friend for more than twenty-five years.

GLOBALIZATION AND ITS DISCONTENTS

CHAPTER I

THE PROMISE
OF GLOBAL
INSTITUTIONS

INTERNATIONAL BUREAUCRATS—THE faceless symbols of the world economic order—are under attack everywhere. Formerly uneventful meetings of obscure technocrats discussing mundane subjects such as concessional loans and trade quotas have now become the scene of raging street battles and huge demonstrations. The protests at the Seattle meeting of the World Trade Organization in 1999 were a shock. Since then, the movement has grown stronger and the fury has spread. Virtually every major meeting of the International Monetary Fund, the World Bank, and the World Trade Organization is now the scene of conflict and turmoil. The death of a protestor in Genoa in 2001 was just the beginning of what may be many more casualties in the war against globalization.

Riots and protests against the policies of and actions by institutions of globalization are hardly new. For decades, people in the developing world have rioted when the austerity programs imposed on their countries proved to be too harsh, but their protests were largely unheard in the West. What is new is the wave of protests in the developed countries.

It used to be that subjects such as structural adjustment loans (the programs that were designed to help countries adjust to and weather crises) and banana quotas (the limits that some European countries

3

impose on the importing of bananas from countries other than their former colonies) were of interest to only a few. Now sixteen-year-old kids from the suburbs have strong opinions on such esoteric treaties as GATT (the General Agreement on Tariffs and Trade) and NAFTA (the North American Free Trade Area, the agreement signed in 1992 between Mexico, United States, and Canada that allows for the freer movement of goods, services, and investment—but not people—among those countries). These protests have provoked an enormous amount of soul-searching from those in power. Even conservative politicians such as France's president, Jacques Chirac, have expressed concern that globalization is not making life better for those most in need of its promised benefits.[1] It is clear to almost everyone that something has gone horribly wrong. Almost overnight, globalization has become the most pressing issue of our time, something debated from boardrooms to op-ed pages and in schools all over the world.

WHY HAS GLOBALIZATION—a force that has brought so much good—become so controversial? Opening up to international trade has helped many countries grow far more quickly than they would otherwise have done. International trade helps economic development when a country's exports drive its economic growth. Export-led growth was the centerpiece of the industrial policy that enriched much of Asia and left millions of people there far better off. Because of globalization many people in the world now live longer than before and their standard of living is far better. People in the West may regard low-paying jobs at Nike as exploitation, but for many people in the developing world, working in a factory is a far better option than staying down on the farm and growing rice.

Globalization has reduced the sense of isolation felt in much of the developing world and has given many people in the developing countries access to knowledge well beyond the reach of even the wealthiest in any country a century ago. The antiglobalization protests themselves are a result of this connectedness. Links between activists in different parts of the world, particularly those links forged through Internet communication, brought about the pressure that resulted in the international landmines treaty—despite the opposition of many powerful governments. Signed by 121 countries as of 1997, it reduces the likelihood that children and other innocent victims will be maimed by mines. Similar, well-orchestrated public pressure forced the international community to forgive the debts of some of the poorest countries. Even when there are negative sides to globalization, there are often benefits. Opening up the Jamaican milk market to U.S. imports in 1992 may have hurt local dairy farmers but it also meant poor children could get milk more cheaply. New foreign firms may hurt protected state-owned enterprises but they can also lead to the introduction of new technologies, access to new markets, and the creation of new industries.

Foreign aid, another aspect of the globalized world, for all its faults still has brought benefits to millions, often in ways that have almost gone unnoticed: guerrillas in the Philippines were provided jobs by a World Bank–financed project as they laid down their arms; irrigation projects have more than doubled the incomes of farmers lucky enough to get water; education projects have brought literacy to the rural areas; in a few countries AIDS projects have helped contain the spread of this deadly disease.

Those who vilify globalization too often overlook its benefits. But the proponents of globalization have been, if anything, even more unbalanced. To them, globalization (which typically is associated with accepting triumphant capitalism, American style) *is* progress; developing countries must accept it, if they are to grow and to fight poverty effectively. But to many in the developing world, globalization has not brought the promised economic benefits.

A growing divide between the haves and the have-nots has left increasing numbers in the Third World in dire poverty, living on less than a dollar a day. Despite repeated promises of poverty reduction made over the last decade of the twentieth century, the actual number of people living in poverty has actually increased by almost 100 million.[2] This occurred at the same time that total world income actually increased by an average of 2.5 percent annually.

In Africa, the high aspirations following colonial independence have been largely unfulfilled. Instead, the continent plunges deeper into misery, as incomes fall and standards of living decline. The hard-won improvements in life expectancy gained in the past few decades have begun to reverse. While the scourge of AIDS is at the center of this decline, poverty is also a killer. Even countries that have abandoned African socialism, managed to install reasonably honest governments, balanced their budgets, and kept inflation down find that they simply cannot attract private investors. Without this investment, they cannot have sustainable growth.

If globalization has not succeeded in reducing poverty, neither has it succeeded in ensuring stability. Crises in Asia and in Latin America have threatened the economies and the stability of all developing countries. There are fears of financial contagion spreading around the world, that the collapse of one emerging market currency will mean that others fall as well. For a while, in 1997 and 1998, the Asian crisis appeared to pose a threat to the entire world economy.

Globalization and the introduction of a market economy has not produced the promised results in Russia and most of the other economies making the transition from communism to the market. These countries were told by the West that the new economic system would bring them unprecedented prosperity. Instead, it brought unprecedented poverty: in many respects, for most of the people, the market economy proved even worse than their Communist leaders had predicted. The contrast between Russia's transition, as engineered by the international economic institutions, and that of China, designed by itself, could not be greater: While in 1990 China's gross domestic product (GDP) was 60 percent that of Russia, by the end of the decade the numbers had been reversed. While Russia saw an unprecedented increase in poverty, China saw an unprecedented decrease.

The critics of globalization accuse Western countries of hypocrisy, and the critics are right. The Western countries have pushed poor countries to eliminate trade barriers, but kept up their own barriers, preventing developing countries from exporting their agricultural products and so depriving them of desperately needed export income. The United States was, of course, one of the prime culprits, and this was an issue about which I felt intensely. When I was chairman of the Council of Economic Advisers, I fought hard against this hypocrisy. It not only hurt the developing countries; it also cost Americans, both as consumers, in the higher prices they paid, and as taxpayers, to finance the huge subsidies, billions of dollars. My struggles were, all too often, unsuccessful. Special commercial and financial interests prevailed—and when I moved over to the World Bank, I saw the consequences to the developing countries all too clearly.

But even when not guilty of hypocrisy, the West has driven the globalization agenda, ensuring that it garners a disproportionate share of the benefits, at the expense of the developing world. It was not just that the more advanced industrial countries declined to open up their markets to the goods of the developing countries—for instance, keeping their quotas on a multitude of goods from textiles to sugar—while insisting that those countries open up their markets to the goods of the wealthier countries; it was not just that the more advanced industrial countries continued to subsidize agriculture, making it difficult for the developing countries to compete, while insisting that the developing countries eliminate their subsidies on industrial goods. Looking at the "terms of trade"—the prices which developed and less developed countries get for the products they produce—after the last trade agreement in 1995 (the eighth), the *net* effect was to lower the prices some of the poorest countries in the world received relative to what they paid for their imports.* The result was that some of the poorest countries in the world were actually made worse off.

Western banks benefited from the loosening of capital market controls in Latin America and Asia, but those regions suffered when inflows of speculative hot money (money that comes into and out of a country, often overnight, often little more than betting on whether a currency is going to appreciate or depreciate) that had poured into countries suddenly reversed. The abrupt outflow of money left behind collapsed currencies and weakened banking systems. The Uruguay Round also strengthened intellectual property rights.

---

*This eighth agreement was the result of negotiations called the *Uruguay Round* because the negotiations began in 1986 in Punta del Este, Uruguay. The round was concluded in Marrakech on December 15, 1993, when 117 countries joined in this trade liberalization agreement. The agreement was finally signed for the United States by President Clinton on December 8, 1994. The World Trade Organization came into formal effect on January 1, 1995, and over 100 nations had signed on by July. One provision of the agreement entailed converting the GATT into the WTO.

American and other Western drug companies could now stop drug companies in India and Brazil from "stealing" their intellectual property. But these drug companies in the developing world were making these life-saving drugs available to their citizens at a fraction of the price at which the drugs were sold by the Western drug companies. There were thus two sides to the decisions made in the Uruguay Round. Profits of the Western drug companies would go up. Advocates said this would provide them more incentive to innovate; but the increased profits from sales in the developing world were small, since few could afford the drugs, and hence the incentive effect, at best, might be limited. The other side was that thousands were effectively condemned to death, because governments and individuals in developing countries could no longer pay the high prices demanded. In the case of AIDS, the international outrage was so great that drug companies had to back down, eventually agreeing to lower their prices, to sell the drugs at cost in late 2001. But the underlying problems—the fact that the intellectual property regime established under the Uruguay Round was not balanced, that it overwhelmingly reflected the interests and perspectives of the producers, as opposed to the users, whether in developed or developing countries—remain.

Not only in trade liberalization but in every other aspect of globalization even seemingly well-intentioned efforts have often backfired. When projects, whether agriculture or infrastructure, recommended by the West, designed with the advice of Western advisers, and financed by the World Bank or others have failed, unless there is some form of debt forgiveness, the poor people in the developing world still must repay the loans.

If, in too many instances, the benefits of globalization have been less than its advocates claim, the price paid has been greater, as the environment has been destroyed, as political processes have been corrupted, and as the rapid pace of change has not allowed countries time for cultural adaptation. The crises that have brought in their wake massive unemployment have, in turn, been followed by longer-term problems of social dissolution—from urban violence in Latin America to ethnic conflicts in other parts of the world, such as Indonesia.

These problems are hardly new—but the increasingly vehement

worldwide reaction against the policies that drive globalization is a significant change. For decades, the cries of the poor in Africa and in developing countries in other parts of the world have been largely unheard in the West. Those who labored in the developing countries knew something was wrong when they saw financial crises becoming more commonplace and the numbers of poor increasing. But they had no way to change the rules or to influence the international financial institutions that wrote them. Those who valued democratic processes saw how "conditionality"—the conditions that international lenders imposed in return for their assistance—undermined national sovereignty. But until the protestors came along there was little hope for change and no outlets for complaint. *Some* of the protestors went to excesses; *some* of the protestors were arguing for higher protectionist barriers against the developing countries, which would have made their plight even worse. But despite these problems, it is the trade unionists, students, environmentalists—ordinary citizens—marching in the streets of Prague, Seattle, Washington, and Genoa who have put the need for reform on the agenda of the developed world.

Protestors see globalization in a very different light than the treasury secretary of the United States, or the finance and trade ministers of most of the advanced industrial countries. The differences in views are so great that one wonders, are the protestors and the policy makers talking about the same phenomena? Are they looking at the same data? Are the visions of those in power so clouded by special and particular interests?

What is this phenomenon of globalization that has been subject, at the same time, to such vilification and such praise? Fundamentally, it is the closer integration of the countries and peoples of the world which has been brought about by the enormous reduction of costs of transportation and communication, and the breaking down of artificial barriers to the flows of goods, services, capital, knowledge, and (to a lesser extent) people across borders. Globalization has been accompanied by the creation of new institutions that have joined with existing ones to work across borders. In the arena of international civil society, new groups, like the Jubilee movement pushing for debt reduction for the poorest countries, have joined long-established organizations like the International Red Cross. Globalization is powerfully driven by international corporations, which move not only capital and goods across borders but also technology. Globalization has also led to renewed attention to long-established international *intergovernmental* institutions: the United Nations, which attempts to maintain peace; the International Labor Organization (ILO), originally created in 1919, which promotes its agenda around the world under its slogan "decent work"; and the World Health Organization (WHO), which has been especially concerned with improving health conditions in the developing world.

Many, perhaps most, of these aspects of globalization have been welcomed everywhere. No one wants to see their child die, when knowledge and medicines are available somewhere else in the world. It is the more narrowly defined *economic* aspects of globalization that have been the subject of controversy, and the international institutions that have written the rules, which mandate or push things like liberalization of capital markets (the elimination of the rules and regulations in many developing countries that are designed to stabilize the flows of volatile money into and out of the country).

To understand what went wrong, it's important to look at the three main institutions that govern globalization: the IMF, the World Bank, and the WTO. There are, in addition, a host of other institutions that play a role in the international economic system—a number of regional banks, smaller and younger sisters to the World Bank, and a large number of UN organizations, such as the UN Development Program or the UN Conference on Trade and Development (UNCTAD). These organizations often have views that are markedly different from the IMF and the World Bank. The ILO, for example, worries that the IMF pays too little attention to workers' rights, while the Asian Development Bank argues for "competitive pluralism," whereby developing countries will be provided with alternative views of development strategies, including the "Asian model"—in which governments, while relying on markets, have taken an active role in creating, shaping, and guiding markets, including promoting new technologies, and in which firms take considerable responsibility for the social welfare of their employees—which the Asian Development Bank sees as distinctly different from the American model pushed by the Washington-based institutions.

In this book, I focus mostly on the IMF and the World Bank, largely because they have been at the center of the major economic issues of the last two decades, including the financial crises and the transition of the former Communist countries to market economics. The IMF and the World Bank both originated in World War II as a result of the UN Monetary and Financial Conference at Bretton Woods, New Hampshire, in July 1944, part of a concerted effort to finance the rebuilding of Europe after the devastation of World War II and to save the world from future economic depressions. The proper name of the World Bank—the International Bank for Reconstruction and Development—reflects its original mission; the last part, "Development," was added almost as an afterthought. At the time, most of the countries in the developing world were still colonies, and what meager economic development efforts could or would be undertaken were considered the responsibility of their European masters.

The more difficult task of ensuring global economic stability was assigned to the IMF. Those who convened at Bretton Woods had the global depression of the 1930s very much on their minds. Almost three quarters of a century ago, capitalism faced its most severe crisis to date. The Great Depression enveloped the whole world and led to unprecedented increases in unemployment. At the worst point, a quarter of America's workforce was unemployed. The British economist John Maynard Keynes, who would later be a key participant at Bretton Woods, put forward a simple explanation, and a correspondingly simple set of prescriptions: lack of sufficient aggregate demand explained economic downturns; government policies could help stimulate aggregate demand. In cases where monetary policy is ineffective, governments could rely on fiscal policies, either by increasing expenditures or cutting taxes. While the models underlying Keynes's analysis have subsequently been criticized and refined, bringing a deeper understanding of why market forces do not work quickly to adjust the economy to full employment, the basic lessons remain valid.

The International Monetary Fund was charged with preventing another global depression. It would do this by putting international pressure on countries that were not doing their fair share to maintain global aggregate demand, by allowing their own economies to go into a slump. When necessary it would also provide liquidity in the form of loans to those countries facing an economic downturn and unable to stimulate aggregate demand with their own resources.

In its original conception, then, the IMF was based on a recognition that markets often did not work well—that they could result in massive unemployment and might fail to make needed funds available to countries to help them restore their economies. The IMF was founded on the belief that there was a need for *collective action at the global level* for economic stability, just as the United Nations had been founded on the belief that there was a need for collective action at the global level for political stability. The IMF is a *public* institution, established with money provided by taxpayers around the world. This is important to remember because it does not report directly to either the citizens who finance it or those whose lives it affects. Rather, it reports to the ministries of finance and the central banks of the governments of the world. They assert their control through a complicated voting arrangement based largely on the economic power of the countries at the end of World War II. There have been some minor adjustments since, but the major developed countries run the show, with only one country, the United States, having effective veto. (In this sense, it is similar to the UN, where a historical anachronism determines who holds the veto—the victorious powers of World War II—but at least there the veto power is shared among five countries.)

Over the years since its inception, the IMF has changed markedly. Founded on the belief that markets often worked badly, it now champions market supremacy with ideological fervor. Founded on the belief that there is a need for international pressure on countries to have more expansionary economic policies—such as increasing expenditures, reducing taxes, or lowering interest rates to stimulate the economy—today the IMF typically provides funds only if countries engage in policies like cutting deficits, raising taxes, or raising interest rates that lead to a contraction of the economy. Keynes would be rolling over in his grave were he to see what has happened to his child.

The most dramatic change in these institutions occurred in the 1980s, the era when Ronald Reagan and Margaret Thatcher preached free market ideology in the United States and the United Kingdom. The IMF and the World Bank became the new missionary institutions, through which these ideas were pushed on the reluctant poor countries that often badly needed their loans and grants. The ministries of finance in poor countries were willing to become converts, if necessary, to obtain the funds, though the vast majority of government officials, and, more to the point, people in these countries often remained skeptical. In the early 1980s, a purge occurred inside the World Bank, in its research department, which guided the Bank's thinking and direction. Hollis Chenery, one of America's most distinguished development economists, a professor at Harvard who had made fundamental contributions to research in the economics of development and other areas as well, had been Robert McNamara's confidant and adviser. McNamara had been appointed president of the World Bank in 1968. Touched by the poverty that he saw throughout the Third World, McNamara had redirected the Bank's effort at its elimination, and Chenery assembled a first-class group of economists from around the world to work with him. But with the changing of the guard came a new president in 1981, William Clausen, and a new chief economist, Ann Krueger, an international trade specialist, best known for her work on "rent seeking"—how special interests use tariffs and other protectionist measures to increase their incomes at the expense of others. While Chenery and his team had focused on how markets failed in developing countries and what governments could do to improve markets and reduce poverty, Krueger saw government as the problem. Free markets were the solution to the problems of developing countries. In the new ideological fervor, many of the first-rate economists that Chenery had assembled left.

Although the missions of the two institutions remained distinct, it was at this time that their activities became increasingly intertwined.

In the 1980s, the Bank went beyond just lending for projects (like roads and dams) to providing broad-based support, in the form of *structural adjustment loans;* but it did this only when the IMF gave its approval—and with that approval came IMF-imposed conditions on the country. The IMF was supposed to focus on crises; but developing countries were always in need of help, so the IMF became a permanent part of life in most of the developing world.

The fall of the Berlin Wall provided a new arena for the IMF: managing the transition to a market economy in the former Soviet Union and the Communist bloc countries in Europe. More recently, as the crises have gotten bigger, and even the deep coffers of the IMF seemed insufficient, the World Bank was called in to provide tens of billions of dollars of emergency support, but strictly as a junior partner, with the guidelines of the programs dictated by the IMF. In principle, there was a division of labor. The IMF was supposed to limit itself to matters of *macroeconomics* in dealing with a country, to the government's budget deficit, its monetary policy, its inflation, its trade deficit, its borrowing from abroad; and the World Bank was supposed to be in charge of *structural issues*—what the country's government spent money on, the country's financial institutions, its labor markets, its trade policies. But the IMF took a rather imperialistic view of the matter: since almost any structural issue could affect the overall performance of the economy, and hence the government's budget or the trade deficit, it viewed almost everything as falling within its domain. It often got impatient with the World Bank, where even in the years when free market ideology reigned supreme there were frequent controversies about what policies would best suit the conditions of the country. The IMF had the answers (basically, the same ones for every country), didn't see the need for all this discussion, and, while the World Bank debated what should be done, saw itself as stepping into the vacuum to provide the answers.

The two institutions could have provided countries with alternative perspectives on some of the challenges of development and transition, and in doing so they might have strengthened democratic processes. But they were both driven by the collective will of the G-7 (the governments of the seven most important advanced industrial countries),* and especially their finance ministers and treasury secretaries, and too often, the last thing they wanted was a lively democratic debate about alternative strategies.

A half century after its founding, it is clear that the IMF has failed in its mission. It has not done what it was supposed to do—provide funds for countries facing an economic downturn, to enable the country to restore itself to close to full employment. In spite of the fact that our understanding of economic processes has increased enormously during the last fifty years, and in spite of IMF's efforts during the past quarter century, crises around the world have been more frequent and (with the exception of the Great Depression) deeper. By some reckonings, close to a hundred countries have faced crises.[3] Worse, many of the policies that the IMF pushed, in particular, premature capital market liberalization, have contributed to global instability. And once a country was in crisis, IMF funds and programs not only failed to stabilize the situation but in many cases actually made matters worse, especially for the poor. The IMF failed in its original mission of promoting global stability; it has also been no more successful in the new missions that it has undertaken, such as guiding the transition of countries from communism to a market economy.

The Bretton Woods agreement had called for a third international economic organization—a World Trade Organization to govern international trade relations, a job similar to the IMF's governing of international financial relations. Beggar-thy-neighbor trade policies, in which countries raised tariffs to maintain their own economies but at the expense of their neighbors, were largely blamed for the spread of the depression and its depth. An international organization was required not just to prevent a recurrence but to encourage the free flow of goods and services. Although the General Agreement on

*These are the United States, Japan, Germany, Canada, Italy, France, and the UK. Today, the G-7 typically meets together with Russia (the G-8). The seven countries are no longer the seven largest economies in the world. Membership in the G-7, like permanent membership in the UN Security Council, is partly a matter of historical accident.

Tariffs and Trade (GATT) did succeed in lowering tariffs enormously, it was difficult to reach the final accord; it was not until 1995, a half century after the end of the war and two thirds of a century after the Great Depression, that the World Trade Organization came into being. But the WTO is markedly different from the other two organizations. It does not set rules itself; rather, it provides a forum in which trade negotiations go on and it ensures that its agreements are lived up to.

The ideas and intentions behind the creation of the international economic institutions were good ones, yet they gradually evolved over the years to become something very different. The Keynesian orientation of the IMF, which emphasized market failures and the role for government in job creation, was replaced by the free market mantra of the 1980s, part of a new "Washington Consensus"—a consensus between the IMF, the World Bank, and the U.S. Treasury about the "right" policies for developing countries—that signaled a radically different approach to economic development and stabilization.

Many of the ideas incorporated in the consensus were developed in response to the problems in Latin America, where governments had let budgets get out of control while loose monetary policies had led to rampant inflation. A burst of growth in some of that region's countries in the decades immediately after World War II had not been sustained, allegedly because of excessive state intervention in the economy. The ideas that were developed to cope with problems arguably specific to Latin American countries, and which I will outline later in the book, subsequently been deemed applicable to countries around the world. Capital market liberalization has been pushed despite the fact that there is no evidence showing it spurs economic growth. In other cases, the economic policies that evolved into the Washington Consensus and were introduced into developing countries were not appropriate for countries in the early stages of development or early stages of transition.

To take just a few examples, most of the advanced industrial countries—including the United States and Japan—had built up their economies by wisely and selectively protecting some of their industries until they were strong enough to compete with foreign companies. While blanket protectionism has often not worked for countries that have tried it, neither has rapid trade liberalization. Forcing a developing country to open itself up to imported products that would compete with those produced by certain of its industries, industries that were dangerously vulnerable to competition from much stronger counterpart industries in other countries, can have disastrous consequences—socially and economically. Jobs have systematically been destroyed—poor farmers in developing countries simply couldn't compete with the highly subsidized goods from Europe and America—before the countries' industrial and agricultural sectors were able to grow strong and create new jobs. Even worse, the IMF's insistence on developing countries maintaining tight monetary policies has led to interest rates that would make job creation impossible even in the best of circumstances. And because trade liberalization occurred before safety nets were put into place, those who lost their jobs were forced into poverty. Liberalization has thus, too often, not been followed by the promised growth, but by increased misery. And even those who have not lost their jobs have been hit by a heightened sense of insecurity.

Capital controls are another example: European countries banned the free flow of capital until the seventies. Some might say it's not fair to insist that developing countries with a barely functioning bank system risk opening their markets. But putting aside such notions of fairness, it's bad economics; the influx of hot money into and out of the country that so frequently follows after capital market liberalization leaves havoc in its wake. Small developing countries are like small boats. Rapid capital market liberalization, in the manner pushed by the IMF, amounted to setting them off on a voyage on a rough sea, before the holes in their hulls have been repaired, before the captain has received training, before life vests have been put on board. Even in the best of circumstances, there was a high likelihood that they would be overturned when they were hit broadside by a big wave.

The application of mistaken economic theories would not be such a problem if the end of first colonialism and then communism had not given the IMF and the World Bank the opportunity to greatly expand their respective original mandates, to vastly extend their reach. Today these institutions have become dominant players in the world economy. Not only countries seeking their help but also those seeking their "seal of approval" so that they can better access international capital markets must follow their economic prescriptions, prescriptions which reflect their free market ideologies and theories.

The result for many people has been poverty and for many countries social and political chaos. The IMF has made mistakes in all the areas it has been involved in: development, crisis management, and in countries making the transition from communism to capitalism. Structural adjustment programs did not bring sustained growth even to those, like Bolivia, that adhered to its strictures; in many countries, excessive austerity stifled growth; successful economic programs require extreme care in *sequencing*—the order in which reforms occur—and pacing. If, for instance, markets are opened up for competition too rapidly, before strong financial institutions are established, then jobs will be destroyed faster than new jobs are created. In many countries, mistakes in sequencing and pacing led to rising unemployment and increased poverty.[4] After the 1997 Asian crisis, IMF policies exacerbated the crises in Indonesia and Thailand. Free market reforms in Latin America have had one or two successes— Chile is repeatedly cited—but much of the rest of the continent has still to make up for the lost decade of growth following the so-called successful IMF bailouts of the early 1980s, and many today have persistently high rates of unemployment—in Argentina, for instance, at double-digit levels since 1995—even as inflation has been brought down. The collapse in Argentina in 2001 is one of the most recent of a series of failures over the past few years. Given the high unemployment rate for almost seven years, the wonder is not that the citizens eventually rioted, but that they suffered quietly so much for so long. Even those countries that have experienced some limited growth have seen the benefits accrue to the well-off, and especially the *very* well-off—the top 10 percent—while poverty has remained high, and in some cases the income of those at the bottom has even fallen.

Underlying the problems of the IMF and the other international economic institutions is the problem of governance: who decides what they do. The institutions are dominated not just by the wealthiest industrial countries but by commercial and financial interests in those countries, and the policies of the institutions naturally reflect this. The choice heads for these institutions symbolizes the institutions' problem, and too often has contributed to their dysfunction. While almost all of the activities of the IMF and the World Bank today are in the developing world (certainly, all of their lending), they are led by representatives from the industrialized nations. (By custom or tacit agreement the head of the IMF is always a European, that of the World Bank an American.) They are chosen behind closed doors, and it has never even been viewed as a prerequisite that the head should have any experience in the developing world. The institutions are not representative of the nations they serve.

The problems also arise from who *speaks* for the country. At the IMF, it is the finance ministers and the central bank governors. At the WTO, it is the trade ministers. Each of these ministers is closely aligned with particular constituencies *within* their countries. The trade ministries reflect the concerns of the business community—both exporters who want to see new markets opened up for their products and producers of goods which compete with new imports. These constituencies, of course, want to maintain as many barriers to trade as they can and keep whatever subsidies they can persuade Congress (or their parliament) to give them. The fact that the trade barriers raise the prices consumers pay or that the subsidies impose burdens on taxpayers is of less concern than the profits of the producers—and environmental and labor issues are of even less concern, other than as obstacles that have to be overcome. The finance ministers and central bank governors typically are closely tied to the financial community; they come from financial firms, and after their period of government service, that is where they return. Robert Rubin, the treasury secretary during much of the period described in this book, came from the largest investment bank, Goldman Sachs, and returned to the firm, Citigroup, that controlled the largest commercial bank, Citibank. The number-two person at the IMF during this period, Stan Fischer, went straight from the IMF to Citigroup. These individuals naturally see the world through the eyes of the financial community. The decisions of any institution naturally reflect the perspectives and interests of those who make the decisions; not surprisingly, as we shall see repeatedly in the following chapters, the policies of the international economic institutions are all too often closely aligned with the commercial and financial interests of those in the advanced industrial countries.

For the peasants in developing countries who toil to pay off their countries' IMF debts or the businessmen who suffer from higher value-added taxes upon the insistence of the IMF, the current system run by the IMF is one of taxation without representation. Disillusion with the international system of globalization under the aegis of the IMF grows as the poor in Indonesia, Morocco, or Papua New Guinea have fuel and food subsidies cut, as those in Thailand see AIDS increase as a result of IMF-forced cutbacks in health expenditures, and as families in many developing countries, having to pay for their children's education under so-called cost recovery programs, make the painful choice not to send their daughters to school.

Left with no alternatives, no way to express their concern, to press for change, people riot. The streets, of course, are not the place where issues are discussed, policies formulated, or compromises forged. But the protests have made government officials and economists around the world think about alternatives to these Washington Consensus policies as the one and true way for growth and development. It has become increasingly clear not to just ordinary citizens but to policy makers as well, and not just those in the developing countries but those in the developed countries as well, that globalization as it has been practiced has not lived up to what its advocates promised it would accomplish—or to what it can and should do. In some cases it has not even resulted in growth, but when it has, it has not brought benefits to all; the net effect of the policies set by the Washington Consensus has all too often been to benefit the few at the expense of the many, the well-off at the expense of the poor. In many cases commercial interests and values have superseded concern for the environment, democracy, human rights, and social justice.

Globalization itself is neither good nor bad. It has the *power* to do enormous good, and for the countries of East Asia, who have embraced globalization *under their own terms*, at their own pace, it has been an enormous benefit, in spite of the setback of the 1997 crisis. But in much of the world it has not brought comparable benefits. For many, it seems closer to an unmitigated disaster.

The experience of the United States during the nineteenth century makes a good parallel for today's globalization—and the contrast helps illustrate the successes of the past and today's failures. At that time, when transportation and communication costs fell and previously local markets expanded, new national economies formed, and with these new national economies came national companies, doing business throughout the country. But the markets were not left to develop willy-nilly on their own; government played a vital role in shaping the evolution of the economy. The U.S. government obtained wide economic latitude when the courts broadly interpreted the constitutional provision that allows the federal government to regulate interstate commerce. The federal government began to regulate the financial system, set minimum wages and working conditions, and eventually provided unemployment and welfare systems to deal with the problems posed by a market system. The federal government also promoted some industries (the first telegraph line, for example, was laid by the federal government between Baltimore and Washington in 1842) and encouraged others, like agriculture, not just helping set up universities to do research but providing extension services to train farmers in the new technologies. The federal government played a central role not only in promoting American growth. Even if it did not engage in the kinds of active redistribution policies, at least it had programs whose benefits were widely shared—not just those that extended education and improved agricultural productivity, but also land grants that provided a minimum opportunity for all Americans.

Today, with the continuing decline in transportation and communication costs, and the reduction of man-made barriers to the flow of goods, services, and capital (though there remain serious barriers to the free flow of labor), we have a process of "globalization" analogous to the earlier processes in which national economies were formed. Unfortunately, we have no world government, accountable to the people of every country, to oversee the globalization process in a fashion comparable to the way national governments guided the nationalization process. Instead, we have a system that might be called *global governance without global government*, one in which a few institutions—the World Bank, the IMF, the WTO—and a few players—the finance, commerce, and trade ministries, closely linked to certain financial and commercial interests—dominate the scene, but in which many of those affected by their decisions are left almost voiceless. It's time to change some of the rules governing the international economic order, to think once again about how decisions get made at the international level—and in whose interests—and to place less emphasis on ideology and to look more at what works. It is crucial that the successful development we have seen in East Asia be achieved elsewhere. There is an enormous cost to continuing global instability. Globalization can be reshaped, and when it is, when it is properly, fairly run, with all countries having a voice in policies affecting them, there is a possibility that it will help create a new global economy in which growth is not only more sustainable and less volatile but the fruits of this growth are more equitably shared.

CHAPTER 2

BROKEN PROMISES

O N MY FIRST day, February 13, 1997, as chief economist and senior vice president of the World Bank, as I walked into its gigantic, modern, gleaming main building on 19th Street in Washington, DC, the institution's motto was the first thing that caught my eye: *Our dream is a world without poverty.* In the center of the thirteen-story atrium there is a statue of a young boy leading an old blind man, a memorial to the eradication of river blindness (*onchocerciasis*). Before the World Bank, the World Health Organization, and others pooled their efforts, thousands were blinded annually in Africa from this preventable disease. Across the street stands another gleaming monument to public wealth, the headquarters of the International Monetary Fund. The marble atrium inside, graced with abundant flora, serves to remind visiting finance ministers from countries around the world that the IMF represents the centers of wealth and power.

These two institutions, often confused in the public mind, present marked contrasts that underline the differences in their cultures, styles, and missions: one is devoted to eradicating poverty, one to maintaining global stability. While both have teams of economists flying into developing countries for three-week missions, the World

Bank has worked hard to make sure that a substantial fraction of its staff live permanently in the country they are trying to assist; the IMF generally has only a single "resident representative," whose powers are limited. IMF programs are typically dictated from Washington, and shaped by the short missions during which its staff members pore over numbers in the finance ministries and central banks and make themselves comfortable in five-star hotels in the capitals. There is more than symbolism in this difference: one cannot come to learn about, and love, a nation unless one gets out to the countryside. One should not see unemployment as just a statistic, an economic "body count," the unintended casualties in the fight against inflation or to ensure that Western banks get repaid. The unemployed are people, with families, whose lives are affected—sometimes devastated—by the economic policies that outsiders recommend, and, in the case of the IMF, effectively impose. Modern high-tech warfare is designed to remove physical contact: dropping bombs from 50,000 feet ensures that one does not "feel" what one does. Modern economic management is similar: from one's luxury hotel, one can callously impose policies about which one would think twice if one knew the people whose lives one was destroying.

Statistics bear out what those who travel outside the capital see in the villages of Africa, Nepal, Mindanao, or Ethiopia; the gap between the poor and the rich has been growing, and even the number in absolutely poverty—living on less than a dollar a day—has increased. Even where river blindness has been eliminated, poverty endures—this despite all the good intentions and promises made by the developed nations to the developing nations, most of which were once the colonial possessions of the developed nations.

Mind-sets are not changed overnight, and this is as true in the developed as in the developing countries. Giving developing countries their freedom (generally after little preparation for autonomy) often did not change the view of their former colonial masters, who continued to feel that they knew best. The colonial mentality—the "white man's burden" and the presumption that they knew what was best for the developing countries—persisted. America, which came to dominate the global economic scene, had much less of a colonial heritage, yet America's credentials too had been tarred, not so much by its "Manifest Destiny" expansionism as by the cold war, in which principles of democracy were compromised or ignored, in the all-encompassing struggle against communism.

THE NIGHT BEFORE I started at the Bank, I held my last press conference as chairman of the President's Council of Economic Advisers. With the domestic economy so well under control, I felt that the greatest challenges for an economist now lay in the growing problem of world poverty. What could we do about the 1.2 billion people around the world living on less than a dollar a day, or the 2.8 billion people living on less than $2 a day—more than 45 percent of the world's population? What could I do to bring to reality the dream of a world without poverty? How could I embark on the more modest dream of a world with less poverty? I saw my task as threefold: thinking through what strategies might be most effective in promoting growth and reducing poverty; working with governments in the developing countries to put these strategies in place; and doing everything I could within the developed countries to advance the interests and concerns of the developing world, whether it was pushing for opening up their markets or providing more effective assistance. I knew the tasks were difficult, but I never dreamed that one of the major obstacles the developing countries faced was man-made, totally unnecessary, and lay right across the street—at my "sister" institution, the IMF. I had expected that not everyone in the international financial institutions or in the governments that supported them was committed to the goal of eliminating poverty; but I thought there would be an open debate about strategies—strategies which in so many areas seem to be failing, and especially failing the poor. In this, I was to be disappointed.

Ethiopia and the Struggle Between Power Politics and Poverty

After four years in Washington, I had become used to the strange world of bureaucracies and politicians. But it was not until I traveled to Ethiopia, one of the poorest countries in the world, in March 1997, barely a month into the World Bank job, that I became fully immersed in the astonishing world of IMF politics and arithmetic.

Ethiopia's per capita income was $110 a year and the country had suffered from successive droughts and famines that had killed 2 million people. I went to meet Prime Minister Meles Zenawi, a man who had led a seventeen-year guerrilla war against the bloody Marxist regime of Mengistu Haile Mariam. Meles's forces won in 1991 and then the government began the hard work of rebuilding the country. A doctor by training, Meles had formally studied economics because he knew that to bring his country out of centuries of poverty would require nothing less than economic transformation, and he demonstrated a knowledge of economics—and indeed a creativity—that would have put him at the head of any of my university classes. He showed a deeper understanding of economic principles— and certainly a greater knowledge of the circumstances in his country—than many of the international economic bureaucrats that I had to deal with in the succeeding three years.

Meles combined these intellectual attributes with personal integrity: no one doubted his honesty and there were few accusations of corruption within his government. His political opponents came mostly from the long-dominant groups around the capital who had lost political power with his accession, and they raised questions about his commitment to democratic principles. However, he was not an old-fashioned autocrat. Both he and the government were generally committed to a process of decentralization, bringing government closer to the people and ensuring that the center did not lose touch with the separate regions. The new constitution even gave each region the right to vote democratically to secede, ensuring that the political elites in the capital city, whoever they might be, could not risk ignoring the concerns of ordinary citizens in every part of the country, or that one part of the country could not impose its views on the rest. The government actually lived up to its commitment, when Eritrea declared its independence in 1993. (Subsequent events—such as the government's occupation of the university in Addis Ababa in the spring of 2000, with the imprisonment of some students and professors—show the precariousness, in Ethiopia as elsewhere, of basic democratic rights.)

When I arrived in 1997, Meles was engaged in a heated dispute with the IMF, and the Fund had suspended its lending program.

Ethiopia's macroeconomic "results"—upon which the Fund was supposed to focus—could not have been better. There was no inflation; in fact, prices were falling. Output had been growing steadily since he had succeeded in ousting Mengistu.[1] Meles showed that, with the right policies in place, even a poor African country could experience sustained economic growth. After years of war and rebuilding, international assistance was beginning to return to the country. But Meles was having problems with the IMF. What was at stake was not just $127 million of IMF money provided through its so-called Enhanced Structural Adjustment Facility (ESAF) program (a lending program at highly subsidized rates to help very poor countries), but World Bank monies as well.

The IMF has a distinct role in international assistance. It is supposed to review each recipient's macroeconomic situation and make sure that the country is living within its means. If it is not, there is inevitably trouble down the road. In the short run, a country can live beyond its means by borrowing, but eventually a day of reckoning comes, and there is a crisis. The IMF is particularly concerned about inflation. Countries whose governments spend more than they take in in taxes and foreign aid often will face inflation, especially if they finance their deficits by printing money. Of course, there are other dimensions to good macroeconomic policy besides inflation. The term *macro* refers to the *aggregate* behavior, the overall levels of growth, unemployment, and inflation, and a country can have low inflation but no growth and high unemployment. To most economists, such a country would rate as having a disastrous macroeconomic framework. To most economists, inflation is not so much an end in itself, but a means to an end: it is because *excessively* high inflation often leads to low growth, and low growth leads to high unemployment, that inflation is so frowned upon. But the IMF often seems to confuse means with ends, thereby losing sight of what is ultimately of concern. A country like Argentina can get an "A" grade, even if it has double-digit unemployment for years, so long as its budget seems in balance and its inflation seems in control!

If a country does not come up to certain minimum standards, the IMF suspends assistance; and typically, when it does, so do other donors. Understandably, the World Bank and the IMF don't lend to countries unless they have a good macroframework in place. If countries have huge deficits and soaring inflation, there is a risk that money will not be well spent. Governments that fail to manage their overall economy generally typically do a poor job managing foreign aid. But if the macroeconomic indicators—inflation and growth—are solid, as they were in Ethiopia, surely the underlying macroeconomic framework must be good. Not only did Ethiopia have a sound macroeconomic framework but the World Bank had direct evidence of the competence of the government and its commitment to the poor. Ethiopia had formulated a rural development strategy, focusing its attention on the poor, and especially the 85 percent of the population living in the rural sector. It had dramatically cut back on military expenditures—remarkable for a government which had come to power through military means—because it knew that funds spent on weapons were funds that could not be spent on fighting poverty. Surely, this was precisely the kind of government to which the international community should have been giving assistance. But the IMF had suspended its program with Ethiopia, in spite of the good macroeconomic performance, saying it was worried about Ethiopia's budgetary position.

The Ethiopian government had two revenue sources, taxes and foreign assistance. A government's budget is in balance so long as its revenue sources equal its expenditures. Ethiopia, like many developing countries, derived much of its revenues from foreign assistance. The IMF worried that if this aid dried up, Ethiopia would be in trouble. Hence it argued that Ethiopia's budgetary position could only be judged solid if expenditures were limited to the taxes it collected.

The obvious problem with the IMF's logic is that it implies no poor country can ever spend money on anything it gets aid for. If Sweden, say, gives money to Ethiopia to build schools, this logic dictates that Ethiopia should instead put the money into its reserves. (All countries have, or should have, reserve accounts that hold funds for the proverbial rainy day. Gold is the traditional reserve, but today it has been replaced by hard currency and its interest-bearing relatives. The most common way to hold reserves is in U.S. Treasury bills.) But this is not why international donors give aid. In Ethiopia, the donors, who were working independently and not beholden to the IMF, wanted to see new schools and health clinics built, and so did Ethiopia. Meles put the matter more forcefully: He told me that he had not fought so hard for seventeen years to be instructed by some international bureaucrat that he could not build schools and clinics for his people once he had succeeded in convincing donors to pay for them.

The IMF view was not rooted in a long-held concern about project sustainability. Sometimes countries had used aid dollars to construct schools or clinics. When the aid money ran out, there was no money to maintain these facilities. The donors had recognized this problem and built it into their assistance programs in Ethiopia and elsewhere. But what the IMF alleged in the case of Ethiopia went beyond that concern. The Fund contended that international assistance was too unstable to be relied upon. To me, the IMF's position made no sense, and not just because of its absurd implications. I knew that assistance was often far more stable than tax revenues, which can vary markedly with economic conditions. When I got back to Washington, I asked my staff to check the statistics, and they confirmed that international assistance was more stable than tax revenues. Using the IMF reasoning about stable sources of revenue, Ethiopia, and other developing countries, should have counted foreign aid but not included tax revenues in their budgets. And if neither taxes nor foreign assistance were to be included in the revenue side of budgets, *every* country would be considered to be in bad shape.

But the IMF's reasoning was even more flawed. There are a number of appropriate responses to instability of revenues, such as setting aside additional reserves and maintaining flexibility of expenditures. If revenues, from any source, decline, and there are not reserves to draw upon, then the government has to be prepared to cut back expenditures. But for the kinds of assistance that constitute so much of what a poor country like Ethiopia receives, there is a built-in flexibility; if the country does not receive money to build an additional school, it simply does not build the school. Ethiopia's government officials understood what was at issue, they understood the concern about what might happen if *either* tax revenues or foreign assistance should fall, and they had designed policies to deal with these contingencies. What they couldn't understand—and I couldn't understand—is why the IMF couldn't see the logic of their position. And much was at stake: schools and health clinics for some of the poorest people in the world.

In addition to the disagreement over how to treat foreign aid, I also became immediately entangled in another IMF-Ethiopia dispute over early loan repayment. Ethiopia had repaid an American bank loan early, using some of its reserves. The transaction made perfect *economic* sense. In spite of the quality of the collateral (an airplane), Ethiopia was paying a far higher interest rate on its loan than it was receiving on its reserves. I, too, would have advised them to repay, particularly since in the event that funds would later be required, the government could presumably readily obtain funds using the plane as collateral. The United States and the IMF objected to the early repayment. They objected not to the logic of the strategy, but to the fact that Ethiopia had undertaken this course without IMF approval. But why should a sovereign country ask permission of the IMF for every action which it undertakes? One might have understood if Ethiopia's action threatened its ability to repay what was owed the IMF; but quite the contrary, because it was a sensible financial decision, it enhanced the country's ability to repay what was due.

For years, the mantra at the 19th Street headquarters of the IMF in Washington had been accountability and judgment by results. The results of Ethiopia's largely self-determined policies should have demonstrated convincingly that it was a capable master of its own destiny. But the IMF felt countries receiving money from it had an obligation to report everything that might be germane; not to do so was grounds for suspension of the program, regardless of the reasonableness of the action. To Ethiopia, such intrusiveness smacked of a new form of colonialism; to the IMF, it was just standard operating procedure.

There were other sticking points in IMF-Ethiopia relations, concerning Ethiopian financial market liberalization. Good capital markets are the hallmark of capitalism, but nowhere is the disparity between developed and less developed countries greater than in their capital markets. Ethiopia's entire banking system (measured, for instance, by the size of its assets) is somewhat smaller than that of

Bethesda, Maryland, a suburb on the outskirts of Washington with a population of 55,277. The IMF wanted Ethiopia not only to open up its financial markets to Western competition but also to divide its largest bank into several pieces. In a world in which U.S. megafinancial institutions like Citibank and Travelers, or Manufacturers Hanover and Chemical, say they have to merge to compete effectively, a bank the size of North East Bethesda National Bank really has no way to compete against a global giant like Citibank. When global financial institutions enter a country, they can squelch the domestic competition. And as they attract depositors away from the local banks in a country like Ethiopia, they may be far more attentive and generous when it comes to making loans to large multinational corporations than they will to providing credit to small businesses and farmers.

The IMF wanted to do more than just open up the banking system to foreign competition. It wanted to "strengthen" the financial system by creating an auction market for Ethiopia's government Treasury bills—a reform, as desirable as it might be in many countries, which was completely out of tune with that country's state of development. It also wanted Ethiopia to "liberalize" its financial market, that is, allow interest rates to be freely determined by market forces—something the United States and Western Europe did not do until after 1970, when their markets, and the requisite regulatory apparatus, were far more developed. The IMF was confusing ends with means. One of the prime objectives of a good banking system is to provide credit at good terms to those who will repay. In a largely rural country like Ethiopia, it is especially important for farmers to be able to obtain credit at reasonable terms to buy seed and fertilizer. The task of providing such credit is not easy; even in the United States, at critical stages of its development when agriculture was more important, the government took a crucial role in providing needed credit. The Ethiopian banking system was at least seemingly quite efficient, the difference between borrowing and lending rates being far lower than those in other developing countries that had followed the IMF's advice. Still, the Fund was unhappy, simply because it believed interest rates should be freely determined by international market forces, whether those markets were or were not competitive. To the Fund, a liberalized financial system was an end in itself. Its naive faith in markets made it confident that a liberalized financial system would lower interest rates paid on loans and thereby make more funds available. The IMF was so certain about the correctness of its dogmatic position that it had little interest in looking at actual experiences.

Ethiopia resisted the IMF's demand that it "open" its banking system, for good reason. It had seen what happened when one of its East African neighbors gave in to IMF demands. The IMF had insisted on financial market liberalization, believing that competition among banks would lead to lower interest rates. The results were disastrous: the move was followed by the very rapid growth of local and indigenous commercial banks, at a time when the banking legislation and bank supervision were inadequate, with the predictable results—fourteen banking failures in Kenya in 1993 and 1994 alone. In the end, interest rates increased, not decreased. Understandably, the government of Ethiopia was wary. Committed to improving the living standards of its citizens in the rural sector, it feared that liberalization would have a devastating effect on its economy. Those farmers who had previously managed to obtain credit would find themselves unable to buy seed or fertilizer because they would be unable to get cheap credit or would be forced to pay higher interest rates which they could ill afford. This is a country wracked by droughts which result in massive starvation. Its leaders did not want to make matters worse. The Ethiopians worried that the IMF's advice would cause farmers' incomes to fall, exacerbating an already dismal situation.

Faced with Ethiopian reluctance to accede to its demands, the IMF suggested the government was not serious about reform and, as I have said, suspended its program. Happily, other economists in the World Bank and I managed to persuade the Bank management that lending more money to Ethiopia made good sense: it was a country desperately in need, with a first-rate economic framework and a government committed to improving the plight of its poor. World Bank lending tripled, even though it took months before the IMF finally relented on its position. In order to turn the situation around I had, with the invaluable help and support of colleagues, mounted a determined campaign of "intellectual lobbying." In Washington, my colleagues and I held conferences to encourage people at both the IMF and the World Bank to look again at issues of financial sector liberalization in very underdeveloped nations, and the consequences of unnecessarily imposed budgetary austerity in foreign aid–dependent poor countries, as in Ethiopia. I attempted to reach senior managers at the Fund, both directly and through colleagues at the World Bank, and those at the Bank working in Ethiopia made similar efforts to persuade their counterparts at the Fund. I used what influence I could through my connections with the Clinton administration, including talking to America's representative on the Fund. In short, I did everything I could to get the IMF program reinstated.

Assistance was restored, and I would like to think that my efforts helped Ethiopia. I learned, however, that immense time and effort are required to effect change, even from the inside, in an international bureaucracy. Such organizations are opaque rather than transparent, and not only does far too little information radiate from inside to the outside world, perhaps even less information from outside is able to penetrate the organization. The opaqueness also means that it is hard for information from the bottom of the organization to percolate to the top.

The tussle over lending to Ethiopia taught me a lot about how the IMF works. There was clear evidence the IMF was wrong about financial market liberalization and Ethiopia's macroeconomic position, but the IMF had to have its way. It seemingly would not listen to others, no matter how well informed, no matter how disinterested. Matters of substance became subsidiary to matters of process. Whether it made sense for Ethiopia to repay the loan was less important than the fact that it failed to consult the IMF. Financial market liberalization—how best this should be done in a country at Ethiopia's stage of development—was a matter of substance and experts could have been asked for their opinion. The fact that outside experts were not called in to help arbitrate what was clearly a contentious issue is consonant with the style of the IMF, in which the Fund casts itself as the monopoly supplier of "sound" advice. Even matters like the repayment of the loan—though properly not something on which the IMF should have taken a position at all, so long as Ethiopia's action enhanced rather than subtracted from its ability to repay what was owed—could have been referred to outsiders, to see whether the action was "reasonable." But doing so would have been anathema to the IMF. Because so much of its decision making was done behind closed doors—there was virtually no public discussion of the issues just raised—the IMF left itself open to suspicions that power politics, special interests, or other hidden reasons not related to the IMF's mandate and stated objectives were influencing its institutional policies and conduct.

It is hard even for a moderate-sized institution like the IMF to know a great deal about every economy in the world. Some of the best IMF economists were assigned to work on the United States, but when I served as chairman of the Council of Economic Advisers, I often felt that the IMF's limited understanding of the U.S. economy had led it to make misguided policy recommendations for America. The IMF economists felt, for instance, that inflation would start rising in the United States as soon as unemployment fell below 6 percent. At the Council, our models said they were wrong, but they were not terribly interested in our input. We were right, and the IMF was wrong: unemployment in the United States fell to below 4 percent and still inflation did not increase. Based on their faulty analysis of the U.S. economy, the IMF economists came up with a misguided policy prescription: raise interest rates. Fortunately, the Fed paid no attention to the IMF recommendation. Other countries could not ignore it so easily.

But to the IMF the lack of detailed knowledge is of less moment, because it tends to take a "one-size-fits-all" approach. The problems of this approach become particularly acute when facing the challenges of the developing and transition economies. The institution does not really claim expertise in development—its original mandate is supporting global economic stability, as I have said, not reducing poverty in developing countries—yet it does not hesitate to weigh in, and weigh in heavily, on development issues. Development issues are complicated; in many ways developing countries present far greater difficulties than more developed countries. This is because in developing nations, markets are often absent, and when present, often work imperfectly. Information problems abound, and cultural mores may significantly affect economic behavior.

Unfortunately, too often the training of the macroeconomists does not prepare them well for the problems that they have to confront in developing countries. In some of the universities from which the IMF hires regularly, the core curricula involve models in which there is never any unemployment. After all, in the standard competitive model—the model that underlies the IMF's market fundamentalism—demand always equals supply. If the demand for labor equals supply, there is never any *involuntary* unemployment. Someone who is not working has evidently chosen not to work. In this interpretation, unemployment in the Great Depression, when one out of four people was out of work, would be the result of a sudden increase in the desire for more leisure. It might be of some interest to psychologists why there was this sudden change in the desire for leisure, or why those who were supposed to be enjoying this leisure seemed so unhappy, but according to the standard model these questions go beyond the scope of economics. While these models might provide some amusement within academia, they seemed particularly ill suited to understanding the problems of a country like South Africa, which has been plagued with unemployment rates in excess of 25 percent since apartheid was dismantled.

The IMF economists could not, of course, ignore the existence of unemployment. Because under market fundamentalism—in which, *by assumption*, markets work perfectly and demand must equal supply for labor as for every other good or factor—there cannot be unemployment, the problem cannot lie with markets. It must lie elsewhere—with greedy unions and politicians interfering with the workings of free markets, by demanding—and getting—excessively high wages. There is an obvious policy implication—if there is unemployment, wages should be reduced.

But even if the training of the typical IMF macroeconomist had been better suited to the problems of developing countries, it's unlikely that an IMF mission, on a three-week trip to Addis Ababa, Ethiopia's capital, or the capital of any other developing country, could really develop policies appropriate for that country. Such policies are far more likely to be crafted by highly educated, first-rate economists already in the country, deeply knowledgeable about it and working daily on solving that country's problems. Outsiders can play a role, in sharing the experiences of other countries, and in offering alternative interpretations of the economic forces at play. But the IMF did not want to take on the mere role of an adviser, competing with others who might be offering their ideas. It wanted a more central role in shaping policy. And it could do this because its position was based on an ideology—market fundamentalism—that required little, if any, consideration of a country's particular circumstances and immediate problems. IMF economists could ignore the short-term effects their policies might have on the country, content in the belief that *in the long run* the country would be better off; any adverse short-run impacts would be merely pain that was necessary as part of the process. Soaring interest rates might, today, lead to starvation, but market efficiency requires free markets, and eventually, efficiency leads to growth, and growth benefits all. Suffering and pain became part of the process of redemption, evidence that a country was on the right track. To me, sometimes pain *is* necessary, but it is not a virtue in its own right. Well-designed policies can often avoid much of the pain; and some forms of pain—the misery caused by abrupt cuts in food subsidies, for example, which leads to rioting, urban violence, and the dissolution of the social fabric—are counterproductive.

The IMF has done a good job of persuading many that its ideologically driven policies were necessary if countries are to succeed in the long run. Economists always focus on the importance of scarcity and the IMF often says it is simply the messenger of scarcity: countries cannot persistently live beyond their means. One doesn't, of course, need a sophisticated financial institution staffed by Ph.D. economists to tell a country to limit expenditures to revenues. But IMF reform programs go well beyond simply ensuring that countries live within their means.

THERE ARE ALTERNATIVES to IMF-style programs, other programs that may involve a reasonable level of sacrifice, which are not based on market fundamentalism, programs that have had positive outcomes. A good example is Botswana, 2,300 miles south of Ethiopia, a small country of 1.5 million, which has managed a stable democracy since independence.

At the time Botswana became fully independent in 1966 it was a

desperately poor country, like Ethiopia and most of the other countries in Africa, with a per capita annual income of $100. It too was
largely agricultural, lacked water, and had a rudimentary infrastructure. But Botswana is one of the success stories of development.
Although the country is now suffering from the ravages of AIDS, it
averaged a growth rate of more than 7.5 percent from 1961 to 1997.

Botswana was helped by having diamonds, but countries like
Congo Republic (formerly Zaire), Nigeria, and Sierra Leone were
also rich in resources. In those countries, the wealth from this
abundance fueled corruption and spawned privileged elites that
engaged in internecine struggles for control of each country's wealth.
Botswana's success rested on its ability to maintain a political consensus,
based on a broader sense of national unity. That political consensus, necessary to any workable social contract between government and the
governed, had been carefully forged by the government, in collabora-
tion with outside advisers, from a variety of public institutions and
private foundations, including the Ford Foundation. The advisers
helped Botswana map out a program for the country's future. Unlike
the IMF, which largely deals with the finance ministry and central
banks, the advisers openly and candidly explained their policies as
they worked with the government to obtain popular support for the
programs and policies. They discussed the program with senior
Botswana officials, including cabinet ministers and members of Parliament, with open seminars as well as one-to-one meetings.

Part of the reason for this success was that the senior people in
Botswana's government took great care in selecting their advisers.
When the IMF offered to supply the Bank of Botswana with a
deputy governor, the Bank of Botswana did not automatically accept
him. The bank's governor flew to Washington to interview him. He
turned out to do a splendid job. Of course, no success is without
blemishes. On another occasion, the Bank of Botswana allowed the
IMF to pick somebody to be director of research, and that turned
out, at least in the view of some, to be far less successful.

The differences in how the two organizations approached development were reflected not just in performance. While the IMF is vil-
ified almost everywhere in the developing world, the warm
relationship that was created between Botswana and its advisers was

symbolized by the awarding of that country's highest medal to Steve Lewis, who at the time he advised Botswana was a professor of development economics at Williams. (He later became president of Carleton College.)

That vital consensus was threatened two decades ago when Botswana had an economic crisis. A drought threatened the livelihood of the many people engaged in raising cattle and problems in the diamond industry had put a strain on the country's budget and its foreign exchange position. Botswana was suffering exactly the kind of liquidity crisis the IMF had originally been created to deal with— a crisis that could be eased by financing a deficit to forestall recession and hardship. However, while that may have been Keynes's intent when he pushed for the establishment of the IMF, the institution does not now conceive of itself as a deficit financier, committed to maintaining economies at full employment. Rather, it has taken on the pre-Keynesian position of fiscal austerity in the face of a downturn, doling out funds only if the borrowing country conforms to the IMF's views about appropriate economic policy, which almost always entail contractionary policies leading to recessions or worse. Botswana, recognizing the volatility of its two main sectors, cattle and diamonds, had prudently set aside reserve funds for just such a crisis. As it saw its reserves dwindling, it knew that it would have to take further measures. Botswana tightened its belt, pulled together, and got through the crisis. But because of the broad understanding of economic policies that had been developed over the years and the consensus-based approach to policy making, the austerity did not cause the kinds of cleavages in society that have occurred so frequently elsewhere under IMF programs. Presumably, if the IMF had done what it should have been doing—providing funds quickly to countries with good economic policies in times of crisis, without searching around for conditionalities to impose—the country would have been able to wend its way through the crisis with even less pain. (The IMF mission that came in 1981, quite amusingly, found it very difficult to impose new conditions, because Botswana had already done so many of the things that they would have insisted upon.) Since then, Botswana has not turned to the IMF for help.

The assistance of outside advisers—independent of the international financial institutions—had played a role in Botswana's success even earlier. Botswana would not have fared as well as it did if its original contract with the South African diamond cartel had been maintained. Shortly after independence, the cartel paid Botswana $20 million for a diamond concession in 1969, which reportedly returned $60 million in profits a year. In other words, the payback period was four months! A brilliant and dedicated lawyer seconded to the Botswana government from the World Bank argued forcefully for a renegotiation of the contract at a higher price, much to the consternation of the mining interests. De Beers (the South African diamond cartel) tried to tell people that Botswana was being greedy. They used what political muscle they could, through the World Bank, to stop him. In the end, they managed to extract a letter from the World Bank making it clear that the lawyer did not speak for the Bank. Botswana's response: That is precisely why we are listening to him. In the end, the discovery of the second large diamond mine gave Botswana the opportunity to renegotiate the whole relationship. The new agreement has so far served Botswana's interests well, and enabled Botswana and De Beers to maintain good relations.

Ethiopia and Botswana are emblematic of the challenges facing the more successful countries of Africa today: countries with leaders dedicated to the well-being of their people, fragile and in some cases imperfect democracies, attempting to create new lives for their peoples from the wreckage of a colonial heritage that left them without institutions or human resources. The two countries are also emblematic of the contrasts that mark the developing world: contrasts between success and failure, between rich and poor, between hopes and reality, between what is and what might have been.

I BECAME AWARE of this contrast when I first went to Kenya, in the late 1960s. Here was a rich and fertile country, with some of the most valuable land still owned by old colonial settlers. When I arrived, the colonial civil servants were also still there; now they were called advisers.

As I watched developments in East Africa over the ensuing years, and returned for several visits after becoming chief economist of the World Bank, the contrast between the aspirations in the 1960s and the subsequent developments were striking. When I first went, the spirit of *uhuru*, the Swahili word for freedom, and *ujama*, the word for self-help, were in the air. When I returned, the government offices were staffed by well-spoken and well-trained Kenyans; but the economy had been sinking for years. Some of the problems—the seemingly rampant corruption—were of Kenya's own making. But the high interest rates which had resulted from its following IMF advice, as well as other problems, could rightly be blamed at least in part on outsiders.

Uganda had begun the transition in perhaps better shape than any of the others, a relatively rich coffee-growing country, but it lacked trained native administrators and leaders. The British had allowed only two Africans to rise to the level of a master sergeant in their own army. One of them, unfortunately, was a Ugandan named Idi Amin, who ultimately became General Amin in Uganda's army and overthrew Prime Minister Milton Obote in 1971. (Amin enjoyed a certain measure of British confidence thanks to his service in the King's African Rifles in World War II and in Britain's struggle to suppress the Mau-Mau revolt in Kenya.) Amin turned the country into a slaughterhouse; as many as 300,000 people were killed because they were considered opponents of the "President for Life" —as Amin proclaimed himself in 1976. The reign of terror by an arguably psychopathic dictator ended only in 1979 when he was toppled by Ugandan exiles and forces from neighboring Tanzania. Today, the country is on the way to recovery, led by a charismatic leader, Yoweri Museveni, who has instituted major reforms with remarkable success, reducing illiteracy and AIDS. And he is as interesting in talking about political philosophy as he is in talking about development strategies.

BUT THE IMF is not particularly interested in hearing the thoughts of its "client countries" on such topics as development strategy or fiscal austerity. All too often, the Fund's approach to developing countries has had the feel of a colonial ruler. A picture can be worth a thousand words, and a single picture snapped in 1998, shown throughout the world, has engraved itself in the minds of millions, particularly those in the former colonies. The IMF's managing director, Michel Camdessus (the head of the IMF is referred to as its "Managing Director"), a short, neatly dressed former French Treasury bureaucrat, who once claimed to be a Socialist, is standing with a stern face and crossed arms over the seated and humiliated president of Indonesia. The hapless president was being forced, in effect, to turn over economic sovereignty of his country to the IMF in return for the aid his country needed. In the end, ironically, much of the money went not to help Indonesia but to bail out the "colonial power's" private sector creditors. (Officially, the "ceremony" was the signing of a letter of agreement, an agreement effectively dictated by the IMF, though it often still keeps up the pretense that the letter of intent comes from the country's government!)

Defenders of Camdessus claim the photograph was unfair, that he did not realize that it was being taken and that it was viewed out of context. But that is the point—in day-to-day interactions, away from cameras and reporters, this is precisely the stance that the IMF bureaucrats take, from the leader of the organization on down. To those in the developing countries, the picture raised a very disturbing question: Had things really changed since the "official" ending of colonialism a half century ago? When I saw the picture, images of other signings of "agreements" came to mind. I wondered how similar this scene was to those marking the "opening up of Japan" with Admiral Perry's gunboat diplomacy or the end of the Opium Wars or the surrender of maharajas in India.

The stance of the IMF, like the stance of its leader, was clear: it was the font of wisdom, the purveyor of an orthodoxy too subtle to be grasped by those in the developing world. The message conveyed was all too often clear: in the best of cases there was a member of an elite—a minister of finance or the head of a central bank—with whom the Fund might have a meaningful dialogue. Outside of this circle, there was little point in even trying to talk.

A quarter of a century ago, those in the developing countries might rightly have given some deference to the "experts" from the IMF. But just as there has been a shift in the military balance of power, there has been an even more dramatic shift in the intellectual balance of power. The developing world now has its own economists—many of them trained at the world's best academic institutions. These economists have the significant advantage of lifelong familiarity with local politics, conditions, and trends. The IMF is like so many bureaucracies; it has repeatedly sought to extend what it does, beyond the bounds of the objectives originally assigned to it. As IMF's mission creep gradually brought it outside its core area of competency in macroeconomics, into structural issues, such as privatization, labor markets, pension reforms, and so forth, and into broader areas of development strategies, the intellectual balance of power became even more tilted.

The IMF, of course, claims that it never dictates but always negotiates the terms of any loan agreement with the borrowing country. But these are one-sided negotiations in which all the power is in the hands of the IMF, largely because many countries seeking IMF help are in desperate need of funds. Although I had seen this so clearly in Ethiopia and the other developing countries with which I was involved, it was brought home again to me during my visit to South Korea in December 1997, as the East Asia crisis was unfolding. South Korea's economists knew that the policies being pushed on their country by the IMF would be disastrous. While, in retrospect, even the IMF agreed that it imposed excessive fiscal stringency, in prospect, few economists (outside the IMF) thought the policy made sense.[2] Yet Korea's economic officials remained silent. I wondered why they had kept this silence, but did not get an answer from officials inside the government until a subsequent visit two years later, when the Korean economy had recovered. The answer was what, given past experience, I had suspected all along. Korean officials reluctantly explained that they had been scared to disagree openly. The IMF could not only cut off its own funds, but could use its bully pulpit to discourage investments from private market funds by telling private sector financial institutions of the doubts the IMF had about Korea's economy. So Korea had no choice. Even implied criticism by Korea of the IMF program could have a disastrous effect: to the IMF, it would suggest that the government didn't fully understand "IMF economics," that it had reservations, making it less likely that it would actually carry out the program. (The IMF has a special phrase for describing such situations: the country has gone "off track." There is one "right" way, and any deviation is a sign of an impending derailment.) A public announcement by the IMF that negotiations had broken off, or even been postponed, would send a highly negative signal to the markets. This signal would at best lead to higher interest rates and at worst a total cutoff from private funds. Even more serious for some of the poorest countries, which have in any case little access to private funds, is that other donors (the World Bank, the European Union, and many other countries) make access to their funds contingent on IMF approval. Recent initiatives for debt relief have effectively given the IMF even more power, because unless the IMF approves the country's economic policy, there will be no debt relief. This gives the IMF enormous leverage, as the IMF well knows.

The imbalance of power between the IMF and the "client" countries inevitably creates tension between the two, but the IMF's own behavior in negotiations exacerbates an already difficult situation. In dictating the terms of the agreements, the IMF effectively stifles any discussions within a client government—let alone more broadly within the country—about alternative economic policies. In times of crises, the IMF would defend its stance by saying there simply wasn't time. But its behavior was little different in or out of crisis. The IMF's view was simple: questions, particularly when raised vociferously and openly, would be viewed as a challenge to the inviolate orthodoxy. If accepted, they might even undermine its authority and credibility. Government leaders knew this and took the cue: they might argue in private, but not in public. The chance of modifying the Fund's views was tiny, while the chance of annoying Fund leaders and provoking them to take a tougher position on other issues was far greater. And if they were angry or annoyed, the IMF could postpone its loans—a scary prospect for a country facing a crisis. But the fact that the government officials *seemed* to go along with the IMF's recommendation did not mean that they really agreed. And the IMF knew it.

Even a casual reading of the terms of the typical agreements between the IMF and the developing countries showed the lack of trust between the Fund and its recipients. The IMF staff monitored progress, not just on the relevant indicators for sound macromanagement—inflation, growth, and unemployment—but on intermediate variables, such as the money supply, often only loosely connected to the variables of ultimate concern. Countries were put on strict targets—what would be accomplished in thirty days, in sixty days, in ninety days. In some cases the agreements stipulated what laws the country's Parliament would have to pass to meet IMF requirements or "targets"—and by when.

These requirements are referred to as "conditions," and "conditionality" is a hotly debated topic in the development world. Every loan document specifies basic conditions, of course. At a minimum, a loan agreement says the loan goes out on the condition that it will be repaid, usually with a schedule attached. Many loans impose conditions designed to increase the likelihood that they will be repaid. "Conditionality" refers to more forceful conditions, ones that often turn the loan into a policy tool. If the IMF wanted a nation to liberalize its financial markets, for instance, it might pay out the loan in installments, tying subsequent installments to verifiable steps toward liberalization. I personally believe that conditionality, at least in the manner and extent to which it has been used by the IMF, is a bad idea; there is little evidence that it leads to improved economic policy, but it does have adverse political effects because countries resent having conditions imposed on them. Some defend conditionality by saying that any banker imposes conditions on borrowers, to make it more likely that the loan will be repaid. But the conditionality imposed by the IMF and the World Bank was very different. In some cases, it even *reduced* the likelihood of repayment.

For instance, conditions that might weaken the economy in the short run, whatever their merits in the long, run the risk of exacerbating the downturn and thus making it more difficult for the country to repay the short-term IMF loans. Eliminating trade barriers, monopolies, and tax distortions may enhance long-run growth, but the disturbances to the economy, as it strives to adjust, may only deepen its downturn.

While the conditionalities could not be justified in terms of the Fund's fiduciary responsibility, they might be justified in terms of what it might have perceived as its moral responsibility, its obligation to do everything it could to strengthen the economy of the countries that had turned to it for help. But the danger was that even when well intentioned, the myriad of conditions—in some cases over a hundred, each with its own rigid timetable—detracted from the country's ability to address the central pressing problems.

The conditions went beyond economics into areas that properly belong in the realm of politics. In the case of Korea, for instance, the loans included a change in the charter of the Central Bank, to make it more independent of the political process, though there was scant evidence that countries with more independent central banks grow faster[3] or have fewer or shallower fluctuations. There is a widespread feeling that Europe's independent Central Bank exacerbated Europe's economic slowdown in 2001, as, like a child, it responded peevishly to the natural political concerns over the growing unemployment. Just to show that it was independent, it refused to allow interest rates to fall, and there was nothing anyone could do about it. The problems partly arose because the European Central Bank has a mandate to focus on inflation, a policy which the IMF has advocated around the world but one that can stifle growth or exacerbate an economic downturn. In the midst of Korea's crisis, the Korean Central Bank was told not only to be more independent but to focus exclusively on inflation, although Korea had not had a problem with inflation, and there was no reason to believe that mismanaged monetary policy had anything to do with the crisis. The IMF simply used the opportunity that the crisis gave it to push its political agenda. When, in Seoul, I asked the IMF team why they were doing this, I found the answer shocking (though by then it should not have come as a surprise): We always insist that countries have an independent central bank focusing on inflation. This was an issue on which I felt strongly. When I had been the president's chief economic adviser, we beat back an attempt by Senator Connie Mack of Florida to change the charter of the U.S. Federal Reserve Bank to focus exclusively on inflation. The Fed, America's central bank, has a mandate to focus not just on inflation but also on employment and growth. The president opposed the change, and we knew that, if anything, the American people thought the Fed already focused *too much* on inflation. The president made it clear that this was an issue he would fight, and as soon as this was made clear, the proponents backed off. Yet here was the IMF—partially under the influence of the U.S. Treasury—imposing a political condition on Korea that most Americans would have found unacceptable for themselves.

Sometimes, the conditions seemed little more than a simple exercise of power: in its 1997 lending agreement to Korea, the IMF insisted on moving up the date of opening Korea's markets to certain Japanese goods although this could not possibly help Korea address the problems of the crisis. To some, these actions represented "seizing the window of opportunity," using the crisis to leverage in changes that the IMF and World Bank had long been pushing; but to others, these were simply acts of pure political might, extracting a concession, of limited value, simply as a demonstration of who was running the show.

While conditionality did engender resentment, it did not succeed in engendering development. Studies at the World Bank and elsewhere showed not just that conditionality did not *ensure* that money was well spent and that countries would grow faster but that there was little evidence it worked at all. Good policies cannot be bought.

THERE ARE SEVERAL reasons for the failure of conditionality. The simplest has to do with the economists' basic notion of fungibility, which simply refers to the fact that money going in for one purpose frees up other money for another use; the net impact may have nothing to do with the intended purpose. Even if conditions are imposed which ensure that this particular loan is used well, the loan frees up resources elsewhere, which may or may not be used well. A country may have two road projects, one to make it easier for the president to get to his summer villa, the other to enable a large group of farmers to bring their goods to a neighboring port. The country may have funds for only one of the two projects. The Bank may insist that its money go for the project that increases the income of the rural poor; but in providing that money, it enables the government to fund the other.

There were other reasons why the Fund's conditionality did not enhance economic growth. In some cases, they were the wrong conditions: financial market liberalization in Kenya and fiscal austerity in East Asia had adverse effects on the countries. In other cases, the way conditionality was imposed made the conditions politically unsustainable; when a new government came into power, they would be abandoned. Such conditions were seen as the intrusion by the new colonial power on the country's own sovereignty. The policies could not withstand the vicissitudes of the political process.

There was a certain irony in the stance of the IMF. It tried to pretend that it was above politics, yet it was clear that its lending program was, in part, driven by politics. The IMF made an issue of corruption in Kenya and halted its relatively small lending program largely because of the corruption it witnessed there. Yet it maintained a flow of money, billions of dollars, to Russia and Indonesia. To some, it seemed that while the Fund was overlooking grand larceny, it was taking a strong stand on petty theft. It should not have been kinder to Kenya—the theft was indeed large relative to the economy; it should have been tougher on Russia. The issue is not just a matter of fairness or consistency; the world is an unfair place, and no one really expected the IMF to treat a nuclear power the same way that it treated a poor African country of little strategic importance. The point was far simpler: the lending decisions were political—and political judgments often entered into IMF advice. The IMF pushed privatization in part because it believed governments could not, in managing enterprises, insulate themselves from political pressures. The very notion that one could separate economics from politics, or a broader understanding of society, illustrated a narrowness of perspective. If policies imposed by lenders induce riots, as has happened in country after country, then economic conditions worsen, as capital flees and businesses worry about investing more of their money. Such policies are not a recipe either for successful development or for economic stability.

The complaints against the IMF imposition of conditions extended beyond what conditions and how they were imposed, but were directed at how they were arrived at as well. The standard IMF procedure before visiting a client country is to write a draft report first. The visit is only intended to fine-tune the report and its recommendations, and to catch any glaring mistakes. In practice, the draft report is often what is known as boilerplate, with whole paragraphs being borrowed from the report of one country and inserted into another. Word processors make this easier. A perhaps apocryphal story has it that on one occasion a word processor failed to do a "search and replace," and the name of the country from which a report had been borrowed almost in its entirety was left in a document that was circulated. It is hard to know whether this was a one-off occurrence, done under time pressure, but the alleged foulup confirmed in the minds of many the image of "one-size-fits-all" reports.

Even countries not borrowing money from the IMF can be affected by its views. It is not just through conditionality that the Fund imposes its perspectives throughout the world. The IMF has an annual consultation with every country in the world. The consultations, referred to as "Article 4" consultations after the article in its charter that authorized them, are supposed to ensure that each country is adhering to the articles of agreement under which the IMF was established (fundamentally ensuring exchange rate convertibility for trade purposes). Mission creep has affected this report as it has other aspects of IMF activity: the real Article 4 consultations are but a minor part of the entire surveillance process. The report is really the IMF's grading of the nation's economy.

While small countries often had to listen to the Article 4 evaluations, the United States and other countries with developed economies could basically ignore them. For instance, the IMF suffered from inflation paranoia, even when the United States was facing the lowest inflation rates in decades. Its prescription was therefore predictable: increase interest rates to slow down the economy. The IMF simply had no understanding of the changes that were then occurring, and had been occurring over the preceding decade in the U.S. economy that allowed it to enjoy faster growth, lower unemployment, and low inflation all at the same time. Had the IMF's advice been followed, the United States would not have experienced the boom in the American economy over the 1990s—a boom that brought unprecedented prosperity and enabled the country to turn around its massive fiscal deficit into a sizable surplus. The lower unemployment also had profound social consequences—issues to which the IMF paid little attention anywhere. Millions of workers who had been excluded from the labor force were brought in, reducing poverty and welfare roles at an unprecedented pace. This in turn brought down the crime rate. All Americans benefited. The low unemployment rate, in turn, encouraged individuals to take risks, to accept jobs without job security; and that willingness to take risks has proven an essential ingredient in America's success in the so-called New Economy.

The United States ignored the IMF's advice. Neither the Clinton administration nor the Federal Reserve paid much attention to it. The United States could do so with impunity because it was not dependent on the IMF or other donors for assistance, and we knew that the market would pay almost as little attention to it as we did. The market would not punish us for ignoring its advice or reward us for following it. But poor countries around the world are not so lucky. They ignore the Fund's advice only at their peril.

There are at least two reasons why the IMF should consult widely *within* a country as it makes its assessments and designs its programs. Those within the country are likely to know more about the economy than the IMF staffers—as I saw so clearly even in the case of the United States. And for the programs to be implemented in an effective and sustainable manner, there must be a commitment of the country behind the program, based on a broad consensus. Such a consensus can only be arrived at through discussion—the kind of open discussion that, in the past, the IMF shunned. To be fair to the IMF, in the midst of a crisis there is often little time for an open debate, the kind of broad consultation required to build a consensus. But the IMF has been in the African countries for years. If it is a crisis, it is a permanent ongoing crisis. There is time for consultations and consensus building—and in a few cases, such as Ghana, the World Bank (while my predecessor, Michael Bruno, was chief economist) succeeded in doing that, and these have been among the more successful cases of macroeconomic stabilization.

At the World Bank, during the time I was there, there was an increasing conviction that participation mattered, that policies and programs could not be imposed on countries but to be successful had to be "owned" by them, that consensus building was essential, that policies and development strategies had to be adapted to the situation in the country, that there should be a shift from "conditionality" to "selectivity," rewarding countries that had proven track records for using funds well with more funds, trusting them to continue to make good use of their funds, and providing them with strong incentives. This was reflected in the new Bank rhetoric, articulated forcefully by the Bank's president, James D. Wolfensohn: "The country should be put in the driver's seat." Even so, many critics say this process has not gone far enough and that the Bank still expects to remain in control. They worry that the country may be in the driver's seat of a dual-control car, in which the controls are really in the hands of the instructor. Changes in attitudes and operating procedures in the Bank will inevitably be slow, proceeding at different paces in its programs in different countries. But there remains a large gap between where the Bank is on these matters and where the IMF is, both in attitudes and procedures.

As much as it might like, the IMF, in its public rhetoric at least, could not be completely oblivious to the widespread demands for greater participation by the poor countries in the formulation of development strategies and for greater attention to be paid to poverty. As a result, the IMF and the World Bank have agreed to conduct "participatory" poverty assessments in which client countries join the two institutions in measuring the size of the problem as a first step. This was potentially a dramatic change in philosophy—but its full import seemed to escape the IMF. On one recent occasion, recognizing that the Bank was supposed to be taking the lead on poverty projects, just before the initial and, theoretically, consultative IMF mission to a certain client country prepared to depart, the IMF sent an imperious message to the Bank to have a draft of the client country's "participatory" poverty assessment sent to IMF headquarters "asap." Some of us joked that the IMF was confused. It thought the big philosophical change was that in joint Bank–IMF missions, the Bank could actually participate by having a say in what was written. The idea that citizens in a borrowing country might also participate was simply too much! Stories of this kind would be amusing were they not so deeply worrying.

Even if, however, the participatory poverty assessments are not perfectly implemented, they are a step in the right direction. Even if there remains a gap between the rhetoric and the reality, the recognition that those in the developing country ought to have a major voice in their programs is important. But if the gap persists for too long or remains too great, there will be a sense of disillusionment. Already, in some quarters, doubts are being raised, and increasingly loudly. While the participatory poverty assessments have engendered far more public discussion, more participation, than had previously been the case, in many countries expectations of participation and openness have not been fully realized, and there is growing discontent.

In the United States and other successful democracies citizens regard transparency, openness, knowing what government is doing, as an essential part of government accountability. Citizens regard these as *rights*, not favors conferred by the government. The Freedom of Information Act of 1966 has become an important part of American democracy. By contrast, in the IMF style of operation, citizens (an annoyance because they all too often might be reluctant to go along with the agreements, let alone share in the perceptions of what is good economic policy) were not only barred from discussions of agreements; they were not even told what the agreements were. Indeed, the prevailing culture of secrecy was so strong that the IMF kept much of the negotiations and some of the agreements secret from World Bank members even in joint missions! The IMF staff provided information strictly on a "need to know" basis. The "need to know" list was limited to the head of the IMF mission, a few people at IMF headquarters in Washington, and a few people in the client country's government. My colleagues at the Bank frequently complained that even those participating in a mission had to go to the government of the country who "leaked" what was going on. On a few occasions, I met with executive directors (the title for representatives that nations post to the IMF and the World Bank) who had apparently been kept in the dark.

One recent episode shows how far the consequences of lack of transparency can go. The notion that developing countries might have little voice in the international economic institutions is widely recognized. There may be a debate about whether this is just a historical anachronism or a manifestation of *realpolitik*. But we should expect that the U.S. government—including the U.S. Congress—should have some say, at least in how its executive director, the one who represents the United States at the IMF and the World Bank, votes. In 2001, Congress passed and the president signed a law requiring the United States to oppose proposals for the international financial institutions to charge fees for elementary school (a practice that goes under the seeming innocuous name of "cost recovery"). Yet the U.S. executive director simply ignored the law, and the secrecy of the institutions made it difficult for Congress—or anyone else—to see what was going on. Only because of a leak was the matter discovered, generating outrage even among congressmen and women accustomed to bureaucratic maneuvering.

Today, in spite of the repeated discussions of openness and transparency, the IMF still does not formally recognize the citizen's basic "right to know": there is no Freedom of Information Act to which an American, or a citizen of any other country, can appeal to find out what this international *public* institution is doing.

I should be clear: all of these criticisms of how the IMF operates do not mean the IMF's money and time is always wasted. Sometimes money has gone to governments with good policies in place—but not necessarily because the IMF recommended these policies. Then, the money did make a difference for the good. Sometimes, conditionality shifted the debate inside the country in ways that led to better policies. The rigid timetables that the IMF imposed grew partly from a multitude of experiences in which governments promised to make certain reforms, but once they had the money, the reforms were not forthcoming; sometimes, the rigid timetables helped force the pace of change. But all too often, the conditionality did not ensure either that the money was well used or that meaningful, deep, and long-lasting policy changes occurred. Sometimes, conditionality was even counterproductive, either because the policies were not well suited to the country or because the way they were imposed engendered hostility to the reform process. Sometimes, the IMF program left the country just as impoverished but with more debt and an even richer ruling elite.

The international institutions have thus escaped the kind of direct accountability that we expect of public institutions in modern democracies. The time has come to "grade" the international economic institution's performance and to look at some of those programs—and how well, or poorly, they did in promoting growth and reducing poverty.

CHAPTER 3

FREEDOM TO CHOOSE?

FISCAL AUSTERITY, PRIVATIZATION, and market liberalization were the three pillars of Washington Consensus advice throughout the 1980s and 1990s. The Washington Consensus policies were designed to respond to the very real problems in Latin America, and made considerable sense. In the 1980s, the governments of those countries had often run huge deficits. Losses in inefficient government enterprises contributed to those deficits. Insulated from competition by protectionist measures, inefficient private firms forced customers to pay high prices. Loose monetary policy led to inflation running out of control. Countries cannot persistently run large deficits; and sustained growth is not possible with hyperinflation. Some level of fiscal discipline is required. Most countries would be better off with governments focusing on providing essential public services rather than running enterprises that would arguably perform better in the private sector, and so privatization often makes sense. When trade liberalization—the lowering of tariffs and elimination of other protectionist measures—is done in the right way and at the right pace, so that new jobs are created as inefficient jobs are destroyed, there can be significant efficiency gains.

The problem was that many of these policies became ends in themselves, rather than means to more equitable and sustainable growth. In doing so, these policies were pushed too far, too fast, and to the exclusion of other policies that were needed.

The results have been far from those intended. Fiscal austerity pushed too far, under the wrong circumstances, can induce recessions, and high interest rates may impede fledgling business enterprises. The IMF vigorously pursued privatization and liberalization, at a pace and in a manner that often imposed very real costs on countries ill-equipped to incur them.

Privatization

In many developing—and developed—countries, governments all too often spend too much energy doing things they shouldn't do. This distracts them from what they should be doing. The problem is not so much that the government is too big, but that it is not doing the right thing. Governments, by and large, have little business running steel mills, and typically make a mess of it. (Although the most efficient steel mills in the world are those established and run by the Korean and Taiwanese governments, they are an exception.) In general, competing private enterprises can perform such functions more efficiently. This is the argument for privatization—converting state-run industries and firms into private ones. However, there are some important preconditions that have to be satisfied before privatization can contribute to an economy's growth. And the way privatization is accomplished makes a great deal of difference.

Unfortunately, the IMF and the World Bank have approached the issues from a narrow ideological perspective—privatization was to be pursued rapidly. Scorecards were kept for the countries making the transition from communism to the market: those who privatized faster were given the high marks. As a result, privatization often did not bring the benefits that were promised. The problems that arose from these failures have created antipathy to the very idea of privatization.

In 1998 I visited some poor villages in Morocco to see the impact that projects undertaken by the World Bank and nongovernmental organizations (NGOs) were having on the lives of the people there. I saw, for instance, how community-based irrigation projects were increasing farm productivity enormously. One project, however, had failed. An NGO had painstakingly instructed local villagers on raising chickens, an enterprise that the village women could perform as they continued more traditional activities. Originally, the women obtained their seven-day-old chicks from a government enterprise. But when I visited the village, this new enterprise had collapsed. I discussed with villagers and government officials what had gone wrong. The answer was simple: The government had been told by the IMF that it should not be in the business of distributing chicks, so it ceased selling them. It was simply *assumed* that the private sector would immediately fill the gap. Indeed, a new private supplier arrived to provide the villagers with newborn chicks. The death rate of chicks in the first two weeks is high, however, and the private firm was unwilling to provide a guarantee. The villagers simply could not bear the risk of buying chicks that might die in large numbers. Thus, a nascent industry, poised to make a difference in the lives of these poor peasants, was shut down.

The assumption underlying this failure is one that I saw made repeatedly; the IMF simply assumed that markets arise quickly to meet every need, when in fact, many government activities arise because markets have *failed* to provide essential services. Examples abound. Outside the United States, this point often seems obvious. When many European countries created their social security systems and unemployment and disability insurance systems, there were no well-functioning private annuity markets, no private firms that would sell insurance against these risks that played such an important role in individuals' lives. Even when the United States created its social security system, much later, in the depths of the Great Depression as part of the New Deal, private markets for annuities did not work well—and even today one cannot get annuities that insure one against inflation. Again, in the United States, one of the reasons for the creation of the Federal National Mortgage Association (Fannie Mae) was that the private market did not provide mortgages at reasonable terms to low- and middle-income families. In developing countries, these problems are even worse; eliminating the government enterprise may leave a huge gap—and even if eventually the private sector enters, there can be enormous suffering in the meanwhile.

In Côte d'Ivoire, the telephone company was privatized, as is so often the case, *before* either an adequate regulatory or competition framework was put into place. The government was persuaded by the French firm that purchased the state's assets into giving it a monopoly, not only on the existing telephone services but on new cellular services as well. The private firm raised prices so high that, for instance, university students reportedly could not afford Internet connections, essential to prevent the already huge gap in digital access between rich and poor from widening even further.

The IMF argues that it is far more important to privatize quickly; one can deal with the issues of competition and regulation later. But the danger here is that once a vested interest has been created, it has an incentive, and the money, to maintain its monopoly position, squelching regulation and competition, and distorting the political process along the way. There is a natural reason why the IMF has been less concerned about competition and regulation than it might have been. Privatizing an unregulated monopoly can yield more revenue to the government, and the IMF focuses far more on macroeconomic issues, such as the size of the government's deficit, than on structural issues, such as the efficiency and competitiveness of the industry. Whether the privatized monopolies were more efficient in production than government, they were often more efficient in exploiting their monopoly position; consumers suffered as a result.

Privatization has also come not just at the expense of consumers but at the expense of workers as well. The impact on employment has perhaps been both the major argument for and against privatization, with advocates arguing that only through privatization can unproductive workers be shed, and critics arguing that job cuts occur with no sensitivity to the social costs. There is, in fact, considerable truth in both positions. Privatization often turns state enterprises from losses to profits by trimming the payroll. Economists, however, are supposed to focus on overall efficiency. There are social costs associated with unemployment, *which private firms simply do not take into account*. Given minimal job protections, employers can dismiss workers, with little or no costs, including, at best, minimal severance pay. Privatization has been so widely criticized because, unlike so-called Greenfield investments—investments in new firms as opposed to private investors taking over existing firms—privatization often destroys jobs rather than creating new ones.

In industrialized countries, the pain of layoffs is acknowledged and somewhat ameliorated by the safety net of unemployment insurance. In less developed countries, the unemployed workers typically do not become a public charge, since there are seldom unemployment insurance schemes. There can be a large social cost nonetheless—manifested, in its worst forms, by urban violence, increased crime, and social and political unrest. But even in the absence of these problems, there are huge costs of unemployment. They include widespread anxiety even among workers who have managed to keep their jobs, a broader sense of alienation, additional financial burdens on family members who manage to remain employed, and the withdrawal of children from school to help support the family. These kinds of social costs endure long past the immediate loss of a job. They are often especially apparent in the case when a firm is sold to foreigners. Domestic firms may at least be attuned to the social context* and be reluctant to fire workers if they know there are no alternative jobs available. Foreign owners, on the other hand, may feel a greater obligation to their shareholders to maximize stock market value by reducing costs, and less of an obligation to what they will refer to as an "overbloated labor force."

It is important to restructure state enterprises, and privatization is often an effective way to do so. But moving people from low-productivity jobs in state enterprises to unemployment does not increase a country's income, and it certainly does not increase the welfare of the workers. The moral is a simple one, and one to which I shall return repeatedly: Privatization needs to be part of a more comprehensive program, which entails creating jobs *in tandem with* the inevitable job destruction that privatization often entails. Macroeconomic policies, including low interest rates, that help create jobs, have to be put in place. Timing (and sequencing) is everything. These are

*I saw this forcefully in my discussions in Korea. Private owners showed an enormous social conscience in letting their workers go; they felt that there was a social contract, which they were reluctant to abrogate, even if it meant that they themselves would lose money.

not just issues of pragmatics, of "implementation": these are issues of principle.

Perhaps the most serious concern with privatization, as it has so often been practiced, is corruption. The rhetoric of market fundamentalism asserts that privatization will reduce what economists call the "rent-seeking" activity of government officials who either skim off the profits of government enterprises or award contracts and jobs to their friends. But in contrast to what it was supposed to do, privatization has made matters so much worse that in many countries today privatization is jokingly referred to as "briberization." If a government is corrupt, there is little evidence that privatization will solve the problem. After all, the same corrupt government that mismanaged the firm will also handle the privatization. In country after country, government officials have realized that privatization meant that they no longer needed to be limited to annual profit skimming. By selling a government enterprise at below market price, they could get a significant chunk of the asset value for themselves rather than leaving it for subsequent officeholders. In effect, they could steal today much of what would have been skimmed off by future politicians. Not surprisingly, the rigged privatization process was designed to maximize the amount government ministers could appropriate for themselves, not the amount that would accrue to the government's treasury, let alone the overall efficiency of the economy. As we will see, Russia provides a devastating case study of the harm of "privatization at all costs."

Privatization advocates naively persuaded themselves these costs could be overlooked because the textbooks seemed to say that once private property rights were clearly defined, the new owners would ensure that the assets would be efficiently managed. Thus the situation would improve in the long term even if it was ugly in the short term. They failed to realize that without the appropriate legal structures and market institutions, the new owners might have an incentive to strip assets rather than use them as a basis for expanding industry. As a result, in Russia, and many other countries, privatization failed to be as effective a force for growth as it might have been. Indeed, sometimes it was associated with decline and proved to be a powerful force for undermining confidence in democratic and market institutions.

Liberalization

Liberalization—the removal of government interference in financial markets, capital markets, and of barriers to trade—has many dimensions. Today, even the IMF agrees that it has pushed that agenda too far—that liberalizing capital and financial markets contributed to the global financial crises of the 1990s and can wreak havoc on a small emerging country.

The one aspect of liberalization that does have widespread support—at least among the elites in the advanced industrial countries—is trade liberalization. But a closer look at how it has worked out in many developing countries serves to illustrate why it is so often so strongly opposed, as seen in the protests in Seattle, Prague, and Washington, DC.

Trade liberalization is supposed to enhance a country's income by forcing resources to move from less productive uses to more productive uses; as economists would say, utilizing comparative advantage. But moving resources from low-productivity uses to *zero* productivity does not enrich a country, and this is what happened all too often under IMF programs. It is easy to destroy jobs, and this is often the immediate impact of trade liberalization, as inefficient industries close down under pressure from international competition. IMF ideology holds that new, more productive jobs will be created as the old, inefficient jobs that have been created behind protectionist walls are eliminated. But that is simply not the case—and few economists have believed in instantaneous job creation, at least since the Great Depression. It takes capital and entrepreneurship to create new firms and jobs, and in developing countries there is often a shortage of the latter, due to lack of education, and of the former, due to lack of bank financing. The IMF in many countries has made matters worse, because its austerity programs often also entailed such high interest rates—sometimes exceeding 20 percent, sometimes exceeding 50 percent, sometimes even exceeding 100 percent—that job and enter-

prise creation would have been an impossibility even in a good economic environment such as the United States. The necessary capital
for growth is simply too costly.

The most successful developing countries, those in East Asia,
opened themselves to the outside world but did so slowly and in a
sequenced way. These countries took advantage of globalization to
expand their exports and grew faster as a result. But they dropped
protective barriers carefully and systematically, phasing them out only
when new jobs were created. They ensured that there was capital
available for new job and enterprise creation; and they even took an
entrepreneurial role in promoting new enterprises. China is just dis-
mantling its trade barriers, twenty years after its march to the market
began, a period in which it grew extremely rapidly.

Those in the United States and the advanced industrialized countries should have found it easy to grasp these concerns. In the last
two U.S. presidential campaigns, the candidate Pat Buchanan has
exploited American workers' worries about job loss from trade liberalization. Buchanan's themes resonated even in a country with close
to full employment (by 1999, the unemployment rate had fallen to
under 4 percent), coupled with a good unemployment insurance system and a variety of assistance to help workers move from one job to
another. The fact that, even during the booming 1990s, American
workers could be so worried about the threat of liberalized trade to
their jobs should have led to a greater understanding of the plight of
workers in poor developing countries, where they live on the verge
of subsistence, often on $2 a day or less, with no safety net in the
form of savings, much less unemployment insurance, and in an economy with 20 percent or more unemployment.

The fact that trade liberalization all too often fails to live up to its
promise—but instead simply leads to more unemployment—is why
it provokes strong opposition. But the *hypocrisy* of those pushing for
trade liberalization—and the way they have pushed it—has no doubt
reinforced hostility to trade liberalization. The Western countries
pushed trade liberalization for the products that they exported, but
at the same time continued to protect those sectors in which competition from developing countries might have threatened their
economies. This was one of the bases of the opposition to the new

round of trade negotiations that was supposed to be launched in Seattle; previous rounds of trade negotiations had protected the interests of the advanced industrial countries—or more accurately, special interests within those countries—without concomitant benefits for the lesser developed countries. Protestors pointed out, quite rightly, that the earlier rounds of trade negotiations had lowered trade barriers on industrial goods, from automobiles to machinery, exported by the advanced industrial countries. At the same time, negotiators for these countries maintained their nations' subsidies on agricultural goods and kept closed the markets for these goods and for textiles, where many developing countries have a comparative advantage.

In the most recent Uruguay Round of trade negotiations, the subject of trade in services was introduced. In the end, however, markets were opened mainly for the services exported by the advanced countries—financial services and information technology—but not for maritime and construction services, where the developing countries might have been able to gain a toehold. The United States bragged about the benefits it received. But the developing countries did not get a proportionate share of the gains. One World Bank calculation showed that Sub-Saharan Africa, the poorest region in the world, saw its income decline by more than 2 percent as a result of the trade agreement. There were other examples of inequities that increasingly became the subject of discourse in the developing world, though the issues seldom made it into print in the more developed nations. Bolivia not only brought down its trade barriers to the point that they were lower than those in the United States but also cooperated with the United States in virtually eradicating the growth of coca, the basis of cocaine, even though this crop provided a higher income to its already poor farmers than any alternative. The United States responded, however, by keeping its markets closed to the alternative agriculture products, like sugar, that Bolivia's farmers might have produced for export—had America's markets been open to them.

Developing countries get especially angry over this sort of double standard because of the long history of hypocrisy and inequities. In the nineteenth century the Western powers—many of which had grown through using protectionist policies—had pushed unfair trade treaties. The most outrageous, perhaps, followed the Opium Wars, when the United Kingdom and France ganged up against a weak China, and together with Russia and the United States forced it, in the Treaty of Tientsin in 1858, not just to make trade and territorial concessions, ensuring it would export the goods the West wanted at low prices, but to open its markets *to opium*, so that millions in China would become addicted. (One might call this an almost diabolical approach to a "balance of trade.") Today, the emerging markets are not forced open under the threat of the use of military might, but through economic power, through the threat of sanctions or the withholding of needed assistance in a time of crisis. While the World Trade Organization was the forum within which international trade agreements were negotiated, U.S. trade negotiators and the IMF have often insisted on going further, accelerating the pace of trade liberalization. The IMF insists on this faster pace of liberalization as a condition for assistance—and countries facing a crisis feel they have no choice but to accede to the Fund's demands.

Matters are perhaps worse still when the United States acts unilaterally rather than behind the cloak of the IMF. The U.S. Trade Representative or the Department of Commerce, often prodded by special interests within the United States, brings an accusation against a foreign country; there is then a review process—involving only the U.S. government—with a decision made by the United States, after which sanctions are brought against the offending country. The United States sets itself up as prosecutor, judge, and jury. There is a quasi-judicial process, but the cards are stacked: both the rules and the judges favor a finding of guilty. When this arsenal is brought against other industrial countries, Europe and Japan, they have the resources to defend themselves; when it comes to the developing countries, even large ones like India and China, it is an unfair match. The ill will that results is far out of proportion to any possible gain for the United States. The process itself does little to reinforce confidence in a just international trading system.

The rhetoric the United States uses to push its position adds to the image of a superpower willing to throw its weight around for its own special interests. Mickey Kantor, when he was the U.S. Trade Representative in the first Clinton administration, wanted to push China to open its markets faster. The 1994 Uruguay Round negotiations, in which he himself had played a major role, established the WTO and set ground rules for members. The agreement had quite rightly provided a longer adjustment period for developing countries. The World Bank, and every economist, treats China—with its per capita income of $450—not only as a developing country but also as a low-income developing country. But Kantor is a hard negotiator. He insisted that it was a developed country, and should therefore have a quick transition.

Kantor had some leverage because China needed U.S. approval in order to join the WTO. The United States–China agreement that eventually led to China's being admitted to the WTO in November 2001 illustrates two aspects of the contradictions of the U.S. position. While the United States dragged out the bargaining with its unreasonable insistence that China was really a developed country, China began the adjustment process itself. In effect, unwittingly, the United States gave China the extra time it had wanted. But the agreement itself illustrates the double standards and inequity at play here. Ironically, while the United States insisted that China adjust quickly, as if it were a developed country—and because China had used the prolonged bargaining time well, it was able to accede to those demands—the United States also demanded, in effect, that America be treated as if *it* were a less developed country, that it be given not just the ten years of adjustment for lowering its barrier against textile imports that had been part of the 1994 negotiations, but an additional four years.

What is particularly disturbing is how special interests can undermine both U.S. credibility and broader national interests. This was seen most forcefully in April 1999, when Premier Zhu Rongji came to the United States partly to finish off negotiations for China's admission to the World Trade Organization, a move that was essential for the world trading regime—how could one of the largest trading countries be excluded?—but also for the market reforms in China itself. Over the opposition of the U.S. Trade Representative and the State Department, the U.S. Treasury insisted on a provision for faster liberalization of China's financial markets. China was quite rightly worried; it was precisely such liberalization that had led to the financial crises in neighboring countries in East Asia, at such costs. China had been spared because of its wise policies.

This American demand for liberalization of financial markets in China would not help secure global economic stability. It was made to serve the narrow interests of the financial community in the United States, which Treasury vigorously represents. Wall Street rightly believed that China represented a potential vast market for its financial services, and it was important that Wall Street get in, establish a strong toehold, before others. How shortsighted this was! It was clear that China would eventually be opened up. Hurrying the process up by a year or two can surely make little difference, except that Wall Street worries that its competitive advantage may disappear over time, as financial institutions in Europe and elsewhere catch up to the short-term advantages of their Wall Street competitors. But the potential cost was enormous. In the immediate aftermath of the Asian financial crisis, it was impossible for China to accede to Treasury's demands. For China, maintaining stability is essential; it could not risk policies that had proved so destabilizing elsewhere. Zhu Rongji was forced to return to China without a signed agreement. There had long been a struggle inside China between those pushing for and against reform. Those opposing reform argued that the West was seeking to weaken China, and would never sign a fair agreement. A successful end to the negotiations would have helped to secure the positions of the reformers in the Chinese government and added strength to the reform movement. As it turned out, Zhu Rongji and the reform movement for which he stood, were discredited, and the reformists' power and influence were curtailed. Fortunately, the damage was only temporary, but still, the U.S. Treasury had shown how much it was willing to risk to pursue its special agenda.

EVEN THOUGH AN unfair trade agenda was pushed, at least there was a considerable body of theory and evidence that trade liberalization would, if implemented properly, be a good thing. The case for financial market liberalization was far more problematic. Many countries do have financial regulations that serve little purpose other than to impede the flow of capital and these should be stripped away. But all countries regulate their financial markets, and excessive zeal in deregulation has brought on massive problems in capital markets even in developed countries around the world. To cite one example, the infamous savings-and-loan debacle in the United States, while it was a key factor in precipitating the 1991 recession and cost American taxpayers upward of $200 billion, was one of the least expensive (as a percentage of GDP) bailouts that deregulation has brought on, just as the U.S. recession was one of the mildest compared to ones in other economies that suffered similar crises.

While the more advanced industrialized countries, with their sophisticated institutions, were learning the hard lessons of financial deregulation, the IMF was carrying this Reagan-Thatcher message to the developing countries, countries which were particularly ill-equipped to manage what has proven, under the best of circumstances, to be a difficult task fraught with risks. Whereas the more advanced industrial countries did not attempt capital market liberalization until late in their development—European nations waited until the 1970s to get rid of their capital market controls—the developing nations have been encouraged to do so quickly.

The consequences—economic recession—of banking crises brought on by capital market deregulation, while painful for developed countries, were much more serious for developing countries. The poor countries have no safety net to soften the impact of recession. In addition, the limited competition in financial markets meant that liberalization did not always bring the promised benefits of lower interest rates. Instead, farmers sometimes found that they had to pay higher interest rates, making it more difficult for them to buy the seed and fertilizer necessary to eke out their bare subsistence living.

And as bad as premature and badly managed trade liberalization was for developing countries, in many ways capital market liberalization was even worse. Capital market liberalization entails stripping away the regulations intended to control the flow of hot money in and out of the country—short-term loans and contracts that are usually no more than bets on exchange rate movements. This speculative money cannot be used to build factories or create jobs—companies don't make long-term investments using money that can be pulled out on a moment's notice—and indeed, the risk that such hot money brings with it makes long-term investments in a developing country even less attractive. The adverse effects on growth are even greater. To manage the risks associated with these volatile capital flows, countries are routinely advised to set aside in their reserves an amount equal to their short-term foreign-denominated loans. To see what this implies, assume that a firm in a small developing country accepts a short-term $100 million loan from an American bank, paying 18 percent interest. Prudential policy on the part of the country would require that it would add $100 million to reserves. Typically reserves are held in U.S. Treasury bills, which today pay around 4 percent. In effect, the country is simultaneously borrowing from the United States at 18 percent and lending to the United States at 4 percent. The country as a whole has no more resources available for investing. American banks may make a tidy profit and the United States as a whole gains $14 million a year in interest. But it is hard to see how this allows the developing country to grow faster. Put this way, it clearly makes no sense. There is a further problem: a mismatch of incentives. With capital market liberalization, it is firms in a country's private sector that get to decide whether to borrow short-term funds from the American banks, but it is the government that must accommodate itself, adding to its reserves if it wishes to maintain its prudential standing.

The IMF, in arguing for capital market liberalization, relied on simplistic reasoning: Free markets are more efficient, greater efficiency allowed for faster growth. It ignored arguments such as the one just given, and put forward some further specious contentions, for instance, that without liberalization, countries would not be able to attract foreign capital, and especially direct investment. The Fund's economists have never laid claim to being great theorists; its claim to expertise lay in its global experience and its mastery of the data. Yet strikingly, not even the data supported the Fund's conclusions. China, which received the largest amount of foreign investment, did not follow any of the Western prescriptions (other than macrostability)— prudently forestalling full capital market liberalization. Broader statistical studies confirmed the finding that using the IMF's own definitions of liberalization, it did not entail faster growth or higher investment.

While China demonstrated that capital market liberalization was not needed to attract funds, the fact of the matter was that, given the high savings rates in East Asia (30–40% of GDP, in contrast to 18% in the United States and 17–30% in Europe), the region hardly needed additional funds; it already faced a daunting challenge in investing the flow of savings well.

The advocates of liberalization put forth another argument, one that looks particularly laughable in light of the global financial crisis that began in 1997, that liberalization would enhance stability by diversifying the sources of funding. The notion was that in times of downturn, countries could call upon foreigners to make up for a shortfall in domestic funds. The IMF economists were supposed to be practical people, well versed in the ways of the world. Surely, they must have known that bankers prefer to lend to those who do not need their funds; surely they must have seen how it is when countries face difficulties, that foreign lenders pull their money out—exacerbating the economic downturn.

While we shall take a closer look at why liberalization—especially when undertaken prematurely, before strong financial institutions are in place—increased instability, one fact remains clear: instability is not only bad for economic growth, but the costs of the instability are disproportionately borne by the poor.

The Role of Foreign Investment

Foreign investment is not one of the three main pillars of the Washington Consensus, but it is a key part of the new globalization. According to the Washington Consensus, growth occurs through liberalization, "freeing up" markets. Privatization, liberalization, and macrostability are supposed to create a climate to attract investment, including from abroad. This investment creates growth. Foreign business brings with it technical expertise and access to foreign markets, creating new employment possibilities. Foreign companies also have access to sources of finance, especially important in those developing countries where local financial institutions are weak. Foreign direct investment has played an important role in many—but not all—of the most successful development stories in countries such as Singapore and Malaysia and even China.

Having said this, there are some real downsides. When foreign businesses come in they often destroy local competitors, quashing the ambitions of the small businessmen who had hoped to develop homegrown industry. There are many examples of this. Soft drinks manufacturers around the world have been overwhelmed by the entrance of Coca-Cola and Pepsi into their home markets. Local ice cream manufacturers find they are unable to compete with Unilever's ice cream products.

One way to think about it is to recall the controversy in the United States over the large chains of drugstores and convenience stores. When Wal★Mart comes into a community, there are often strong protests from local firms, who fear (rightly) that they will be displaced. Local shopkeepers worry they won't be able to compete with Wal★Mart, with its enormous buying power. People living in small towns worry about what will happen to the character of the community if all local stores are destroyed. These same concerns are a thousand times stronger in developing countries. Although such concerns are legitimate, one has to maintain a perspective: the reason that Wal★Mart is successful is that it provides goods to consumers at lower prices. The more efficient delivery of goods and services to poor individuals within developing countries is all the more important, given how close to subsistence so many live.

But critics raise several points. In the absence of strong (or effectively enforced) competition laws, after the international firm drives out the local competition it uses its monopoly power to raise prices. The benefits of low-prices were short-lived.

Part of what is at stake is a matter of pacing; local businesses claim that, if they are given time, they can adapt and respond to the competition, that they can produce goods efficiently, that preserving local businesses is important for the strengthening of the local community, both economically and socially. The problem, of course, is that all too often policies first described as a temporary protection from foreign competition become permanent.

Many of the multinationals have done less than they might to improve the working conditions in the developing countries. Only gradually have they come to recognize the lessons that they learned all too slowly at home. Providing better working conditions may actually enhance worker productivity, and lower overall costs—or at least not raise costs very much.

Banking is another area where foreign companies often overrun local ones. The large American banks can provide greater security for depositors than do small local banks (unless the local government provides deposit insurance). The U.S. government has been pushing for opening up of financial markets in developing nations. The advantages are clear: the increased competition can lead to improved services. The greater financial strength of the foreign banks can enhance financial stability. Still, the threat foreign banks pose to the local banking sector is very real. Indeed, there was an extended debate in the United States on the same issue. National banking was resisted (until the Clinton administration, under Wall Street influence, reversed the traditional position of the Democratic Party) for fear that funds would flow to the major money centers, like New York, starving the outlying areas of needed funds. Argentina shows the dangers. There, before the collapse in 2001, the domestic banking industry had become dominated by foreign-owned banks, and while the banks easily provide funds to multinationals, and even large domestic firms, small and medium-size firms complained of a lack of access to capital. International banks' expertise—and information base—lies in lending to their traditional clients. Eventually, they may expand into these other niches, or new financial institutions may arise to address these gaps. And the lack of growth—to which the lack of finance contributed—was pivotal in that country's collapse. Within Argentina, the problem was widely recognized; the government took some limited steps to fill the credit gap. But government lending could not make up for the market's failure.

Argentina's experience illustrates some basic lessons. The IMF and the World Bank have been stressing the importance of bank stability. It is easy to create sound banks, banks that do not lose money because of bad loans—simply require them to invest in U.S. Treasury bills. The challenge is not just to create sound banks but also to create sound banks that provide credit for growth. Argentina has shown how the failure to do that may itself lead to macroinstability. Because of a lack of growth it has had mounting fiscal deficits, and as the IMF forced cutbacks in expenditures and increases in taxes, a vicious downward spiral of economic decline and social unrest was set in motion.

Bolivia provides yet another example where foreign banks have contributed to macroeconomic instability. In 2001, a foreign bank that loomed large in the Bolivian economy suddenly decided, given the increased global risks, to pull back on lending. The sudden change in the credit supply helped plunge the economy into an even deeper economic downturn than falling commodity prices and the global economic slowdown were already bringing about.

There are additional concerns with respect to the intrusion of foreign banks. Domestic banks are more sensitive to what used to be called "window guidance"—subtle forms of influence by the central bank, for example, to expand credit when the economy needs stimulus and contract it when there are signs of overheating. Foreign banks are far less likely to be responsive to such signals. Similarly, domestic banks are far more likely to be responsive to pressure to address basic holes in the credit system—unserved and underserved groups, such as minorities and disadvantaged regions. In the United States, with one of the most developed credit markets, these gaps were felt to be so important that the Community Reinvestment Act (CRA) was passed in 1977, which imposed requirements on banks to lend to these underserved groups and areas. The CRA has been an important, if controversial, way of achieving critical social goals.

Finance, however, is not the only area in which foreign direct investment has been a mixed blessing. In some cases, new investors persuaded (often with bribes) governments to grant them special privileges, such as tariff protection. In many cases, the U.S., French, or governments of other advanced industrial countries weighed in—reinforcing the view within developing countries that it was perfectly appropriate for governments to meddle in and presumably receive payments from the private sector. In some cases, the role of government seemed relatively innocuous (although not necessarily uncorrupt). When U.S. Secretary of Commerce Ron Brown traveled abroad, he was accompanied by U.S. business people trying to make contacts with and gain entry into these emerging markets. Presumably, the chances of getting a seat on the plane were enhanced if one made significant campaign contributions.

In other cases, one government was called in to countervail the weight of another. In Côte d'Ivoire while the French government supported the French Telecom's attempt to exclude competition from an independent (American) cell phone company, the U.S. government pushed the claims of the American firm. But in many cases, governments went well beyond the realm of what was reasonable. In Argentina, the French government reportedly weighed in pushing for a rewriting of the terms of concessions for a water utility (Aguas Argentinas), after the French parent company (Suez Lyonnaise) that had signed the agreements found them less profitable than it had thought.

Perhaps of greatest concern has been the role of governments, including the American government, in pushing nations to live up to agreements that were vastly unfair to the developing countries, and often signed by corrupt governments in those countries. In Indonesia, at the 1994 meeting of leaders of APEC (Asia-Pacific Economic Cooperation) held at Jakarta, President Clinton encouraged American firms to come into Indonesia. Many did so, and often at highly favorable terms (with suggestions of corruption "greasing" the wheels—to the disadvantage of the people of Indonesia). The World Bank similarly encouraged private power deals there and in other countries, such as Pakistan. These contracts entailed provisions where the government was committed to purchasing large quantities of electricity at very high prices (the so-called take or pay clauses). The private sector got the profits; the government bore the risk. That was bad enough. But when the corrupt governments were overthrown (Mohammed Suharto in Indonesia in 1998, Nawaz Sharif in Pakistan in 1999), the U.S. government put pressure on the governments to fulfill the contract, rather than default or at least renegotiate the terms of the contract. There is, in fact, a long history of "unfair" contracts, which Western governments have used their muscle to enforce.[1]

There is more to the list of legitimate complaints against foreign direct investment. Such investment often flourishes only because of special privileges extracted from the government. While standard economics focuses on the *distortions* of incentives that result from such privileges, there is a far more insidious aspect: often those privileges are the result of corruption, the bribery of government officials. The foreign direct investment comes only at the price of undermining democratic processes. This is particularly true for investments in mining, oil, and other natural resources, where foreigners have a real incentive to obtain the concessions at low prices.

Moreover, such investments have other adverse effects—and often do not promote growth. The income that mining concessions brings can be invaluable but development is a transformation of society. An investment in a mine—say in a remote region of a country—does little to assist the development transformation, beyond the resources that it generates. It can help create a dual economy, an economy in which there are pockets of wealth. But a dual economy is not a developed economy. Indeed, the inflow of resources can sometimes actually impede development, through a mechanism that is called the "Dutch Disease." The inflow of capital leads to an appreciation of the currency, making imports cheap and exports expensive. The name comes from the Netherlands experience following the discovery of gas in the North Sea. Natural gas sales drove the Dutch currency up, seriously hurting the country's other export industries. It presented a challenging but solvable problem for that country; but for developing countries, the problem may be especially difficult.

Worse still, the availability of resources can alter incentives: as we saw in chapter 2, rather than devoting energy to creating wealth, in many countries that are well-endowed with resources, efforts are directed at appropriating the income (which economists refer to as "rents") associated with the natural resources.

The international financial institutions tended to ignore the problems I have outlined. Instead, the IMF's prescription for job creation—when it focused on that issue—was simple: Eliminate government intervention (in the form of oppressive regulation), reduce taxes, get inflation as low as possible, and invite foreign entrepreneurs in. In a sense, even here policy reflected the colonial mentality described in the previous chapter: of course, the developing countries would have to rely on foreigners for entrepreneurship. Never mind the remarkable successes of Korea and Japan, in which foreign investment played no role. In many cases, as in Singapore, China, and Malaysia, which kept the abuses of foreign investment in check, foreign direct investment played a critical role, not so much for the capital (which, given the high savings rate, was not really needed) or even for the entrepreneurship, but for the access to markets and new technology that it brought along.

Sequencing and Pacing

Perhaps of all the IMF's blunders, it is the mistakes in sequencing and pacing, and the failure to be sensitive to the broader social context, that have received the most attention—forcing liberalization before safety nets were put in place, before there was an adequate regulatory framework, before the countries could withstand the adverse consequences of the sudden changes in market sentiment that are part and parcel of modern capitalism; forcing policies that led to job destruction before the essentials for job creation were in place; forcing privatization before there were adequate competition and regulatory frameworks. Many of the sequencing mistakes reflected fundamental misunderstandings of both economic and political processes, misunderstandings that were particularly associated with those who believed in market fundamentalism. They argued, for instance, that once private property rights were established, all else would follow naturally—including the institutions and the kinds of legal structures that make market economies work.

Behind the free market ideology there is a model, often attributed to Adam Smith, which argues that market forces—the profit motive—drive the economy to efficient outcomes *as if by an invisible hand*. One of the great achievements of modern economics is to show the sense in which, and the conditions under which, Smith's conclusion is correct. It turns out that these conditions are highly restrictive.[2] Indeed, more recent advances in economic theory—ironically occurring precisely during the period of the most relentless pursuit of the Washington Consensus policies—have shown that whenever information is imperfect and markets incomplete, which is to say always, *and especially in developing countries*, then the invisible hand works most imperfectly. Significantly, there are desirable government interventions which, in principle, can improve upon the efficiency of the market. These restrictions on the conditions under which markets result in efficiency are important—many of the key activities of government can be understood as responses to the resulting market failures. If information were perfect, we now know, there would be little role for financial markets—and little role for financial market regulation. If competition were automatically perfect, there would be no role for antitrust authorities.

The Washington Consensus policies, however, were based on a simplistic model of the market economy, the competitive equilibrium model, in which Adam Smith's invisible hand works, and works perfectly. Because in this model there is no need for government—that is, free, unfettered, "liberal" markets work perfectly—the Washington Consensus policies are sometimes referred to as "neo-liberal," based on "market fundamentalism," a resuscitation of the laissez-faire policies that were popular in some circles in the nineteenth century. In the aftermath of the Great Depression and the recognition of other failings of the market system, from massive inequality to unlivable cities marred by pollution and decay, these free market policies have been widely rejected in the more advanced industrial countries, though within these countries there remains an active debate about the appropriate balance between government and markets.

EVEN IF SMITH'S invisible hand theory were relevant for advanced industrialized countries, the required conditions are not satisfied in developing countries. The market system requires clearly established property rights and the courts to enforce them; but often these are absent in developing countries. The market system requires competition and perfect information. But competition is limited and information is far from perfect—and well-functioning competitive markets can't be established overnight. The theory says that an efficient market economy requires that *all* of the assumptions be satisfied. In some cases, reforms in one area, without accompanying reforms in others, may actually make matters worse. This is the issue of sequencing. Ideology ignores these matters; it says simply move as quickly to a market economy as you can. But economic theory and history show how disastrous it can be to ignore sequencing.

The mistakes in trade, capital market liberalization, and privatization described earlier represent sequencing errors on a grand scale. The smaller-scale sequencing mistakes are even less noticed in the Western press. They constitute the day-to-day tragedies of IMF policies that affect the already desperately poor in the developing world. For example, many countries have marketing boards that purchase agricultural produce from the farmers and market it domestically and internationally. They often are a source of inefficiency and corruption, with farmers getting only a fraction of the ultimate price. Even though it makes little sense for the government to be engaged in this business, if the government suddenly gets out of it, it does not mean a vibrant competitive private sector will emerge automatically.

Several West African countries got out of the marketing board business under pressure from the IMF and World Bank. In some cases, it seemed to work; but in others, when the marketing board disappeared, a system of local monopolies developed. Limited capital restricted entry into this market. Few peasants could afford to buy a truck to carry their produce to market. They couldn't borrow the requisite funds either, given the lack of well-functioning banks. In some cases, people were able to get trucks to transport their goods, and the market did function initially; but then this lucrative business became the provenance of the local mafia. In either situation, the net benefits that the IMF and the World Bank promised did not materialize. Government revenue was lowered, the peasants were little if any better off than before, and a few local businessmen (mafiosi and politicians) were much better off.

Many marketing boards also engage in a policy of uniform pricing—paying farmers the same price no matter where they are located. While seemingly "fair," economists object to this policy because it effectively requires those farmers near markets to subsidize those far away. With market competition, farmers farther away from the place where the goods are actually sold receive lower prices; in effect, they bear the costs of transporting their goods to the market. The IMF forced one African country to abandon its uniform pricing before an adequate road system was in place. The price received by those in more isolated places was suddenly lowered markedly, as they had to bear the costs of transportation. As a result, incomes in some of the poorest rural regions in the country plummeted, and widespread hardship ensued. The IMF pricing scheme may have had some slight benefits in terms of increased efficiency, but we have to weigh these benefits against the social costs. Proper sequencing and pacing might have enabled one to gradually achieve the efficiency gains without these costs.

There is a more fundamental criticism of the IMF/Washington Consensus approach: It does not acknowledge that development requires a transformation of society. Uganda grasped this in its radical elimination of all school fees, something that budget accountants focusing solely on revenues and costs simply could not understand. Part of the mantra of development economics today is a stress on universal primary education, including educating girls. Countless studies have shown that countries, like those in East Asia, which have invested in primary education, including education of girls, have done better. But in some very poor countries, such as those in Africa, it has been very difficult to achieve high enrollment rates, especially for girls. The reason is simple: poor families have barely enough to survive; they see little direct benefit from educating their daughters, and the education systems have been oriented to enhancing opportunities mainly through jobs in the urban sector considered more suitable for boys. Most countries, facing severe budgetary constraints, have followed the Washington Consensus advice that fees should be charged. Their reasoning: statistical studies showed that small fees had little impact on school enrollment. But Uganda's President Museveni thought otherwise. He knew that he had to create a culture in which the expectation was that everyone went to school. And he knew he couldn't do that so long as there were any fees charged. So he ignored the advice of the outside experts and simply abolished all school fees. Enrollments soared. As each family saw others sending all of their children to school, it too decided to send its girls to school. What the simplistic statistical studies ignored is the power of *systemic* change.

If IMF strategies had simply failed to accomplish the full potential of development, that would have been bad enough. But the failures in many places have set back the development agenda, by unnecessarily corroding the very fabric of society. It is inevitable that the process of development and rapid change puts enormous stresses on society. Traditional authorities are challenged, traditional relationships are reassessed. That is why successful development pays careful attention to social stability—a major lesson not only of the story of Botswana in the previous chapter but also of Indonesia in the next, where the IMF insisted on abolishing subsidies for food and kerosene (the fuel used for cooking by the poor) just as IMF policies had exacerbated the country's recession, with incomes and wages falling and unemployment soaring. The riots that ensued tore the country's social fabric, exacerbating the ongoing depression. Abolishing the subsidies was not only bad social policy; it was bad economic policy.

These were not the first IMF-inspired riots, and had the IMF advice been followed more broadly, there surely would have been more. In 1995, I was in Jordan for a meeting with the crown prince and other senior government officials, when the IMF argued for cutting food subsidies to improve the government's budget. They had almost succeeded in getting agreement when King Hussein intervened and put a stop to it. He enjoyed his post, was doing a marvelous job, and wanted to keep it. In the highly volatile Middle East, food-inspired riots could well have overturned the government, and with that the fragile peace in the region. Weighed against the meager possible improvement in the budget situation, these events would have been far more harmful to the goal of prosperity. The IMF's narrow economic view made it impossible for it to consider these issues in their broader context.

Such riots are, however, like the tip of an iceberg: they bring to everyone's attention the simple fact that the social and political context cannot be ignored. But there were other problems. While in the 1980s Latin America needed to have its budgets brought into better balance and inflation brought under control, excessive austerity led to high unemployment, without an adequate safety net, which in turn contributed to high levels of urban violence, an environment hardly conducive to investment. Civil strife in Africa has been a major factor setting back its development agenda. Studies at the World Bank show that such strife is systematically related to adverse economic factors, including unemployment that can be produced by excessive austerity. Moderate inflation may not be ideal for creating an environment for investment, but violence and civil strife are even worse.

We recognize today that there is a "social contract" that binds citizens together, and with their government. When government policies abrogate that social contract, citizens may not honor their "contracts" with each other, or with the government. Maintaining that social contract is particularly important, and difficult, in the midst of the social upheavals that so frequently accompany the development transformation. In the green eye–shaded calculations of the IMF macroeconomics there is, too often, no room for these concerns.

Trickle–Down Economics

Part of the social contract entails "fairness," that the poor share in the gains of society as it grows, and that the rich share in the pains of society in times of crisis. The Washington Consensus policies paid little attention to issues of distribution or "fairness." If pressed, many of its proponents would argue that the best way to help the poor is to make the economy grow. They believe in trickle-down economics. *Eventually*, it is asserted, the benefits of that growth *trickle down* even to the poor. Trickle-down economics was never much more than just a belief, an article of faith. Pauperism seemed to grow in nineteenth-century England even though the country as a whole prospered. Growth in America in the 1980s provided the most recent dramatic example: while the economy grew, those at the bottom saw their real incomes decline. The Clinton administration had argued strongly against trickle-down economics; it believed that there had to be active programs to help the poor. And when I left the White House to go to the World Bank, I brought with me the same skepticism of trickle-down economics; if this had not worked in the United States, why would it work in developing countries? While it is true that sustained reductions in poverty cannot be attained without robust economic growth, the converse is not true: growth need not benefit all. It is not true that "a rising tide lifts all boats." Sometimes, a quickly rising tide, especially when accompanied by a storm, dashes weaker boats against the shore, smashing them to smithereens.

In spite of the obvious problems confronting trickle-down economics, it has a good intellectual pedigree. One Nobel Prize winner, Arthur Lewis, argued that inequality was good for development and economic growth, since the rich save more than the poor, and the key to growth was capital accumulation. Another Nobel Prize winner, Simon Kuznets, argued that while in the initial stages of development inequality increased, later on the trend was reversed.[3]

THE HISTORY OF the past fifty years has, however, not supported these theories and hypotheses. As we will see in the next chapter, East Asian countries—South Korea, China, Taiwan, Japan—showed that high savings did not require high inequality, that one could achieve rapid growth without a substantial increase in inequality. Because the governments did not believe that growth would automatically benefit the poor, and because they believed that greater *equality* would actually enhance growth, governments in the region took active steps to ensure that the rising tide of growth did lift most boats, that wage inequalities were kept in bounds, that some educational opportunity was extended to all. Their policies led to social and political stability, which in turn contributed to an economic environment in which businesses flourished. Tapping new reservoirs of talent provided the energy and human skills that contributed to the dynamism of the region.

Elsewhere, where governments adopted the Washington Consensus policies, the poor have benefited less from growth. In Latin America, growth has not been accompanied by a reduction in inequality, or even a reduction in poverty. In some cases poverty has actually increased, as evidenced by the urban slums that dot the landscape. The IMF talks with pride about the progress Latin America has made in market reforms over the past decade (though somewhat more quietly after the collapse of the star student Argentina in 2001, and the recession and stagnation that have afflicted many of the "reform" countries during the past five years), but has said less about the numbers in poverty.

Clearly, growth alone does not always improve the lives of all a country's people. Not surprisingly, the phrase "trickle-down" has disappeared from the policy debate. But, in a slightly mutated form, the idea is still alive. I call the new variant *trickle-down-plus*. It holds that growth is necessary and *almost* sufficient for reducing poverty—implying that the best strategy is simply to focus on growth, while mentioning issues like female education and health. But proponents of trickle-down-plus failed to implement policies that would effectively address either broader concerns of poverty or even specific issues such as the education of women. In practice, the advocates of trickle-down-plus continued with much the same policies as before, with much the same adverse effects. The overly stringent "adjustment policies" in country after country forced cutbacks in education and health: in Thailand, as a result, not only did female prostitution increase but expenditures on AIDS were cut way back; and what had been one of the world's most successful programs in fighting aids had a major setback.

The irony was that one of the major proponents of trickle-down-plus was the U.S. Treasury under the Clinton administration. Within the administration, in domestic politics, there was a wide spectrum of views, from New Democrats, who wanted to see a more limited role for government, to Old Democrats, who looked for more government intervention. But the central view, reflected in the annual Economic Report of the President (prepared by the Council of Economic Advisers), argued strongly against trickle-down economics—or even trickle-down-plus. Here was the U.S. Treasury pushing policies on other countries that, had they been advocated for the United States, would have been strongly contested *within the administration*, and almost surely defeated. The reason for this seeming inconsistency was simple: The IMF and the World Bank were part of Treasury's turf, an arena in which, with few exceptions, they were allowed to push their perspectives, just as other departments, within their domains, could push theirs.

PRIORITIES AND STRATEGIES

It is important not only to look at what the IMF puts on its agenda, but what it leaves off. Stabilization is on the agenda; job creation is off. Taxation, and its adverse effects, are on the agenda; land reform is off. There is money to bail out banks but not to pay for improved education and health services, let alone to bail out workers who are thrown out of their jobs as a result of the IMF's macroeconomic mismanagement.

Many of the items that were not on the Washington Consensus might bring both higher growth and greater equality. Land reform itself illustrates the choices at stake in many countries. In many developing countries, a few rich people own most of the land. The vast majority of the people work as tenant farmers, keeping only half, or less, of what they produce. This is termed *sharecropping*. The share-cropping system weakens incentives—where they share equally with the landowners, the effects are the same as a 50 percent tax on poor farmers. The IMF rails against high tax rates that are imposed against the rich, pointing out how they destroy incentives, but nary a word is spoken about these hidden taxes. Land reform, done properly, peacefully, and legally, ensuring that workers get not only land but access to credit, and the extension services that teach them about new seeds and planting techniques, could provide an enormous boost to output. But land reform represents a fundamental change in the structure of society, one that those in the elite that populates the finance ministries, those with whom the international financial institutions interact, do not necessarily like. If these institutions were really concerned about growth and poverty alleviation, they would have paid considerable attention to the issue: land reform preceded several of the most successful instances of development, such as those in Korea and Taiwan.

Another neglected item was financial sector regulation. Focusing on the Latin American crisis of the early 1980s, the IMF maintained that crises were caused by imprudent fiscal policies and loose monetary policies. But crises around the world had revealed a third source of instability, inadequate financial sector regulation. Yet the IMF pushed for reducing regulations—until the East Asia crisis forced it to change course. If land reform and financial sector regulation were underemphasized by the IMF and the Washington Consensus, in many places inflation was overemphasized. Of course, in regions like Latin America where inflation had been rampant, it deserved attention. But an *excessive* focus on inflation by the IMF led to high interest rates and high exchange rates, creating unemployment but not growth. Financial markets may have been pleased with the low inflation numbers, but workers—and those concerned with poverty—were not happy with the low growth and the high unemployment numbers.

Fortunately, poverty reduction has become an increasingly important development priority. We saw earlier that the trickle-down-plus strategies have not worked. Still, it is true that, on average, countries that have grown faster have done a better job of reducing poverty, as China and East Asia amply demonstrate. It is also true that poverty eradication requires resources, resources that can only be obtained with growth. Thus the existence of a correlation between growth and poverty reduction should come as no surprise. But this correlation does not prove that trickle-down strategies (or trickle-down-plus) constitute the best way to attack poverty. On the contrary, the statistics show that some countries have grown without reducing poverty, and some countries have been much more successful in reducing poverty, at any given growth rate, than others. The issue is not whether one is in favor of or against growth. In some ways, the growth/poverty debate seemed pointless. After all, almost everyone believes in growth.

The question has to do with the impact of *particular policies*. Some policies promote growth but have little effect on poverty; some promote growth but actually increase poverty; and some promote growth and reduce poverty at the same time. The last are called pro-poor growth strategies. Sometimes there are policies which are "win-win," policies like land reform or better access to education for the poor which hold out the promise of enhanced growth and greater equality. But many times there are trade-offs. Sometimes trade liberalization might enhance growth, but at the same time, at least in the short run, there will be increased poverty—especially if it is done rapidly—as some workers are thrown out of a job. And sometimes, there are lose-lose policies, policies for which there is little if any gain in growth but a significant increase in inequality. For many countries, capital market liberalization represents an example. The growth-poverty debate is about development strategies—strategies that look for policies that reduce poverty as they promote growth, that shun policies that increase poverty with little if any gain in growth, and that, in assessing situations where there are trade-offs, put a heavy weight on the impact on the poor.

Understanding the choices requires understanding the causes and nature of poverty. It is not that the poor are lazy; they often work harder, with longer hours, than those who are far better off. Many are caught in a series of vicious spirals: lack of food leads to ill health, which limits their earning ability, leading to still poorer health. Barely surviving, they cannot send their children to school, and without an education, their children are condemned to a life of poverty. Poverty is passed along from one generation to another. Poor farmers cannot afford to pay the money for the fertilizers and high-yielding seeds that would increase their productivity.

This is but one of many vicious cycles facing the poor. Partha Dasgupta of Cambridge University has emphasized another. In poor countries, like Nepal, the impoverished have no source of energy other than the neighboring forests; but as they strip the forests for the bare necessities of heating and cooking, the soil erodes, and as the environment degrades, they are condemned to a life of ever-increasing poverty.

Along with poverty come feelings of powerlessness. For its 2000 *World Development Report*, the World Bank interviewed thousands of poor in an exercise that was called *The Voices of the Poor*. Several themes—hardly unexpected—emerge. The poor feel that they are voiceless, and that they do not have control over their own destiny. They are buffeted by forces beyond their control.

And the poor feel insecure. Not only is their income uncertain—changes in economic circumstances beyond their control can lead to lower real wages and a loss of jobs, dramatically illustrated by the East Asia crisis—but they face health risks and continual threats of violence, sometimes from other poor people trying against all odds to meet the needs of their family, sometimes from police and others in positions of authority. While those in developed countries fret about the inadequacies of health insurance, those in developing countries must get by without any form of insurance—no unemployment insurance, no health insurance, no retirement insurance. The only safety net is provided by family and community, which is why it is so important, in the process of development, to do what one can to preserve these bonds.

To ameliorate the insecurity—whether the capriciousness of an exploitative boss or the capriciousness of a market increasingly buffeted by international storms—workers have fought for greater job security. But as hard as workers have fought for "decent jobs," the IMF has fought for what it euphemistically called "labor market flexibility," which sounds like little more than making the labor market work better but as applied has been simply a code name for lower wages, and less job protection.

Not all the downsides of the Washington Consensus policies for the poor could have been foreseen, but by now they are clear. We have seen how trade liberalization *accompanied by high interest rates* is an almost certain recipe for job destruction and unemployment creation—at the expense of the poor. Financial market liberalization *unaccompanied by an appropriate regulatory structure* is an almost certain recipe for economic instability—and may well lead to higher, not lower interest rates, making it harder for poor farmers to buy the seeds and fertilizer that can raise them above subsistence. Privatization, *unaccompanied by competition policies and oversight to ensure that monopoly powers are not abused*, can lead to higher, not lower, prices for consumers. Fiscal austerity, *pursued blindly*, in the wrong circumstances, can lead to high unemployment and a shredding of the social contract.

If the IMF underestimated the risks to the poor of its development strategies, it also underestimated the long-term social and political costs of policies that devastated the middle class, enriching a few at the top, and overestimated the benefits of its market fundamentalist policies. The middle classes have traditionally been the group that has pushed for the rule of law, that has pushed for universal public education, that has pushed for the creation of a social safety net. These are essential elements of a healthy economy and the erosion of the middle class has led to a concomitant erosion of support for these important reforms.

At the same time that it underestimated the costs of its programs, the IMF overestimated the benefits. Take the problem of unemployment. To the IMF and others who believe that when markets function normally demand must equal supply, unemployment is a symptom of an interference in the free workings of the market. Wages are too high (for instance, because of union power). The obvious remedy to unemployment was to lower wages; lower wages will increase the demand for labor, bringing more people onto employment rolls. While modern economic theory (in particular, theories based on asymmetric information and incomplete contracts) has explained why even with highly competitive markets, including labor markets, unemployment can persist—so the argument that says that unemployment must be due to unions or government minimum wages is simply wrong—there is another criticism of the strategy of lowering wages. Lower wages *might* lead some firms to hire a few more workers; but the number of newly hired workers may be relatively few, and the misery caused by the lower wages on all the other workers might be very grave. Employers and owners of capital might be quite happy, as they see their profits soar. These will endorse the IMF/market fundamentalist model with its policy prescriptions with enthusiasm! Asking people in developing countries to pay for schools is another example of this narrow worldview. Those who said charges should be imposed argued that there would be little effect on enrollment and that the government needed the revenue badly. The irony here was that the simplistic models miscalculated the impact on enrollment of eliminating school fees; by failing to take into account the *systemic* effects of policy, not only did they fail to take into account the broader impacts on society, they even failed in the more narrow attempts to estimate accurately the consequences for school enrollment.

If the IMF had an overly optimistic view of the markets, it had an overly pessimistic view of government; if government was not the root of all evil, it certainly was more part of the problem than the solution. But the lack of concern about the poor was not just a matter of views of markets and government, views that said that markets would take care of everything and government would only make matters worse; it was also a matter of values—how concerned we should be about the poor and who should bear what risks.

THE RESULTS OF the policies enforced by Washington Consensus have not been encouraging: for most countries embracing its tenets development has been slow, and where growth has occurred, the benefits have not been shared equally; crises have been mismanaged; the transition from communism to a market economy (as we shall see) has been a disappointment. Inside the developing world, the questions run deep. Those who followed the prescriptions, endured the austerity, are asking: When do we see the fruits? In much of Latin America, after a short burst of growth in the early 1990s, stagnation and recession have set in. The growth was not sustained—some might say not sustainable. Indeed, at this juncture, the growth record of the so-called post-reform era looks no better, and in some countries much worse, than in the pre-reform import substitution period (when countries used protectionist policies to help domestic industries compete against imports) of the 1950s and 1960s. The average annual growth rate in the region in the 1990s, at 2.9 percent on annual average after the reforms, was just more than half that in the 1960s at 5.4 percent. In retrospect, the growth strategies of the 1950s and 1960s were not sustained (critics would say they were unsustainable); but the slight upsurge in growth in the early 1990s also did not last (these also, critics would say, were unsustainable). Indeed, critics of the Washington Consensus point out that the burst of growth in the early nineties was little more than a catch-up, not even making up for the lost decade of the eighties, the decade after the last major crisis, during which growth stagnated. Throughout the region people are asking, has reform failed, or has globalization failed? The distinction is perhaps artificial—globalization was at the center of the reforms. Even in the countries that have managed some growth, such as Mexico, the benefits have accrued largely to the upper 30 percent, and have been even more concentrated in the top 10 percent. Those at the bottom have gained little; many are even worse off.

The Washington consensus reforms have exposed countries to greater risk, and the risks have been borne disproportionately by those least able to cope with them. Just as in many countries the pacing and sequencing of reforms has resulted in job destruction outmatching job creation, so too has the exposure to risk outmatched the ability to create institutions for coping with risk, including effective safety nets.

There were, of course, important messages in the Washington Consensus, including lessons about fiscal and monetary prudence, lessons which were well understood by the countries that succeeded; but most did not have to learn them from the IMF.

Sometimes the IMF and the World Bank have unfairly taken the blame for the messages they deliver—no one likes to be told that they have to live within their means. But the criticism of the international economic institutions goes deeper: while there was much that was good on their development agenda, even reforms that are desirable in the long run have to be implemented carefully. It's now widely accepted that pacing and sequencing cannot be ignored. But even more important, there is more to development than these lessons suggest. There *are* alternative strategies—strategies that differ not only in emphases but even in policies; strategies, for instance, which include land reform but do not include capital market liberalization, which provide for competition policies before privatization, which ensure that job creation accompanies trade liberalization.

These alternatives made use of markets, but recognized that there was an important role for government as well. They recognized the importance of reform, but that reforms needed to be paced and sequenced. They saw change not just as a matter of economics, but as part of a broader evolution of society. They recognized that for long-term success, there had to be broad support of the reforms, and if there was to be broad support, the benefits had to be broadly distributed.

We have already called attention to some of these successes: the limited successes in Africa, for instance, in Uganda, Ethiopia, and Botswana; and the broader successes in East Asia, including China. In chapter 5, we shall take a closer look at some of the successes in transition, such as Poland. The successes show that development and transition are possible; the successes in development are well beyond that which almost anyone imagined a half century ago. The fact that so many of the success cases followed strategies that were markedly different from those of the Washington Consensus is telling.

Each time and each country is different. Would other countries have met the same success if they had followed East Asia's strategy? Would the strategies which worked a quarter of a century ago work in today's global economy? Economists can disagree about the answers to these questions. But countries need to consider the alternatives and, through democratic political processes, make these choices for themselves. It should be—and it should have been—the task of the international economic institutions to provide the countries the wherewithal to make these *informed* choices on their own, with an understanding of the consequences and risks of each. The essence of freedom is the right to make a choice—and to accept the responsibility that comes with it.

CHAPTER 4.

THE EAST ASIA CRISIS

*How IMF Policies Brought the World
to the Verge of a Global Meltdown*

WHEN THE THAI baht collapsed on July 2, 1997, no one
knew that this was the beginning of the greatest economic crisis since the Great Depression—one that
would spread from Asia to Russia and Latin America and threaten the
entire world. For ten years the baht had traded at around 25 to the
dollar; then overnight it fell by about 25 percent. Currency speculation spread and hit Malaysia, Korea, the Philippines, and Indonesia,
and by the end of the year what had started as an exchange rate disaster threatened to take down many of the region's banks, stock markets, and even entire economies. The crisis is over now, but countries
such as Indonesia will feel its effects for years. Unfortunately, the IMF
policies imposed during this tumultuous time worsened the situation. Since the IMF was founded precisely to avert and deal with
crises of this kind, the fact that it failed in so many ways led to a
major rethinking of its role, with many people in the United States
and abroad calling for an overhaul of many of the Fund's policies and
the institution itself. Indeed, in retrospect, it became clear that the
IMF policies not only exacerbated the downturns but were partially
responsible for the onset: excessively rapid financial and capital market liberalization was probably the single most important cause of the
crisis, though mistaken policies on the part of the countries them-

selves played a role as well. Today the IMF acknowledges many, but not all, of its mistakes—its officials realize how dangerous, for instance, excessively rapid capital market liberalization can be—but its change in views comes too late to help the countries afflicted.

The crisis took most observers by surprise. Not long before the crisis, even the IMF had forecast strong growth. Over the preceding three decades East Asia had not only grown faster and done better at reducing poverty than any other region of the world, developed or less developed, but it had also been more stable. It had been spared the ups and downs that mark all market economies. So impressive was its performance that it was widely described as the "East Asia Miracle." Indeed, reportedly, so confident had the IMF been about the region that it assigned a loyal staff member as director for the region, as an easy preretirement posting.

When the crisis broke out, I was surprised at how strongly the IMF and the U.S. Treasury seemed to criticize the countries— according to the IMF, the Asian nations' institutions were rotten, their governments corrupt, and wholesale reform was needed. These outspoken critics were hardly experts on the region, but what they said contradicted so much of what I knew about it. I had been traveling to and studying the area for three decades. I had been asked by the World Bank, by Lawrence Summers himself when he was its vice president for research, to participate in a major study of the East Asia Miracle, to head the team looking at the financial markets. Almost two decades before, as the Chinese began their transition to a market economy, I had been called upon by them to discuss their development strategy. In the White House, I continued my close involvement, heading, for instance, the team that wrote the annual economic report for APEC (the Asia-Pacific Economic Cooperation, the group of countries around the Pacific rim, whose annual meetings of heads of states had come increasingly into prominence as the economic importance of the region grew). I participated actively in the National Security Council in the debates about China—and indeed, when tensions over the administration's "containment" policy got too heated, I was the cabinet member sent to meet with China's premier, Zhu Rongji, to calm the waters. I was one of the few foreigners ever invited to join the country's top leaders at their yearly August retreat for policy discussions.

How, I wondered, if these countries' institutions were so rotten, had they done so well for so long? The difference in perspectives, between what I knew about the region and what the IMF and the Treasury alleged, made little sense, until I recalled the debate that had raged over the East Asia Miracle itself. The IMF and the World Bank had almost consciously avoided studying the region, though presumably, because of its success, it would have seemed natural for them to turn to it for lessons for others. It was only under pressure from the Japanese that the World Bank had undertaken the study of economic growth in East Asia (the final report was titled *The East Asian Miracle*) and then only after the Japanese had offered to pay for it. The reason was obvious: The countries had been successful not only in spite of the fact that they had not followed most of the dictates of the Washington Consensus, but *because* they had not. Though the experts' findings were toned down in the final published report, the World Bank's Asian Miracle study laid out the important roles that the government had played. These were far from the minimalist roles beloved of the Washington Consensus.

There were those, not just in the international financial institutions but in academia, who asked, was there really a miracle? "All" that East Asia had done was to save heavily and invest well! But this view of the "miracle" misses the point. No other set of countries around the world had managed to save at such rates *and* invest the funds well. Government policies played an important role in enabling the East Asian nations to accomplish both things simultaneously.[1]

When the crisis broke out, it was almost as if many of the region's critics were glad: their perspective had been vindicated. In a curious disjunction, while they were loath to credit the region's governments with any of the successes of the previous quarter century, they were quick to blame the governments for the failings.

Whether one calls it a miracle or not is beside the point: the increases in incomes and the reductions in poverty in East Asia over the last three decades have been unprecedented. No one visiting these countries can fail to marvel at the developmental transformation, the changes not only in the economy but also in society, reflected in every statistic imaginable. Thirty years ago, thousands of backbreaking rickshaws were pulled for a pittance; today, they are only a tourist attraction, a photo opportunity for the camera-snapping tourists flocking to the region. The combination of high savings rates, government investment in education, and state-directed industrial policy all served to make the region an economic powerhouse. Growth rates were phenomenal for decades and the standard of living rose enormously for tens of millions of people. The benefits of growth were shared widely. There were problems in the way the Asian economies developed, but overall, the governments had devised a strategy that worked, a strategy which had but one item in common with the Washington Consensus policies—the importance of macrostability. As in the Washington Consensus, trade was important, but the emphasis was on promoting exports, not removing impediments to imports. Trade was eventually liberalized, but only gradually, as new jobs were created in the export industries. While the Washington Consensus policies emphasized rapid financial and capital market liberalization, the East Asian countries liberalized only gradually—some of the most successful, like China, still have a long way to go. While the Washington Consensus policies emphasized privatization, government at the national and local levels helped create efficient enterprises that played a key role in the success of several of the countries. In the Washington Consensus view, industrial policies, in which governments try to shape the future direction of the economy, are a mistake. But the East Asian governments took that as one of their central responsibilities. In particular, they believed that if they were to close the income gap between themselves and the more developed countries, they had to close the knowledge and technology gap, so they designed education and investment policies to do that. While the Washington Consensus policies paid little attention to inequality, believing that such policies were important for maintaining social cohesion, and that social cohesion was necessary to provide a climate favorable to investment and growth. Most broadly, while the Washington Consensus policies emphasized a minimalist role for government, in East Asia, governments helped shape and direct markets.

When the crisis began, those in the West did not realize its severity. Asked about aid for Thailand, President Bill Clinton dismissed the collapse of the baht as "a few glitches in the road" to economic prosperity.[2] The confidence and imperturbability of Clinton was shared by the financial leaders of the world, as they met in September 1997 in Hong Kong for the annual meeting of the IMF and World Bank. IMF officials there were so sure of their advice that they even asked for a change in its charter to allow it to put *more* pressure on developing countries to liberalize their capital markets. Meanwhile, the leaders of the Asian countries, and especially the finance ministers I met with, were terrified. They viewed the hot money that came with liberalized capital markets as the source of their problems. They knew that major trouble was ahead: a crisis would wreak havoc on their economies and their societies, and they feared that IMF policies would prevent them from taking the actions that they thought might stave off the crisis, at the same time that the policies they would insist upon should a crisis occur would worsen the impacts on their economy. They felt, however, powerless to resist. They even knew what could and should be done to prevent a crisis and minimize the damage—but knew that the IMF would condemn them if they undertook those actions and they feared the resulting withdrawal of international capital. In the end, only Malaysia was brave enough to risk the wrath of the IMF; and though Prime Minister Mahathir's policies—trying to keep interest rates low, trying to put brakes on the rapid flow of speculative money out of the country—were attacked from all quarters, Malaysia's downturn was shorter and shallower than that of any of the other countries.[3]

At the Hong Kong meeting, I suggested to the ministers of the Southeast Asian countries with whom I met that there were some concerted actions which they could take together; if they all imposed capital controls—controls intended to prevent the damage as the speculative money rushed out of their countries—in a coordinated way, they might be able to withstand the pressures that would undoubtedly be brought down upon them by the international financial community, and they could help insulate their economies from the turmoil. They talked about getting together later in the year to map out a plan. But hardly had their bags been unpacked from the trip to Hong Kong than the crisis spread, first to Indonesia, and then, in early December, to South Korea. Meanwhile, other countries around the world had been attacked by currency speculators—from Brazil to Hong Kong—and withstood the attack, but at high cost.

There are two familiar patterns to these crises. The first is illustrated by South Korea, a country with an impressive track record. As it emerged from the wreckage of the Korean War, South Korea formulated a growth strategy which increased per capita income eightfold in thirty years, reduced poverty dramatically, achieved universal literacy, and went far in closing the gap in technology between itself and the more advanced countries. At the end of the Korean War, it was poorer than India; by the beginning of the 1990s, it had joined the Organization for Economic Cooperation and Development (OECD), the club of the advanced industrialized countries. Korea had become one of the world's largest producers of computer chips, and its large conglomerates, Samsung, Daewoo, and Hyundai, produced goods known throughout the world. But whereas in the early days of its transformation it had tightly controlled its financial markets, under pressure from the United States it had reluctantly allowed its firms to borrow abroad. But by borrowing abroad, the firms exposed themselves to the vagaries of the international market: in late 1997, rumors flashed through Wall Street that Korea was in trouble. It would not be able to roll over the loans from Western banks that were coming due, and it did not have the reserves to pay them off. Such rumors can be self-fulfilling prophecies. I heard these rumors at the World Bank well before they made the newspapers— and I knew what they meant. Quickly, the banks which such a short time earlier were so eager to lend money to Korean firms decided not to roll over their loans. When they all decided not to roll over their loans, their prophecy came true: Korea *was* in trouble.

The second was illustrated by Thailand. There, a speculative attack (combined with high short-term indebtedness) was to blame. Speculators, believing that a currency will devalue, try to move out of the currency and into dollars; with free convertibility—that is, the ability to change local currency for dollars or any other currency—this can easily be done. But as traders sell the currency, its value is weakened—confirming their prophecy. Alternatively, and more commonly, the government tries to support the currency. It sells dollars from its reserves (money the country holds, often in dollars, against a rainy day), buying up the local currency, to sustain its value. But eventually, the government runs out of hard currency. There are no more dollars to sell. The currency plummets. The speculators are satisfied. They have bet right. They can move back into the currency—and make a nice profit. The magnitude of the returns can be enormous. Assume a speculator goes to a Thai bank, borrows 24 billion baht, which, at the original exchange rate, can be converted into $1 billion. A week later the exchange rate falls; instead of there being 24 baht to the dollar, there are now 40 baht to the dollar. He takes $600 million, converting it back to baht, getting 24 billion baht to repay the loan. The remaining $400 million is his profit—a tidy return for one week's work, and the investment of little of his own money. Confident that the exchange rate would not appreciate (that is, go from 24 baht to the dollar to, say, 20 to the dollar), there was hardly any risk; at worst, if the exchange rate remained unchanged, he would lose one week's interest. As perceptions that a devaluation is imminent grow, the chance to make money becomes irresistible and speculators from around the world pile in to take advantage of the situation.

If the crises had a familiar pattern, so too did the IMF's responses: it provided huge amounts of money (the total bailout packages, including support from G-7 countries, was $95 billion)[4] so that the countries could sustain the exchange rate. It thought that if the market believed that there was enough money in the coffers, there would be no point in attacking the currency, and thus "confidence" would be restored. The money served another function: it enabled the countries to provide dollars to the firms that had borrowed from Western bankers to repay the loans. It was thus, in part, a bailout to the international banks as much as it was a bailout to the country; the lenders did not have to face the full consequences of having made bad loans. And in country after country in which the IMF money was used to sustain the exchange rate temporarily at an unsustainable level, there was another consequence: rich people inside the country took advantage of the opportunity to convert their money into dollars at the favorable exchange rate and whisk it abroad. As we shall note in the next chapter, the most egregious example occurred in

Russia, after the IMF lent it money in July 1998. But this phenome-non, which is sometimes given the more neutral sounding name of "capital flight," also played a key role in the previous important crisis, in Mexico during 1994–95.

The IMF combined the money with conditions, in a package which was supposed to rectify the problems that caused the crisis. It is these other ingredients, as much as the money, that are supposed to persuade markets to roll over their loans, and to persuade speculators to look elsewhere for easy targets. The ingredients typically include higher interest rates—in the case of East Asia, much, much higher interest rates—plus cutbacks in government spending and increases in taxes. They also include "structural reforms," that is, changes in the structure of the economy which, it is believed, lies behind the coun-try's problems. In the case of East Asia, not only were conditions imposed that mandated hikes in interest rates and cutbacks in spend-ing; additional conditions required countries to make political as well as economic changes, major reforms, such as increased openness and transparency and improved financial market regulation, as well as minor reforms, like the abolition of the clove monopoly in Indonesia.

The IMF would claim that imposing these conditions was the responsible thing to do. It was providing billions of dollars; it had a responsibility to make sure not just that it was repaid but that the countries "did the right thing" to restore their economic health. If structural problems had *caused* the macroeconomic crisis, those prob-lems had to be addressed. The breadth of the conditions meant that the countries accepting Fund aid had to give up a large part of their economic sovereignty. Some of the objection to the IMF programs was based on this, and the resulting undermining of democracy; and some were based on the fact that the conditions did not (and arguably were not designed to) restore the economies' health. But, as we noted in chapter 2, some of the conditions had nothing to do with the problem at hand.

The programs—with all of their conditions and with all of their money—failed. They were supposed to arrest the fall in the exchange rates; but these continued to fall, with hardly a flicker of recognition by the markets that the IMF had "come to the rescue." In each case, embarrassed by the failure of its supposed medicine to work, the IMF charged the country with failing to take the necessary reforms seriously. In each case, it announced to the world that there were fundamental problems that had to be addressed before a true recovery could take place. Doing so was like crying fire in a crowded theater: investors, more convinced by the diagnosis of the problems than by the prescriptions, fled.[5] Rather than restoring confidence that would lead to an inflow of capital into the country, IMF criticism exacerbated the stampede of capital out. Because of this, and the other reasons to which I turn shortly, the perception throughout much of the developing world, one I share, is that the IMF itself had become a part of the countries' problem rather than part of the solution. Indeed, in several of the crisis countries, ordinary people as well as many government officials and business people continue to refer to the economic and social storm that hit their nations simply as "the IMF"—the way one would say "the plague" or "the Great Depression." History is dated by "before" and "after" the IMF, just as countries that are devastated by an earthquake or some other natural disaster date events by "before" or "after" the earthquake.

As the crisis progressed, unemployment soared, GDP plummeted, banks closed. The unemployment rate was up fourfold in Korea, threefold in Thailand, tenfold in Indonesia. In Indonesia, almost 15 percent of males working in 1997 had lost their jobs by August 1998, and the economic devastation was even worse in the urban areas of the main island, Java. In South Korea, urban poverty almost tripled, with almost a quarter of the population falling into poverty; in Indonesia, poverty doubled. In some countries, like Thailand, people thrown out of jobs in the cities could return to their rural homes. However, this put increasing pressure on those in the rural sector. In 1998, GDP in Indonesia fell by 13.1 percent, in Korea by 6.7 percent, and in Thailand by 10.8 percent. Three years after the crisis, Indonesia's GDP was still 7.5 percent below that before the crisis, Thailand's 2.3 percent lower.

In some cases, fortunately, outcomes were less bleak than was widely anticipated. Communities in Thailand worked together to ensure that their children's education was not interrupted, with people voluntarily contributing to help keep their neighbors' kids in school. They also made sure that everyone had enough food, and because of this the incidence of malnutrition did not increase. In Indonesia, a World Bank program seemed to succeed in arresting the anticipated adverse effects on education. It was poor urban workers—hardly well off by any standards—who were made most destitute by the crisis. The erosion of the middle class, caused by usurious interest rates which threw small businesses into bankruptcy, will have the longest lasting effects on the social, political, and economic life of the region.

Deteriorating conditions in one country helped bring down its neighbors. The slowdown in the region had global repercussions: global economic growth slowed, and with the slowing of global growth, commodity prices fell. From Russia to Nigeria, the many emerging countries that depended on natural resources were in deep, deep trouble. As investors who had risked their money in these countries saw their wealth plummeting, and as *their* bankers called in their loans, they had to cut back their investments in other emerging markets. Brazil, dependent neither on oil nor on trade with the countries in deep trouble, with economic features far different from these countries, was brought into the unfolding global financial crisis by the generalized fear of foreign investors and the retrenchment in their lending. Eventually, almost every emerging market, even Argentina, which the IMF had long held up as the poster child of reform, largely for its success in bringing down inflation, was affected.

HOW IMF/U.S. TREASURY POLICIES
LED TO THE CRISIS

The disturbances capped a half decade of an American-led global triumph of market economics following the end of the cold war. This period saw international attention focus on newly emerging markets, from East Asia to Latin America, and from Russia to India. Investors saw these countries as a paradise of high returns and seemingly low risk. In the short space of seven years, private capital flows from the developed to the less developed countries increased sevenfold while public flows (foreign aid) stayed steady.[6]

International bankers and politicians were confident that this was the dawn of a new era. The IMF and the U.S. Treasury believed, or at least argued, that full capital account liberalization would help the region grow even faster. The countries in East Asia had no need for additional capital, given their high savings rate, but still capital account liberalization was pushed on these countries in the late eighties and early nineties. I believe that capital account liberalization was *the single most important factor leading to the crisis*. I have come to this conclusion not just by carefully looking at what happened in the region, but by looking at what happened in the almost one hundred other economic crises of the last quarter century. Because economic crises have become more frequent (and deeper), there is now a wealth of data through which one can analyze the factors contributing to crises.[7] It has also become increasingly clear that all too often capital account liberalization represents risk without a reward. Even when countries have strong banks, a mature stock market, and other institutions that many of the Asian countries did not have, it can impose enormous risks.

Probably no country could have withstood the sudden change in investor sentiment, a sentiment that reversed this huge inflow to a huge outflow as investors, both foreign and domestic, put their funds elsewhere. Inevitably, such large reversals would precipitate a crisis, a recession, or worse. In the case of Thailand, this reversal amounted to 7.9 percent of GDP in 1997, 12.3 percent of GDP in 1998, and 7 percent of GDP in the first half of 1999. It would be equivalent to a reversal in capital flows for the United States of an average $765 billion per year between 1997 and 1999. While developing countries' ability to withstand the reversal was weak, so too was their ability to cope with the consequences of a major downturn. Their remarkable economic performance—no major economic recession in three decades—meant that the East Asian countries had not developed unemployment insurance schemes. But even had they turned their mind to the task, it would not have been easy: in the United States, unemployment insurance for those who are self-employed in agriculture is far from adequate, and this is precisely the sector that dominates in the developing world.

The complaint against the IMF, however, runs deeper: it is not just that the Fund pushed the liberalization policies which led to the crisis, but that they pushed these policies even though there was little evidence that such policies promoted growth, and there was ample evidence that they imposed huge risks on developing countries.

Here was a true irony—if such a gentle word can be used. In October 1997, at the very beginning of the crisis, the Fund was advocating the expansion of precisely those polices which underlay the increasing frequency of crises. As an academic, I was shocked that the IMF and the U.S. Treasury would push this agenda with such force, in the face of a virtual absence of theory and evidence suggesting that it was in the economic interests of either the developing countries or global economic stability—and in the presence of evidence to the contrary. Surely, one might have argued, there must be *some* basis for their position, beyond serving the naked self-interest of financial markets, which saw capital market liberalization as just another form of market access—more markets in which to make more money. Recognizing that East Asia had little need for additional capital, the advocates of capital market liberalization came up with an argument that even at the time I thought was unconvincing, but in retrospect looks particularly strange—that it would enhance the countries' economic stability! This was to be achieved by allowing greater diversification of sources of funding.[8] It is hard to believe that these advocates had not seen the data that showed that capital flows were pro-cyclical. That is to say that capital flows out of a country in a recession, precisely when the country needs it most, and flows in during a boom, exacerbating inflationary pressures. Sure enough, just at the time the countries needed outside funds, the bankers asked for their money back.

Capital market liberalization made the developing countries subject to both the rational and the irrational whims of the investor community, to their irrational exuberance and pessimism. Keynes was well aware of the often seemingly irrational changes in sentiments. In *The General Theory of Employment, Interest and Money* (1935), he referred to these huge and often inexplicable swings in moods as "animal spirits." Nowhere were these spirits more evident than in East Asia. Slightly before the crisis, Thai bonds paid only 0.85 percent higher interest than the safest bonds in the world, that is, they were regarded as extremely safe. A short while later, the risk premium on Thai bonds had soared.

There was a second, hardly more credible argument that the advocates of capital market liberalization put forward—again without evidence. They contended that capital market controls impeded economic efficiency and that, as a result, countries would grow better without these controls. Thailand provides a case in point for why this argument was so flawed. Before liberalization, Thailand had severe limitations on the extent to which banks could lend for speculative real estate. It had imposed these limits because it was a poor country that wanted to grow, and it believed that investing the country's scarce capital in manufacturing would both create jobs and enhance growth. It also knew that throughout the world, speculative real estate lending is a major source of economic instability. This type of lending gives rise to bubbles (the soaring of prices as investors clamor to reap the gain from the seeming boom in the sector); these bubbles always burst; and when they do, the economy crashes. The pattern is familiar, and was the same in Bangkok as it was in Houston: as real estate prices rise, banks feel they can lend more on the basis of the collateral; as investors see prices going up, they want to get in on the game before it's too late—and the bankers give them the money to do it. Real estate developers see quick profits by putting up new buildings, until excess capacity results. The developers can't rent their space, they default on their loans, and the bubble bursts.

The IMF, however, contended that the kinds of restraints that Thailand had imposed to prevent a crisis interfered with the efficient market allocation of resources. If the market says, build office buildings, commercial construction *must be* the highest return activity. If the market says, as it *effectively* did after liberalization, build empty office buildings, then so be it; again, according to IMF logic, the market *must* know best. While Thailand was desperate for more public investment to strengthen its infrastructure and relatively weak secondary and university education systems, billions were squandered on commercial real estate. These buildings remain empty today, testimony to the risks posed by excessive market exuberance and the pervasive market failures that can arise in the presence of inadequate government regulation of financial institutions.[9]

The IMF, of course, was not alone in pushing for liberalization. The U.S. Treasury, which, as the IMF's largest shareholder and the only one with veto power has a large role in determining IMF policies, pushed liberalization too.

I was in President Clinton's Council of Economic Advisers in 1993 when South Korea's trade relations with the United States came up for discussion. The negotiations included a host of minor issues—such as opening up South Korea's markets to American sausages—and the important issue of financial and capital market liberalization. For three decades, Korea enjoyed remarkable economic growth without significant international investment. Growth had come based on the nation's own savings and on its own firms managed by its own people. It did not need Western funds and had demonstrated an alternative route for the importation of modern technology and market access. While its neighbors, Singapore and Malaysia, had invited in multinational companies, South Korea had created its own enterprises. Through good products and aggressive marketing, South Korean companies had sold their goods around the world. South Korea recognized that continued growth and integration in the global markets would require some liberalization, or deregulation, in the way its financial and capital markets were run. South Korea was also aware of the dangers of poor deregulation: it had seen what happened in the United States, where deregulation had culminated in the 1980s savings-and-loan debacle. In response, South Korea had carefully charted out a path of liberalization. This path was too slow for Wall Street, which saw profitable opportunities and did not want to wait. While Wall Streeters defended the principles of free markets and a limited role for government, they were not above asking help from government to push their agenda for them. And as we shall see, the Treasury Department responded with force.

At the Council of Economic Advisers we weren't convinced that South Korean liberalization was an issue of U.S. *national* interest, though obviously it would help the *special* interests of Wall Street. Also we were worried about the effect it would have on global stability. We wrote a memorandum, or "think piece," to lay out the issues, stimulate a debate, and help focus attention on the matter. We prepared a set of criteria for evaluating which market-opening measures are most vital to U.S. national interests. We argued for a system of *prioritization*. Many forms of "market access" are of little benefit to the United States. While some specific groups might benefit a great deal, the country as a whole would gain little. Without prioritization, there was a risk of what happened during the previous Bush administration: one of the supposedly great achievements in opening up Japan's market was that Toys "R" Us could sell Chinese toys to Japanese children—good for Japanese children and Chinese workers, but of little benefit to America. Though it is hard to believe that such a mild-mannered proposal could be greeted with objections, it was. Lawrence Summers, at the time undersecretary of the Treasury, adamantly opposed the exercise, saying such prioritization was unnecessary. It was the responsibility of the National Economic Council (NEC) to coordinate economic policy, to balance the economic analysis of the Council of Economic Advisers with the political pressures that were reflected in the various agencies, and decide what issues to take to the president for final decision.

The NEC, then headed by Robert Rubin, decided the issue was of insufficient importance to be brought to the president for consideration. The real reason for the opposition was only too transparent. Forcing Korea to liberalize faster would not create many jobs in America, nor would it likely lead to significant increases in American GDP. Any system of privatization would therefore not put these measures high on the agenda.[10] But worse, it was not even clear that the United States would, as a whole, even benefit, and it was clear that Korea might in fact be worse off. The U.S. Treasury, which argued to the contrary both that it was important for the United States and that it would not lead to instability, prevailed. In the final analysis, such matters are the Department of the Treasury's province, and it would be unusual for the position of the Treasury to be overridden. The fact that the debate was conducted behind closed doors meant that other voices could not be heard; perhaps if they had, if there had been more transparency in American decision making, the outcome would have been different. Instead, Treasury won, and the United

States, Korea, and the global economy lost. Treasury would probably claim that the liberalization itself was not at fault; the problem was that liberalization was done in the wrong way. But that was precisely one of the points that the Council of Economic Advisers raised: It was very likely that a quick liberalization would be done poorly.

THE FIRST ROUND OF MISTAKES

There is little doubt that IMF and Treasury policies contributed to an environment that enhanced the likelihood of a crisis by encouraging, in some cases insisting on, an unwarrantedly rapid pace toward financial and capital market liberalization. However, the IMF and Treasury made their most profound mistakes in their initial response to the crisis. Of the many failures outlined below, today there is widespread agreement on all but the criticism of IMF monetary policy.

At the onset, the IMF seemed to have misdiagnosed the problem. It had handled crises in Latin America, caused by profligate government spending and loose monetary policies that led to huge deficits and high inflation; and while it may not have handled those crises well—the region experienced a decade of stagnation after the so-called successful IMF programs, and even the creditors had eventually to absorb large losses—it at least had a game plan that had a certain coherency. East Asia was vastly different from Latin America; governments had surpluses and the economy enjoyed low inflation, but corporations were deeply indebted.

The diagnosis made a difference for two reasons. First, in the highly inflationary environment of Latin America, what was needed was a decrease in the excess demand. Given the impending recession in East Asia, the problem was not excess demand but insufficient demand. Dampening demand could only make matters worse.

Second, if firms have a low level of indebtedness, high interest rates, while painful, can still be absorbed. With high levels of indebtedness, imposing high interest rates, even for short periods of time, is like signing a death warrant for many of the firms—and for the economy.

In fact, while the Asian economies did have some weaknesses that needed to be addressed, they were no worse than those in many other countries, and surely nowhere near as bad as the IMF suggested. Indeed, the rapid recovery of Korea and Malaysia showed that, in large measure, the downturns were not unlike the dozens of recessions that have plagued market economies in the advanced industrial countries in the two hundred years of capitalism. The countries of East Asia not only had an impressive record of growth, as we have already noted, but they had had fewer downturns over the previous three decades than any of the advanced industrial countries. Two of the countries had had only one year of negative growth; two had had no recession in thirty years. In these and other dimensions, there was more to praise in East Asia than to condemn; and if East Asia was vulnerable, it was a newly acquired vulnerability—largely the result of the capital and financial market liberalization for which the IMF was itself partly culpable.

Hooverite Contractionary Policies: An Anomaly in the Modern World

For more than seventy years there has been a standard recipe for a country facing a severe economic downturn. The government must stimulate aggregate demand, either by monetary or fiscal policy—cut taxes, increase expenditures, or loosen monetary policy. When I was chairman of the Council of Economic Advisers, my main objective was to maintain the economy at full employment and maximize long-term growth. At the World Bank, I approached the problems of the countries in East Asia with the same perspective, evaluating policies to see which would be most effective in both the short and long term. The crisis economies of East Asia were clearly threatened with a major downturn and needed stimulation. The IMF pushed exactly the opposite course, with consequences precisely of the kind that one would have predicted.

At the time of the onset of the crisis, East Asia was in rough macrobalance—with low inflationary pressures and government budgets in balance or surplus. This had two obvious implications. First, the collapse of the exchange rate and the stock markets, the breaking of the real estate bubbles, accompanied by falling investment and consumption, would send it into a recession. Second, the economic collapse would result in collapsing tax revenues, and leave a budget gap. Not since Herbert Hoover have responsible economists argued that one should focus on the actual deficit rather than the structural deficit, that is, the deficit that would have been there had the economy been operating at full employment. Yet this is precisely what the IMF advocated.

Today, the IMF admits that the fiscal policy it recommended was excessively austere.[11] The policies made the recession far worse than it needed to be. During the crisis, however, in the *Financial Times* the IMF's first deputy managing director Stanley Fischer defended the IMF's policies, writing, in effect, that *all* the IMF was asking of the countries was to have a balanced budget![12] Not for sixty years have respectable economists believed that an economy going into a recession should have a balanced budget.

I felt intensely about this issue of balanced budgets. While I was at the Council of Economic Advisers, one of our major battles was over the balanced budget amendment to the Constitution. This amendment would have required the federal government to limit its expenditures to its revenues. We, *and Treasury,* were against it because we believed that it was bad economic policy. In the event of a recession, it would be all the more difficult to use fiscal policy to help the economy recover. As the economy goes into a recession, tax revenues decrease, and the amendment would have required the government to cut back expenditures (or increase taxes), which would have depressed the economy further.

Passing the amendment would have been tantamount to the government walking away from one of its central responsibilities, maintaining the economy at full employment. Despite the fact that expansionary fiscal policy was one of the few ways out of recession, and despite the administration's opposition to the balanced budget amendment, the U.S. Treasury and the IMF advocated the equivalent of a balanced budget amendment for Thailand, Korea, and other East Asian countries.

Beggar-Thyself Policies

Of all the mistakes the IMF committed as the East Asian crisis spread from one country to another in 1997 and 1998, one of the hardest to fathom was the Fund's failure to recognize the important interactions among the policies pursued in the different countries. Contractionary policies in one country not only depressed that country's economy but had adverse effects on its neighbors. By continuing to advocate contractionary policies the IMF exacerbated the *contagion*, the spread of the downturn from one country to the next. As each country weakened, it reduced its imports from its neighbors, thereby pulling its neighbors down.

The beggar-thy-neighbor policies of the 1930s are generally thought to have played an important role in the spread of the Great Depression. Each country hit by a downturn tried to bolster its own economy by cutting back on exports and thus shifting consumer demand to its own products. A country would cut back on exports by imposing tariffs and by making competitive devaluations of its currency, which made its own goods cheaper and other countries' more expensive. However, as each country cut back on imports, it succeeded in "exporting" the economic downturn to its neighbors. Hence the term *beggar-thy-neighbor*.

The IMF devised a strategy that had an effect which was even worse than the beggar-thy-neighbor policies that had devastated countries around the world during the depression of the 1930s. Countries were told that when facing a downturn they must cut back on their trade deficit, and even build a trade surplus. This might be logical if the central objective of a country's macroeconomic policy were to repay foreign creditors. By building up a war chest of foreign currency, a country will be better able to pay its bills—never mind the cost to those inside the country or elsewhere. Today, unlike the 1930s, enormous pressure is put on a country not to increase tariffs or other trade barriers in order to decrease imports, even if it faces a recession. The IMF also inveighed strongly against further devaluation. Indeed, the whole point of the bailouts was to *prevent* a further decrease in the exchange rate. This itself might seem peculiar, given the IMF's otherwise seeming faith in markets: why not let market mechanisms determine exchange rates, just as they determine other prices? But intellectual consistency has never been the hallmark of the IMF, and its single-minded worries about inflation being set off by devaluation have always prevailed. With tariffs and devaluations ruled out, there were but two ways to build a trade surplus. One was to increase exports; but this is not easy, and cannot be done quickly, particularly when the economies of your major trading partners are weak and your own financial markets are in disarray, so exporters cannot obtain finance to expand. The other was to reduce imports—by cutting incomes, that is, inducing a major recession. Unfortunately for the countries, and the world, this was the only option left. And this is what happened in East Asia in the late 1990s: contractionary fiscal and monetary policies combined with mis-guided financial policies led to massive economic downturns, cut-ting incomes, which reduced imports and led to huge trade surpluses, giving the countries the resources to pay back foreign creditors.

If one's objective was to increase the size of reserves, the policy was a success. But at what expense to the people in the country, and their neighbors! Hence the name of these policies—"beggar-thyself." The consequence for any country's trading partners was exactly the same as if beggar-thy-neighbor policies had actually been pursued. Each country's imports were cut back, which is the same as other countries' exports being cut. From the neighbors' perspectives, they couldn't care less *why* exports were cut; what they saw was the conse-quence, a reduction of sales abroad. Thus the downturn was exported around the region. Only this time, there was not even the saving grace that as the downturn was exported, the domestic economy was strengthened. As the downturn spread around the world, slower growth in the region led to a collapse in commodity prices, like oil, and the collapse in those prices wrought havoc in oil-producing countries like Russia.

Of all the failures of the IMF, this is perhaps the saddest, because it represented the greatest betrayal of its entire raison d'être. It did worry about contagion—contagion from one capital market to another transmitted through the fears of investors—though as we saw in the last section, the policies it had pushed had made the countries far more vulnerable to the volatility of investor sentiment. A collapse in the exchange rate in Thailand might make investors in Brazil worry about markets there. The buzzword was *confidence*. A lack of confidence in one country could spread to a lack of confidence in emerging markets. But more generally, the IMF's performance as market psychologist left something to be desired. Creating deep recessions with massive bankruptcies and/or pointing out deep-seated problems in the best performing region of the emerging markets are policies hardly designed to restore confidence. But even had it done better in restoring confidence, questions should have been raised: in focusing on protecting investors, it had forgotten about those in the countries it was supposed to be helping; in focusing on financial variables, like exchange rates, it had almost forgotten about the real side of the economy. It had lost sight of its original mission.

Strangling an Economy with High Interest Rates

Today, the IMF agrees that the *fiscal* policies (those relating to the levels of government deficits) it pushed were excessively contractionary, but it does not own up to the mistakes of monetary policy. When the Fund entered East Asia, it forced countries to raise interest rates to what, in conventional terms, would be considered astronomical levels. I remember meetings where President Clinton was frustrated that the Federal Reserve Bank, headed by Alan Greenspan, an appointee from past administrations, was about to raise interest rates one-quarter or one-half percentage point. He worried that it would destroy "his" recovery. He felt he had been elected on a platform of "It's the economy, stupid," and "Jobs, Jobs, Jobs" and he didn't want the Fed to hurt his plans. He knew that the Fed was concerned with inflation, but thought those fears were excessive—a sentiment which I shared, and which the subsequent events bore out. The president worried about the adverse effect interest rate increases would have on unemployment, and the economic recovery just getting underway. And this in the country with one of the best business environments in the world. Yet in East Asia, IMF bureaucrats, who were even less politically accountable, forced interest rate increases not ten but fifty times greater—interest rate increases of more than 25 percentage points. If Clinton worried about the adverse effects of a half-point increase on an economy experiencing a nascent recovery, he would have been apoplectic about the effect of those huge increases in interest rates on an economy plunging into a recession. Korea first raised its interest rates to 25 percent, but was told that to be serious it must allow interest rates to go still higher. Indonesia raised its interest rates in a preemptive move before the crisis, but was told that that was not good enough. Nominal interest rates soared.

The reasoning behind these policies was simple, if not simplistic. If a country raised interest rates, it would make it more attractive for capital to flow into that country. Capital flows into the country would help support the exchange rate and thus stabilize the currency. End of argument.

At first glance, this appears logical. However, consider the case of South Korea as an example. Recall that in South Korea the crisis was started by foreign banks refusing to roll over their short-term loans. They refused because they worried about South Korean firms' ability to repay. Bankruptcy—default—was at the center of the discussion. But in the IMF model—as in the models of most of the macroeconomics textbooks written two decades ago—bankruptcy plays no role. To discuss monetary policy and finance without bankruptcy is like *Hamlet* without the Prince of Denmark. At the heart of the analysis of the macroeconomy *should* have been an analysis of what an increase in interest rates would do to the chances of default and to the amount that creditors can recover in the event of default. Many of the firms in East Asia were highly indebted, and had huge debt equity ratios. Indeed, the excessive leverage had repeatedly been cited as one of South Korea's weaknesses, *even by the IMF*. Highly leveraged companies are particularly sensitive to interest rate increases, especially to the extremely high levels urged by the IMF. At very high interest rate levels, a highly leveraged company goes bankrupt quickly. Even if it does not go bankrupt, its equity (net worth) is quickly depleted as it is forced to pay huge amounts to creditors.

The Fund recognized that the underlying problems in East Asia were weak financial institutions and overleveraged firms; yet it pushed high interest rate policies that actually exacerbated those problems. The consequences were precisely as predicted: The high interest rates increased the number of firms in distress, and thereby increased the number of banks facing nonperforming loans.[13] This weakened the banks further. The increased distress in the corporate and financial sectors exacerbated the downturn that the contractionary policies were inducing through the reduction in aggregate demand. The IMF had engineered a simultaneous contraction in aggregate demand *and* supply.

In defending its policies, the IMF said they would help restore market confidence in the affected countries. But clearly countries in deep recession did not inspire confidence. Consider a Jakarta businessman who has put almost all of his wealth into East Asia. As the regional economy plummets—as contractionary policies take hold and amplify the downturn—he suddenly realizes that his portfolio is hardly sufficiently diversified, and shifts investment to the booming U.S. stock market. Local investors, just like international investors, were not interested in pouring money into an economy going into a tailspin. Higher interest rates did not attract more capital into the country. On the contrary, the higher rates made the recession worse and actually drove capital *out* of the country.

The IMF came up with another defense, of no more validity. They argued that if interest rates were not greatly increased, the exchange rate would collapse, and this would be devastating to the economy, as those who had dollar-denominated debts would not be able to pay them. But the fact was that, for reasons that should have been apparent, raising interest rates did not stabilize the currency; the countries were thus forced to lose on both accounts. Moreover, the IMF never bothered to look at the details of what was going on inside the countries. In Thailand, for instance, it was the already bankrupt real estate firms and those that lent to them who had the most foreign-denominated debt. Further devaluations might have harmed the foreign creditors but would not have made these firms any more dead. In effect, the IMF made the small businesses and other innocent bystanders pay for those who had engaged in excessive dollar borrowing—and to no avail.

When I pleaded with the IMF for a change in policies, and pointed out the disaster that would ensue if the current course were to be continued, there was a curt reply: If I were proven correct, the Fund would change its policies. I was appalled by this wait-and-see attitude. All economists know there are long lags in policy. The benefits of changing course will not be felt for six to eighteen months, while enormous damage could be done in the meantime.

That damage was done in East Asia. Because many firms were highly leveraged, many were forced into bankruptcy. In Indonesia, an estimated 75 percent of all businesses were put into distress, while in Thailand close to 50 percent of bank loans became nonperforming. Unfortunately, it is far easier to destroy a firm than to create a new one. Lowering interest rates would not un-bankrupt a firm that had been forced into bankruptcy: its net worth would still have been wiped out. The IMF's mistakes were costly, and slow to reverse.

Naive geopolitical reasoning, vestiges of Kissinger-style *realpolitik* compounded the consequences of these mistakes. In 1997, Japan offered $100 billion to help create an Asian Monetary Fund, in order to finance the required stimulative actions. But Treasury did everything it could to squelch the idea. The IMF joined in. The reason for the IMF's position was clear: While the IMF was a strong advocate of competition in markets, it did not want competition in its own domain, and the Asian Monetary Fund would provide that. The U.S. Treasury's motivations were similar. As the only shareholder of the IMF with veto power, the United States had considerable say in IMF policies. It was widely known that Japan disagreed strongly with the IMF's actions—I had repeated meetings with senior Japanese officials in which they expressed misgivings about IMF policies that were almost identical to my own.[14] With Japan, and possibly China, as the likely major contributors to the Asian Monetary Fund, their voices would predominate, providing a real challenge to American "leadership"—and control.

The importance of control—including control over the media—was brought home forcefully in the early days of the crisis. When World Bank Vice President for East Asia Jean Michel Severino pointed out in a widely discussed speech that several countries in the region were going into a deep recession, or even depression, he received a strong verbal tongue-lashing from Summers. It was simply unacceptable to use the R (for recession) or D (for depression) words, even though by then it was clear that Indonesia's GDP was likely to fall between 10 to 15 percent, a magnitude that clearly warranted the use of those harsh terms.

Eventually, Summers, Fischer, Treasury, and the IMF could not ignore the depression. Japan once again made a generous offer to help under the Miyazawa Initiative, named after Japan's finance minister. This time the offer was scaled down to $30 billion, and was accepted. But even then the United States argued that the money should be spent not to stimulate the economy through fiscal expansion, but for corporate and financial restructuring—effectively, to help bail out American and other foreign banks and other creditors. The squashing of the Asian Monetary Fund is still resented in Asia and many officials have spoken to me angrily about the incident. Three years after the crisis, the countries of East Asia finally got together to begin, quietly, the creation of a more modest version of the Asian Monetary Fund, under the innocuous name of the Chang Mai Initiative, named after the city in northern Thailand where it was launched.

THE SECOND ROUND OF MISTAKES: BUMBLING RESTRUCTURING

As the crisis worsened, the need for "restructuring" became the new mantra. Banks that had bad loans on their books should be shut down, companies that owed money should be closed or taken over by their creditors. The IMF focused on this rather than simply performing the role it was supposed to fill: providing liquidity to finance needed expenditures. Alas, even this focus on restructuring failed, and much of what the IMF did helped push the sinking economies down further.

Financial Systems

The East Asia crisis was, first and foremost, a crisis of the financial system, and this needed to be dealt with. The financial system can be compared to the brain of the economy. It allocates scarce capital among competing uses by trying to direct it to where it is most effective, in other words, where it yields the highest returns. The financial system also monitors the funds to ensure that they are used in the way promised. If the financial system breaks down, firms cannot get the working capital they need to continue existing levels of production, let alone finance expansion through new investment. A crisis can give rise to a vicious circle wherein banks cut back on their finance, leading firms to cut back on their production, which in turn leads to lower output and lower incomes. As output and incomes plummet, profits fall, and some firms are even forced into bankruptcy. When firms declare bankruptcy, banks' balance sheets become worse, and the banks cut back lending even further, exacerbating the economic downturn.

If enough firms fail to repay their loans, banks may even collapse. A collapse of even a single large bank can have disastrous consequences. Financial institutions determine creditworthiness. This information is highly specific, cannot easily be transmitted, and is embedded in the records and institutional memory of the bank (or other financial institution). When a bank goes out of business, much of the creditworthiness information it has on its borrowers is destroyed, and that information is expensive to recreate. Even in more advanced countries, a typical small or medium-sized enterprise may obtain credit from at most two or three banks. When a bank goes out of business in good times, many of its customers will have difficulty finding an alternative supplier of credit overnight. In developing countries, where sources of finance are even more limited, if the bank that a business relies upon fails, finding a new source of funds—especially during an economic downturn—may be nearly impossible.

Fears of this vicious circle have induced governments throughout the world to strengthen their financial systems through prudent regulation. Repeatedly, free marketeers have bridled against these regulations. When their voices have been heeded the consequences have been disastrous, whether in Chile in 1982–83, in which Chilean gross domestic product fell by 13.7 percent and one in five workers was unemployed, or the United States in the Reagan era, where, as we noted earlier, deregulation led to the savings-and-loan debacle, costing American taxpayers $200 billion.

A recognition of the importance of maintaining credit flows has similarly guided policy makers in trying to deal with the problems of financial restructuring. Fears about the adverse effects of this "destruction of informational capital" partially explain why the United States, during the S&L debacle, closed down very few banks outright. Most of the weak banks were taken over by or merged into other banks, and customers hardly knew of the switch. In this way, the information capital was preserved. Even so, the S&L crisis was an important contributing factor to the 1991 recession.

Inducing a Bank Run

Although financial system weaknesses were far more pervasive in East Asia than in the United States, and the IMF's rhetoric continually focused on these weaknesses as underlying the East Asia crisis, the IMF failed to understand how financial markets work and their impact on the rest of the economy. Its crude macromodels never embraced a broad picture of financial markets at the aggregate level, but were even more deficient at the microlevel—that is, at the level of the firm. The Fund did not adequately take into account the corporate and financial distress to which its so-called stabilization policies, including the high interest rates, contributed so strongly.

As they approached the problem of restructuring, IMF teams in East Asia focused on shutting down weak banks; it was as if they had a Darwinian model of competition in mind, so the weak banks *must* not survive. There was some basis for their position. Elsewhere, allowing weak banks to continue to operate *without tight supervision* resulted in their making highly risky loans. They gambled by making high-risk, high-return loans—if they were lucky, the loans would be repaid, and the higher interest rates would bring them back to solvency. If they were unlucky, they would go out of business—with the government picking up the pieces—but that is what would happen to them in any case if they did not embark on the risky loan strategy. But too often, such risky loans indeed turn out to be bad loans, and when the day of reckoning comes, the government faces an even bigger bailout than if the bank had been shut down earlier. This was one of the lessons that had emerged so clearly from the U.S. savings-and-loan debacle: the refusal of the Reagan administration to deal with the problem for years meant that when the crisis could no longer be ignored, the cost to the taxpayer was far larger. But the IMF overlooked another critical lesson: the importance of keeping credit flowing.

Its strategy for financial restructuring involved triage—separating out the really sick banks, which should be closed immediately, from the healthy banks. A third group were those that were sick but reparable. Banks are required to have a certain ratio of capital to their outstanding loans and other assets; this ratio is termed the *capital adequacy ratio*. Not surprisingly, when many loans are nonperforming, many banks fail to meet their capital adequacy ratio. The IMF insisted that banks either shut down or *quickly* meet this capital adequacy ratio. But this insistence on banks quickly meeting capital adequacy standards exacerbated the downturn. The Fund made the kind of mistake that we warn students about in the first course in economics, called "the fallacy of composition." When only one bank has a problem, then insisting on its meeting its capital adequacy standards makes sense. But when many, or most, banks are in trouble, that policy can be disastrous. There are two ways of increasing the ratio of capital to loans: increasing capital or reducing loans. In the midst of a downturn, especially of the magnitude of that in East Asia, it is hard to raise new capital. The alternative is to reduce outstanding loans. But as each bank calls in its loans, more and more firms are put into distress. Without adequate working capital, they are forced to cut back on their production, cutting into the demand for products from other firms. The downward spiral is exacerbated. And with more firms in distress, the capital adequacy ratio of banks can even be worsened. The attempt to improve the financial position of the banks backfired.

With a large number of banks shut down, and with those managing to survive facing an increasingly large number of loans in distress, and unwilling to take on new customers, more and businesses found themselves without access to credit. Without credit, the one glimmer of hope for a recovery would be squashed. The depreciation of the currency meant that exports should have boomed, as the goods from the region became cheaper, by 30 percent or more. But while export volumes increased, they did not increase nearly as much as expected, and for a simple reason: to expand exports, firms needed to have working capital to produce more. As banks shut down and cut back on their lending, firms could not even get the working capital required to maintain production, let alone to expand.

Nowhere was the IMF's lack of understanding of financial markets so evident as in its policies toward closing banks in Indonesia. There, some sixteen private banks were closed down, and notice was given that other banks might be subsequently shut down as well; but depositors, except for those with very small accounts, would be left to fend for themselves. Not surprisingly, this engendered a run on the remaining private banks, and deposits were quickly shifted to state banks, which were thought to have an implicit government guarantee. The effects on the Indonesia banking system, and economy, were disastrous, compounding the mistakes in fiscal and monetary policy already discussed, and almost sealing that country's fate: a depression had become inevitable.

In contrast, South Korea ignored outside advice, and recapitalized its two largest banks rather than closing them down. This is part of why Korea recovered relatively quickly.

Corporate Restructuring

While attention focused on financial restructuring, it was clear that the problems in the financial sector could not be resolved unless the problems in the corporate sector were effectively addressed. With 75 percent of the firms in Indonesia in distress, and half of the loans in Thailand nonperforming, the corporate sector was entering a stage of paralysis. Firms that are facing bankruptcy are in a state of limbo: it is not clear who really owns them, the current owners or the creditors. Issues of ownership are not fully resolved until the firm emerges from bankruptcy. But without clear owners, there is always a temptation for current management and the old owners to strip assets, and such asset stripping did occur. In the United States and other countries, when companies go into bankruptcy, trustees are appointed by the courts to prevent this. But in Asia there were neither the legal frameworks nor the personnel to implement trusteeships. It was thus imperative that bankruptcies and corporate distress be resolved quickly, before stripping could occur. Unfortunately, IMF's misguided economics, having contributed to the mess through the high interest rates which forced so many firms into distress, conspired with ideology and special interests to dampen the pace of restructuring.

The IMF's strategy for corporate restructuring—restructuring the firms that were effectively in bankruptcy—was no more successful than its strategy for restructuring banks. It confused *financial* restructuring—entailing straightening out who really owns the firm, the discharge of debt or its conversion to equity—with *real* restructuring, the nuts-and-bolts decisions: what the firm should produce, how it should produce its output, and how it should be organized. In the presence of the massive economic downturn, there were real macrobenefits from rapid financial restructuring. Individual participants in the bargaining surrounding bankruptcy workouts would fail to take into account these systemic benefits. It might pay them to drag their feet—and bankruptcy negotiations are often protracted, taking more than a year or two. When only a few firms in an economy are bankrupt, this delay has little social cost; when many firms are in distress, the social cost can be enormous, as the macroeconomic downturn is prolonged. It is thus imperative that the government do whatever it can to facilitate a quick resolution.

I took the view that the government should play an active role in pushing this financial restructuring, ensuring that there were real owners. My view was that once ownership issues were resolved, the new owners should set about the task of deciding the issues of real restructuring. The IMF took the opposite view, saying that the government should *not* take an active role in financial restructuring, but push for real restructuring, selling assets, for instance, to reduce South Korea's *seeming* excess capacity in chips and bringing in outside (typically foreign) management. I saw no reason to believe that international bureaucrats, trained in macromanagement, had any special insight into corporate restructuring in general, or the chip industry in particular. While restructuring is, in any case, a slow process, the governments of Korea and Malaysia took an active role, and succeeded within a remarkably short period of time, two years, in completing the financial restructuring of a remarkably large fraction of the firms in distress. By contrast, restructuring in Thailand, which followed the IMF strategy, languished.

THE MOST GRIEVOUS MISTAKES:
RISKING SOCIAL AND POLITICAL TURMOIL

The social and political consequences of mishandling the Asian crisis may never be measured fully. When the IMF's managing director Michel Camdessus, and G-22 finance ministers and central bank governors (the finance ministers and central bank governors from the major industrial countries, plus the major Asian economies, including Australia) met in Kuala Lumpur, Malaysia, in early December 1997, I warned of the danger of social and political unrest, especially in countries where there has been a history of ethnic division (as in Indonesia, where there had been massive ethnic rioting some thirty years earlier), if the excessively contractionary monetary and fiscal policies that were being imposed continued. Camdessus calmly responded that they needed to follow Mexico's example; they had to take the painful measures if they were to recover. Unfortunately, my forecasts turned out to be all too right. Just over five months after I warned of the impending disaster, riots broke out. While the IMF had provided some $23 billion to be used to support the exchange rate and bail out creditors, the far, far smaller sums required to help the poor were not forthcoming. In American parlance, there were billions and billions for corporate welfare, but not the more modest millions for welfare for ordinary citizens. Food and fuel subsidies for the poor in Indonesia were drastically cut back, and riots exploded the next day. As had happened thirty years earlier, the Indonesian businessmen and their families became the victims.

It was not just that IMF policy might be regarded by softheaded liberals as inhumane. Even if one cared little for those who faced starvation, or the children whose growth would be stunted by malnutrition, it was simply bad economics. Riots do not restore business confidence. They drive capital out of a country; they do not attract capital into a country. And riots are predictable—like any social phenomenon, not with certainty, but with a high probability. It was clear Indonesia was ripe for such social upheaval. The IMF itself should have known this; around the world, the IMF has inspired riots when its policies cut off food subsidies.

After the riots in Indonesia, the IMF reversed its position; food subsidies were restored. But again, the IMF showed that it had not learned the basic lesson of "irreversibility." Just as a firm that was bankrupted by the high interest rates does not become "un-bankrupted" when the interest rates were lowered, a society that is rendered asunder by riots induced by cutting out food subsides just as it is plunging into depression is not brought together when the food subsidies are restored. Indeed, in some quarters, the bitterness is all the greater: if the food subsidies could have been afforded, why were they taken away in the first place?

I had the opportunity to talk to Malaysia's prime minister after the riots in Indonesia. His country had also experienced ethnic riots in the past. Malaysia had done a lot to prevent their recurrence, including putting in a program to promote employment for ethnic Malays. Mahathir knew that all the gains in building a multiracial society could be lost, had he let the IMF dictate its policies to him and his country and then riots had broken out. For him, preventing a severe recession was not just a matter of economics, it was a matter of the survival of the nation.

RECOVERY: VINDICATION OF THE IMF POLICIES?

As this book goes to press, the crisis is over. Many Asian countries are growing again, their recovery slightly stalled by the global slowdown that began in 2000. The countries that managed to avoid a recession in 1998, Taiwan and Singapore, fell into one in 2001; Korea is doing far better. With a worldwide downturn affecting the United States and Germany as well, no one talked about weak institutions and poor governments as the cause of recessions; now, they seemed to have remembered that such fluctuations have always been part of market economies.

But although some at the IMF believe their interventions were successful, it's widely agreed that serious mistakes were made. Indeed, the nature of the recovery shows this. Almost every economic downturn comes to an end. But the Asian crisis was more severe than it should have been, recovery took longer than it needed to, and prospects for future growth are not what they should be.

On Wall Street, a crisis is over as soon as financial variables begin to turn around. So long as exchange rates are weakening or stock prices falling, it is not clear where the bottom lies. But once the bottom has been reached, the losses are at least capped and the worst is known. However, to truly measure recovery, stabilization of exchange rates or interest rates is not enough. People do not live off exchange rates or interest rates. Workers care about jobs and wages. Although the unemployment rate and real wages may have bottomed out, that is not enough for the worker who remains unemployed or who has seen his income fall by a quarter. There is no true recovery until workers return to their jobs and wages are restored to pre-crisis levels. Today, incomes in the countries of East Asia affected by the crisis are still 20 percent below what they would have been had their growth continued at the pace of the previous decade. In Indonesia, output in 2000 was still 7.5 percent lower than in 1997, and even Thailand, the IMF's best pupil, had not attained its pre-crisis level, let alone made up for the lost growth. This is not the first instance of the IMF declaring victory prematurely: Mexico's crisis in 1995 was declared over as soon as the banks and international lenders started to get repaid; but five years after the crisis, workers were just getting back to where they were beforehand. The very fact that the IMF focuses on financial variables, not on measure of real wages, unemployment, GDP, or broader measures of welfare, is itself telling.

The question of how best to manage a recovery is difficult, and the answer clearly depends on the cause of the problem. For many downturns, the best prescription is the standard Keynesian one: expansionary fiscal and monetary policy. The problems in East Asia were more complicated, because *part* of the problem was weaknesses in finance—weak banks and firms with excess leverage. But a deepening recession makes these problems worse. Pain is not a virtue in its own right; pain by itself does not help the economy; and the pain caused by IMF policies, deepening recession, made recovery more difficult. Sometimes, as in Latin America, in Argentina, Brazil, and a host of other countries during the 1970s, crises are caused by profligate governments spending beyond their means, and in those cases, the government will need to cut back expenditures or increase taxes—decisions which are painful, at least in the political sense. But because East Asia had neither loose monetary policies nor profligate public sectors—inflation was low and stable, and budgets prior to the crisis were in surplus—those were not the right measures for dealing with East Asia's crisis.

The problem with the IMF's mistakes is that they are likely to be long-lasting. The IMF often talked as if what the economy needed was a good purgative. Take the pain; the deeper the pain, the stronger the subsequent growth. In the IMF theory, then, a country concerned about its *long-run* prospects—say twenty years from now—should swallow hard and accept a deep downturn. People today would suffer, but their children at least would be better off. Unfortunately, the evidence does not support the IMF's theory. An economy which has a deep recession may grow faster as it recovers, but it never makes up for the lost time. The deeper today's recession, the lower the likely income even twenty years from now. It is not, as the IMF claims, that they are likely to be better off. The effects of a recession are long-lasting. There is an important implication: The deeper the recession today, not only is output lower today, but the lower output is likely to be for years to come. In a way, this is good news, since it means that the best medicine for today's health of the economy and the best medicine for tomorrow's coincide. It implies that economic policy should be directed at minimizing the depth and duration of any economic downturn. Unfortunately, this was neither the intention nor the impact of the IMF prescriptions.

Malaysia and China

By contrasting what happened in Malaysia and in China, two nations that chose not to have IMF programs, with the rest of East Asia, which did, the negative effects of the IMF policies will show clearly. Malaysia was severely criticized during the crisis by the international financial community. Though Prime Minister Mahathir's rhetoric and human rights policies often leave much to be desired, many of his economic policies were a success.

Malaysia was reluctant to join the IMF program, partly because officials there did not want to be dictated to by outsiders but also because they had little confidence in the IMF. Early on in the 1997 crisis, IMF chief Michael Camdessus announced that Malaysia's banks were in a weak position. An IMF/World Bank team was quickly dispatched to look at the country's banking system. While there was a high level of nonperforming loans (15%), Malaysia's Central Bank had imposed strong regulations which had resulted in banks making adequate provisions for these losses. Moreover, Malaysia' strong regulatory stance had prevented banks from exposure to foreign exchange volatility (the danger of borrowing in dollars and lending in ringgit), and had even limited the foreign indebtedness of the companies to which these banks lent (precautionary prescriptions which were, at the time, not part of the IMF standard package).

The standard way to assess the strength of a banking system is to subject it, in simulation exercises, to stress tests and evaluate its response under different economic circumstances. The Malaysian banking system fared quite well. Few banking systems could survive a long recession, or a depression, and Malaysia's was no exception; but Malaysia's banking system was remarkably strong. During one of my many visits to Malaysia, I saw the discomfort of the IMF staffers writing the report: how to formulate it without contradicting the managing director's assertions and yet remain consistent with the evidence.

Within Malaysia itself, the issue of the appropriate response to the crisis was hotly debated. Finance Minister Anwar Ibrahim proposed "an IMF program without the IMF," that is, raising interest rates and cutting back on expenditures. Mahathir remained skeptical. Eventually, he dumped his finance minister and economic policies were reversed.

As the regional crisis grew into a global crisis, and international capital markets went into a seizure, Mahathir acted again. In September 1998, Malaysia pegged the ringgit at 3.80 to the dollar, cut interest rates, and decreed that all offshore ringgit be repatriated by the end of the month. The government also imposed tight limits on transfers of capital abroad by residents in Malaysia and froze the repatriation of foreign portfolio capital for twelve months. These measures were announced as short term, and were carefully designed to make it clear that the country was not hostile to long-term foreign investment. Those who had invested money in Malaysia and had profits were allowed to take them out. On September 7, 1998, in a now-famous column in *Fortune* magazine, the noted economist Paul Krugman urged Mahathir to impose capital controls. But he was in the minority. Malaysia's Central Bank governor Ahmad Mohamed Don and his deputy, Fong Weng Phak, both resigned, reportedly because they disagreed with the imposition of the controls. Some economists—those from Wall Street joined by the IMF—predicted disaster when the controls were imposed, saying foreign investors would be scared off for years to come. They expected foreign investment to plummet, the stock market to fall, and a black market in the ringgit, with its accompanying distortions, to form. And, they warned, while the controls would lead to a drying up of capital *inflows*, they would be ineffective in stopping capital *outflows*. Capital flight would occur anyway. Pundits predicted that the economy would suffer, growth would be halted, the controls would never be lifted, and that Malaysia was postponing addressing the underlying problems. Even Treasury Secretary Robert Rubin, usually of such quiet demeanor, joined in the communal tongue-lashing.

In fact, the outcome was far different. My team at the World Bank worked with Malaysia to convert the capital controls into an exit tax. Since rapid capital flows into or out of a country cause large disturbances, they generate what economists call "large externalities"—effects on other, ordinary people not involved in these capital flows. Such flows lead to massive disturbances to the overall economy. Government has the right, even the obligation, to take measures to address such disturbances. In general, economists believe that market-based interventions such as taxes are more effective and have fewer adverse side effects than direct controls, so we at the World Bank encouraged Malaysia to drop direct controls and impose an exit tax. Moreover, the tax could be gradually lowered, so that there would be no large disturbance when the interventions were finally removed.

Things worked just as planned. Malaysia removed the tax just as it had promised, one year after the imposition of controls. In fact, Malaysia had once before imposed temporary capital controls, and had removed them as soon as things stabilized. This historical experience was ignored by those who attacked the country so roundly. In the one-year interim, Malaysia had restructured its banks and corporations, proving the critics, who had said that it was only with the discipline that comes from free capital markets that governments ever do anything serious, wrong once again. Indeed, it had made far more progress in that direction than Thailand, which followed the IMF prescriptions. In retrospect, it was clear that Malaysia's capital controls allowed it to recover more quickly, with a shallower downturn,[15] and with a far smaller legacy of national debt burdening future growth. The controls allowed it to have lower interest rates than it could otherwise have had; the lower interest rates meant that fewer firms were put into bankruptcy, and so the magnitude of publicly funded corporate and financial bailout was smaller. The lower interest rates meant too that recovery could occur with less reliance on fiscal policy, and consequently less government borrowing. Today, Malaysia stands in a far better position than those countries that took IMF advice. There was little evidence that the capital controls discouraged foreign investors. Foreign investment actually increased.[16] Because investors are concerned about economic stability, and because Malaysia had done a far better job in maintaining that stability than many of its neighbors, it was able to attract investment.

CHINA WAS THE other country that followed an independent course. It is no accident that the two large developing countries spared the ravages of the global economic crisis—India and China— both had capital controls. While developing world countries with liberalized capital markets actually saw their incomes decline, India grew at a rate in excess of 5 percent and China at close to 8 percent. This is all the more remarkable given the overall slowdown in world growth, and in trade in particular, during that period. China achieved this by following the prescriptions of economic orthodoxy. These were not the Hooverite IMF prescriptions, but the standard prescriptions that economists have been teaching for more than half a century: When faced with an economic downturn, respond with expansionary macroeconomic policy. China seized the opportunity to combine its short-run needs with long-run growth objectives. The rapid growth over the preceding decade, anticipated to continue into the next century, created enormous demands on infrastructure. There were large opportunities for public investments with high returns, including projects underway that were sped up, and projects that were already designed but had been put on the shelf for lack of funds. The standard medicines worked, and China averted a growth slowdown.

While making economic policy decisions, China was aware of the link between macrostability and its microeconomy. It knew that it needed to continue restructuring its corporate and financial sector. However, it also recognized that an economic slowdown would make it all the more difficult to proceed with a reform agenda. An economic slowdown would throw more firms into distress and make more loans nonperforming, thereby weakening the banking system. An economic slowdown would also increase unemployment, and rising unemployment would make the social costs of restructuring the state enterprises much higher. And China recognized the links between economics and political and social stability. It had in its recent history all too often experienced the consequences of instability, and wanted none of that. In all respects, China fully appreciated the *systemic* consequences of macroeconomic policies, consequences that the IMF policies habitually overlooked.

This is not to say that China is out of the woods. The restructuring of its banking and state-owned enterprises still represents a challenge for it in the years ahead. But these are challenges that can be far better addressed in the context of a strong macroeconomy.

Though the differences in individual circumstances make the reasons either for the occurrence of a crisis or for quick recovery hard to ascertain, I think it is no accident that the only major East Asian country, China, to avert the crisis took a course directly opposite that advocated by the IMF, and that the country with the shortest downturn, Malaysia, also explicitly rejected an IMF strategy.

Korea, Thailand, and Indonesia

Korea and Thailand provide further contrasts. After a short period of policy vacillation from July through October 1997, Thailand followed IMF prescriptions almost perfectly. Yet more than three years after the beginning of the crisis, it was still in recession, with a GDP approximately 2.3 percent below the pre-crisis level. Little corporate restructuring had taken place, and close to 40 percent of the loans were still nonperforming.

In contrast, Korea did not close down banks according to the standard IMF prescription, and the Korean government, like Malaysia's, took a more active role in restructuring corporations. Moreover, Korea kept its exchange rate low, rather than letting it rebound. This was ostensibly to enable it to reestablish its reserves, since by buying dollars for its reserves it depressed the value of the won. Actually, Korea kept the exchange rate low in order to sustain exports and limit imports. Moreover, Korea did not follow the IMF's advice concerning *physical* restructuring. The IMF acted as if it knew more about the global chip industry than these firms who had made it their business, and argued that Korea should quickly get rid of the excess capacity. Korea, smartly, ignored this advice. As the demand for chips recovered, the economy recovered. Had the IMF's advice been followed, the recovery would have been far more muted.

In evaluating the recoveries, most analysts put Indonesia aside, simply because the economy has been dominated by political events and social turmoil. However, the political and social turmoil are themselves attributable in no small measure to IMF policies, as we have seen. No one will know whether there could have been a more graceful transition from Suharto, but few would doubt that it could have been more tumultuous.

Effects on the Future

Despite the many hardships, the East Asian crisis has had salutary effects. East Asian countries will undoubtedly develop better financial regulatory systems, and better financial institutions overall. Though its firms had already demonstrated a remarkable ability to compete in the global marketplace, Korea is likely to emerge with a more competitive economy. Some of the worst aspects of corruption, the so-called crony capitalism, will have been checked.

However, the manner in which the crisis was addressed—particularly the use of high interest rates—is likely to have a significantly adverse effect on the region's intermediate, and possibly long-term, economic growth. There is a certain irony in the central reason for this. Weak, underregulated financial institutions are bad because they lead to bad resource allocations. While East Asia's banks were far from perfect, over the preceding three decades their achievements in allocating the enormous flows of capital were, in fact, quite impressive—this was what sustained their rapid growth. Although the intention of those pushing for "reforms" in East Asia was to improve the ability of the financial system to allocate resources, in fact, the IMF's policies are likely to have impaired the *overall* efficiency of the market.

Around the world, very little new investment is financed by raising new equity (selling shares of stock in a company). Indeed, the only countries with widely diversified share ownership are the United States, the United Kingdom, and Japan, all of which have strong legal systems and strong shareholder protections. It takes time to develop these legal institutions, and few countries have succeeded in doing so. In the meantime, firms around the world must rely on debt. But debt is inherently risky. IMF strategies, such as capital market liberalization and raising interest rates to exorbitant levels when a crisis occurs, make borrowing even riskier. To respond rationally, firms will engage in lower levels of borrowing and force themselves to rely more heavily on retained earnings. Thus growth in the future will be constrained, and capital will not flow as freely as it otherwise would to the most productive uses. In this way, IMF policies lead to less efficient resource allocation, particularly capital allocation, which is the scarcest resource in developing countries. The IMF does not take this impairment into account because its models do not reflect the realities of how capital markets actually work, including the impact of the imperfections of information on capital markets.

EXPLAINING THE MISTAKES

While the IMF now agrees it made serious mistakes in its fiscal policy advice, in how it pushed bank restructuring in Indonesia, in perhaps pushing capital market liberalization prematurely, and in underestimating the importance of the interregional impacts, by which the downfall of one country contributed to that of its neighbors, it has not admitted to the mistakes in its monetary policy, nor has it even sought to explain why its models failed to predict the course of events so miserably. It has not sought to develop an alternative intellectual frame—implying that in the next crisis, it may well make the same mistakes. (In January 2002, the IMF chalked up one more failure to its credit—Argentina. Part of the reason is its insistence once again on contractionary fiscal policy.)

Part of the explanation of the *magnitude* of the failures has to do with hubris: no one likes to admit a mistake, especially a mistake of this magnitude or with these consequences. Neither Fischer nor Summers, neither Rubin nor Camdessus, neither the IMF nor the U.S. Treasury wanted to think that their policies were misguided. They stuck to their positions, in spite of what I viewed as overwhelming evidence of their failure. (When the IMF finally decided to support lower interest rates and reversed its support for fiscal contraction in East Asia, it said it was because the time was right. I would suggest that it reversed courses partly due to public pressure.)

But in Asia other theories abound, including a conspiracy theory that I do not share which views the policies either as a deliberate attempt to weaken East Asia—the region of the world that had shown the greatest growth over the previous forty years—or at least to enhance the incomes of those on Wall Street and the other money centers. One can understand how this line of thinking developed: The IMF first told countries in Asia to open up their markets to hot short-term capital. The countries did it and money flooded in, but just as suddenly flowed out. The IMF then said interest rates should be raised and there should be a fiscal contraction, and a deep recession was induced. As asset prices plummeted, the IMF urged affected countries to sell their assets even at bargain basement prices. It said the companies needed solid foreign management (conveniently ignoring that these companies had a most enviable record of growth over the preceding decades, hard to reconcile with bad management) and that this would only happen if the companies were sold to foreigners—not just managed by them. The sales were handled by the same foreign financial institutions that had pulled out their capital, precipitating the crisis. These banks then got large commissions from their work selling the troubled companies or splitting them up, just as they had got large commissions when they had originally guided the money into the countries in the first place. As the events unfolded, cynicism grew even greater: some of these American and other financial companies didn't do much restructuring; they just held the assets until the economy recovered, making profits from buying at the fire sale prices and selling at more normal prices.

I believe that there is a simpler set of explanations—the IMF was not participating in a conspiracy, but it was reflecting the interests and ideology of the Western financial community. Modes of operation which were secretive insulated the institution and its policies from the kind of intensive scrutiny that might have forced it to use models and adopt policies that were appropriate to the situation in East Asia. The failures in East Asia bear much in common with those in development and in transition, and in chapters 8 and 9 we will take a closer look at the common causes.

AN ALTERNATIVE STRATEGY

In response to the complaints I continue to raise about the IMF-Treasury strategy, my critics have rightly asked what I would have done. This chapter has already hinted at the basic strategy: Maintain the economy at as close to full employment as possible. Attaining that objective, in turn, entails an expansionary (or at least not contractionary) monetary and fiscal policy, the exact mix of which would depend on the country in question. I agreed with the IMF on the importance of financial restructuring—addressing the problems of weak banks—but I would have approached it totally differently, with a primary objective of maintaining the flow of finance, and a standstill on existing debt repayment: a debt restructuring, such as that which eventually worked for Korea Maintaining the flow of finance, in turn, would require greater efforts at restructuring existing institutions. And a key part of corporate restructuring would entail the implementation of a special bankruptcy provision aimed at the quick resolution of distress resulting from the macroeconomic disturbances that were well beyond the normal. The U.S. bankruptcy code has provisions which allow for relatively quick reorganization of a firm (rather than liquidation), called *Chapter 11*. Bankruptcy induced by macroeconomic disturbances, as in East Asia, call for an even faster resolution—in what I refer to as a *super-Chapter 11*.

With or without such a provision, strong intervention of government was required. But the intervention of the government would have aimed at financial restructuring—establishing clear ownership of firms, enabling them to reenter credit markets. That would have enabled them to take full advantage of the opportunities for export that resulted from their lower exchange rate. It would have eliminated the incentive for asset stripping; it would have provided them with strong incentives to engage in any real restructuring that was required—and the new owners and managers would have been in a far better position to guide this restructuring than international or domestic bureaucrats, who, as the expression goes, had never met a payroll. Such financial restructuring did not require huge bailouts. The disillusionment with the large bailout strategy is now almost universal. I cannot be sure that my ideas would have worked, but there is little doubt in my mind that the chance of success with this strategy was far greater than with the IMF's plan, which failed in ways that were perfectly predictable, at huge costs.

The IMF did not learn quickly from its failures in East Asia. With slight variants, it repeatedly tried the large bailout strategy. With the failures in Russia, Brazil, and Argentina, it has become clear that an alternative strategy is required, and there is today increasing support for at least some of the key elements of the approach I have just described. Today, five years after the onset of the crisis, the IMF and the G-7 are all talking about giving greater emphasis to bankruptcy and standstills (short-term freezes on payments), and even the temporary use of capital controls. We will return to these reforms later, in chapter 9.

THE ASIAN CRISIS has brought many changes that will stand the countries in good stead in the future. Corporate governance and accounting standards have improved—in some cases putting these countries toward the top of the emerging markets. The new constitution in Thailand promises a stronger democracy (including a provision embracing the citizens' "right to know," not even included in the U.S. Constitution), promising a level of transparency certainly beyond that of the international financial institutions. Many of these changes put in place conditions for even more robust growth in the future.

But offsetting these gains are some real losses. The way the IMF approached the crisis has left in most of the countries a legacy of private and public debt. It has not only frightened firms off the excessively high debt that characterized Korea, but even off more cautious debt levels: the exorbitant interest rates forcing thousands of firms into bankruptcy showed how even moderate levels of debt could be highly risky. As a result, firms will have to rely more on self-finance. In effect, capital markets will work less efficiently—a casualty too of the IMF's ideological approach to improving market efficiency. And most important, growth of living standards will be slowed.

The IMF policies in East Asia had exactly the consequences that have brought globalization under attack. The failures of the international institutions in poor developing countries were long-standing; but these failures did not grab the headlines. The East Asia crisis made vivid to those in the more developed world some of the dissatisfaction that those in the developing world had long felt. What took place in Russia through most of the 1990s provides some even more arresting examples why there is such discontent with international institutions, and why they need to change.

CHAPTER 5

WHO LOST RUSSIA?

W ITH THE FALL of the Berlin Wall in late 1989, one of the most important economic transitions of all time began. It was the second bold economic and social experiment of the century.[1] The first was Russia's transition to communism seven decades earlier. Over the years, the failures of this first experiment became apparent. As a consequence of the 1917 Revolution and the Soviet hegemony over a large part of Europe after World War II, some 8 percent of the world's population that lived under the Soviet Communist system forfeited both political freedom and economic prosperity. The second transition in Russia as well as in Eastern and Southeastern Europe is far from over, but this much is clear: in Russia it has fallen far short of what the advocates of the market economy had promised, or hoped for. For the majority of those living in the former Soviet Union, economic life under capitalism has been even worse than the old Communist leaders had said it would be. Prospects for the future are bleak. The middle class has been devastated, a system of crony and mafia capitalism has been created, and the one achievement, the creation of a democracy with meaningful freedoms, including a free press, appears fragile at best, particularly as formerly independent TV stations are shut down one by one. While those in Russia must bear much of the blame for what has happened, the Western advisers, especially from the United States and the IMF, who marched in so quickly to preach the gospel of the market economy, must also take some blame. At the very least, they provided support to those who led Russia and many of the other economies down the paths they followed, arguing for a new religion—market fundamentalism—as a substitute for the old one—Marxism—which had proved so deficient.

Russia is an ever-unfolding drama. Few anticipated the sudden dissolution of the Soviet Union and few anticipated the sudden resignation of Boris Yeltsin. Some see the oligarchy, the worst excesses of the Yeltsin years, as already curbed; others simply see that some of the oligarchs have fallen from grace. Some see in the increases in output that have occurred in the years since its 1998 crisis as the beginning of a renaissance, one which will lead to the recreation of a middle class; others see it as taking years just to repair the damage of the past decade. Incomes today are markedly lower than they were a decade ago, and poverty is much higher. The pessimists see the country as a nuclear power wavering with political and social instability. The optimists (!) see a semiauthoritarian leadership establishing stability, but at the price of the loss of some democratic freedoms.

Russia experienced a burst of growth after 1998, based on high oil prices and the benefits of the devaluation which the IMF so long opposed. But as oil prices have come down, and the benefits of the devaluation have been reaped, growth too has slowed. Today, the economic prognosis is somewhat less bleak than it was at the time of the 1998 crisis, but it is no less uncertain. The government barely made ends meet when oil prices—the country's main exports—were high. If oil prices fall, as they seem to be as this book goes to press, it could spell real trouble. The best that can be said is that the future remains cloudy.

It is not surprising that the debate over who lost Russia has had such resonance. At one level, the question is clearly misplaced. In the United States it evokes memories of the debate a half century ago about who lost China, when the Communists took over that country. But China was not America's to lose in 1949, nor was Russia America's to lose a half century later. In neither case did America and the Western European countries have control over the political and social evolution. At the same time, it is clear that something has clearly gone wrong, not only in Russia but also in most of the more than twenty countries that emerged from the Soviet empire.

The IMF and other Western leaders claim that matters would have been far worse were it not for their help and advice. We had then, and we have now, no crystal ball to tell us what would happen if alternative policies were pursued. We have no way of running a controlled experiment, going back in time to try an alternative strategy. We have no way of being *certain* of what might have been.

But we do know that certain political and economic judgment calls were made, and we know that the outcomes have been disastrous. In some cases, the link between the policies and the consequences is easy to see: The IMF worried that a devaluation of the ruble would set off a round of inflation. Its insistence on Russia maintaining an overvalued currency and its supporting that with billions of dollars of loans ultimately crushed the economy. (When the ruble was finally devalued in 1998, inflation did not soar as the IMF had feared, and the economy experienced its first significant growth.) In other cases, the links are more complicated. But the experiences of the few countries that followed different policies in managing their transitions help guide us through the maze. It is essential that the world make an informed judgment about the IMF policies in Russia, what drove them and why they were so misguided. Those, myself included, who have had an opportunity to see firsthand how decisions were made and what their consequences were have a special responsibility to provide their interpretations of relevant events.

There is a second reason for a reappraisal. Now, over ten years after the fall of the Berlin Wall, it is clear that the transition to a market economy will be a long struggle, and many, if not most, of the issues that seemed settled only a few years ago will need to be revisited. Only if we understand the mistakes of the past can we hope to design policies that are likely to be effective in the future.

The leaders of the 1917 Revolution recognized that what was at stake was more than a change in economics; it was a change in society in all of its dimensions. So, too, the transition from communism to a market economy was more than just an economic experiment: it was a transformation of societies and of social and political structures.

Part of the reason for the dismal results of the economic transition was the failure to recognize the centrality of these other components.

The first Revolution recognized how difficult the task of transformation was, and the revolutionaries believed that it could not be accomplished by democratic means; it had to be led by the "dictatorship of the proletariat." Some of the leaders of the second revolution in the 1990s at first thought that, freed from the shackles of communism, the Russian people would quickly appreciate the benefits of the market. But some of the Russian market reformers (as well as their Western supporters and advisers) had very little faith or interest in democracy, fearing that if the Russian people were allowed to choose, they would not choose the "correct" (that is *their*) economic model. In Eastern Europe and the former Soviet Union, when these "market reform" benefits failed to materialize in country after country, democratic elections rejected the extremes of market reform, and put social democratic parties or even "reformed" Communist parties, many with former Communists at the helm, into power. It is not surprising that many of the market reformers showed a remarkable affinity to the old ways of doing business: in Russia, President Yeltsin, with enormously greater powers than his counterparts in any Western democracy, was encouraged to circumvent the democratically elected Duma (parliament) and to enact market reforms by decree.[2] It is as if the market Bolsheviks, native true believers, as well as the Western experts and evangelists of the new economic religion who flew into the post-Socialist countries, attempted to use a benign version of Lenin's methods to steer the post-communism, "democratic" transition.

THE CHALLENGES AND OPPORTUNITIES OF TRANSITION

As the transition began in the early 1990s, it presented both great challenges and opportunities. Seldom before had a country deliberately set out to go from a situation where government controlled virtually every aspect of the economy to one where decisions occurred through markets. The People's Republic of China had begun its transition in the late 1970s, and was still far from a full-fledged market economy. One of the most successful transitions had been Taiwan, 100 miles off the shore of mainland China. It had been a Japanese colony since the end of the nineteenth century. With China's 1949 revolution, it became the refuge for the old Nationalist leadership, and from their base in Taiwan, they claimed sovereignty over the entire mainland, keeping the name—"the Republic of China." They had nationalized and redistributed the land, established and then partially privatized an array of major industries, and more broadly created a vibrant market economy. After 1945 many countries, including the United States, moved from wartime mobilization to a peacetime economy. At the time, many economists and other experts feared a major recession would follow wartime demobilization, which entailed not only a change in how decisions were made (ending versions of command economies in which wartime governments made the major decisions about production and returning to private sector management of production) but also an enormous reallocation of production of goods, for example, from tanks to cars. But by 1947, the second full postwar year, production in the United States was 9.6 percent higher than 1944, the last full war year. By the end of the war, 37 percent of GDP (1945) was devoted to defense. With peace, this number was brought down rapidly to 7.4 percent (1947).

There was one important difference between the transition from war to peace, and from communism to a market economy, as I will detail later: Before World War II, the United States had the basic market institutions in place, even though during the war many of these were suspended and superseded by a "command and control" approach. In contrast, Russia needed both resource redeployment *and* the wholesale creation of market institutions.

But Taiwan and China faced similar problems to the economies in transition. Both faced the challenge of a major transformation of their societies, including the establishment of the institutions that underlay a market economy. Both have had truly impressive successes. Rather than prolonged transition recession, they had close to double-digit growth. The radical economic reformers who sought to advise Russia and many of the other countries on transition paid scant attention to these experiences, and the lessons that could be learned. It was not because they believed that Russian history (or the history of the other countries making the transition) made these lessons inapplicable. They studiously ignored the advice of Russian scholars, whether they were experts in its history, economics, or society, for a simple reason: they believed that the *market revolution* which was about to occur made all of the knowledge available from these other disciplines irrelevant. What the market fundamentalists preached was textbook economics—an oversimplified version of market economics which paid scant attention to the dynamics of change.

Consider the problems facing Russia (or the other countries) in 1989. There were institutions in Russia that had names *similar* to those in the West, but they did not perform the same functions. There were banks in Russia, and the banks did garner savings; but they did not make decisions about who got loans, nor did they have the responsibility for monitoring and making sure that the loans were repaid. Rather, they simply provided the "funds," as dictated by the government's central planning agency. There were firms, enterprises producing goods in Russia, but the enterprises did not make decisions: they produced what they were told to produce, with inputs (raw material, labor, machines) that were allocated to them. The major scope for entrepreneurship lay in getting around problems posed by the government: the government would give enterprises quotas on output, without necessarily providing the inputs needed, but in some cases providing more than necessary. Entrepreneurial managers engaged in trades to enable themselves to fulfill their quotas, in the meanwhile getting a few more perks for themselves than they could have enjoyed on their official salaries. These activities—which had always been necessary to make the Soviet system merely function—led to the corruption that would only increase as Russia moved to a market economy.[3] Circumventing what laws were in force, if not breaking them outright, became part of the way of life, a precursor to the breakdown of the "rule of law" which was to mark the transition.

As in a market economy, under the Soviet system there were prices, but the prices were set by government fiat, not by the market. Some prices, such as those for basic necessities, were kept artificially low—enabling even those at the bottom of the income distribution to avoid poverty. Prices for energy and natural resources also were kept artificially low—which Russia could only afford because of its huge reservoirs of these resources.

Old-fashioned economics textbooks often talk about market economics as if it had three essential ingredients: prices, private property, and profits. Together with competition, these provide incentives, coordinate economic decision making, ensuring that firms produce what individuals want at the lowest possible cost. But there has also long been a recognition of the importance of *institutions*. Most important are legal and regulatory frameworks, to ensure that contracts are enforced, that there is an orderly way of resolving commercial disputes, that when borrowers cannot repay what is owed, there are orderly bankruptcy procedures, that competition is maintained, and that banks that take depositors are in a position to give the money back to depositors when they ask. This framework of laws and agencies helps ensure that securities markets operate in a fair manner, that managers do not take advantage of shareholders nor majority shareholders of minority shareholders. In the nations with mature market economies, the legal and regulatory frameworks had been built up over a century and a half, in response to problems encountered in unfettered market capitalism. Bank regulation came into place after massive bank failures; securities regulation after major episodes in which unwary shareholders were cheated. Countries seeking to create a market economy did not have to relive these disasters: they could learn from the experiences of others. But while the market reformers may have mentioned this institutional infrastructure, they gave it short shrift. They tried to take a shortcut to capitalism, creating a market economy without the underlying institutions, and institutions without the underlying institutional infrastructure. Before you set up a stock market, you have to make sure there are real regulations in place. New firms need to be able to raise new capital, and this requires banks that are real banks, not the kinds of banks that characterized the old regime, or banks that simply lend money to government. A real and effective banking system requires strong banking regulations. New firms need to be able to acquire land, and this requires a land market and land registration.

Similarly, in Soviet-era agriculture, farmers used to be given the seeds and fertilizer they needed. They did not have to worry about getting these and other inputs (such as tractors) or marketing their output. Under a market economy, markets for inputs and outputs had to be created, and this required new firms or enterprises. Social institutions are also important. Under the old system in the Soviet Union, there was no unemployment, and hence no need for unemployment insurance. Workers typically worked for the same state enterprise for their entire lives, and the firm provided housing and retirement benefits. In post-1989 Russia, however, if there were to be a labor market, individuals would have to be able to move from firm to firm. But if they could not obtain housing, such mobility would be almost impossible. Hence, a housing market was necessary. A minimal level of social sensitivity means that employers will be reluctant to fire workers if there is nothing for them to fall back on. Hence, there could not be much "restructuring" without a social safety net. Unfortunately, neither a housing market nor a real safety net existed in the new Russia of 1989.

The challenges facing the economies of the former Soviet Union and the other Communist bloc nations in transition were daunting: they had to move from one price system—the distorted price system that prevailed under communism—to a market price system; they had to create markets and the institutional infrastructure that underlies it; and they had to privatize all the property which previously had belonged to the state. They had to create a new kind of entrepreneurship—not just the kind that was good at circumventing government rules and laws—and new enterprises to help redeploy the resources that had previously been so inefficiently used.

No matter how one looked at it, these economies faced hard choices, and there were fierce debates about which choices to make. The most contentious centered on the speed of reform: some experts worried that if they did not privatize quickly, creating a large group of people with a vested interest in capitalism, there would be a reversion to communism. But others worried that if they moved too quickly, the reforms would be a disaster—economic failures compounded by political corruption—opening up the way to a backlash, either from the extreme left or right. The former school was called "shock therapy," the latter "gradualist."

The views of the shock therapists—strongly advocated by the U.S. Treasury and the IMF—prevailed in most of the countries. The gradualists, however, believed that the transition to a market economy would be better managed by moving at a reasonable speed, in good order ("sequencing"). One didn't need to have *perfect* institutions; but, to take one example, privatizing a monopoly before an effective competition or regulatory authority was in place might simply replace a government monopoly with a private monopoly, even more ruthless in exploiting the consumer. Ten years later, the wisdom of the gradualist approach is at last being recognized: the tortoises have overtaken the hares. The gradualist critics of shock therapy not only accurately predicted its failures but also outlined the reasons why it would not work. Their only failure was to underestimate the magnitude of the disaster.

If the challenges posed by transition were great, so were the opportunities. Russia was a rich country. While three quarters of a century of communism may have left its populace devoid of an understanding of market economics, it had left them with a high level of education, especially in technical areas so important for the New Economy. After all, Russia was the first country to send a man into space.

The economic theory explaining the failure of the communism was clear: Centralized planning was doomed to failure, simply because no government agency could glean and process all the relevant information required to make an economy function well. Without private property and the profit motive, incentives—especially managerial and entrepreneurial incentives—were lacking. The restricted trade regime, combined with huge subsidies and arbitrarily set prices, meant the system was rife with distortions.

It followed that replacing centralized planning with a decentralized market system, replacing public ownership with private property, and eliminating or at least reducing the distortions by liberalizing trade, would cause a burst of economic output. The cutback in military expenditures—which had absorbed a huge share of

GDP when the USSR was still in existence, five times larger than in the post–cold war era—provided even more room for increases in standards of living. Instead, however, the standard of living in Russia, and many of the other East European transition countries, fell.

THE "REFORM" STORY

The first mistakes occurred almost immediately as the transition began. In the enthusiasm to get on with a market economy, most prices were freed overnight in 1992, setting in motion an inflation that wiped out savings, and moved the problem of macrostability to the top of the agenda. Everybody recognized that with hyperinflation (inflation at double-digit rates *per month*), it would be difficult to have a successful transition. Thus, the first round of shock therapy—instantaneous price liberalization—necessitated the second round: bringing inflation down. This entailed tightening monetary policy—raising interest rates.

While most of the prices were completely freed, some of the most important prices were kept low—those for natural resources. With the newly declared "market economy," this created an open invitation: If you can buy, say, oil and resell it in the West, you could make millions or even billions of dollars. So people did. Instead of making money by creating new enterprises, they got rich from a new form of the old entrepreneurship—exploiting mistaken government policies. And it was this "rent-seeking" behavior that would provide the basis of the claim by reformers that the problem was not that the reforms had been too quick, but that they had been too slow. If only *all* prices had been freed immediately! There is considerable validity in this argument, but as a defense of the radical reforms it is disingenuous. Political processes never give the technocrat free rein, and for good reason: as we have seen, technocrats often miss out on important economic, social, and political dimensions. Reform, even in well-functioning political and economic systems, is always "messy." Even if it made sense to push for instantaneous liberalization, the more relevant question is, how should one have proceeded with liberalization if one could not succeed in getting important sectors, like energy prices, liberalized quickly?

Liberalization and stabilization were two of the pillars of the radical reform strategy. Rapid privatization was the third. But the first two pillars put obstacles in the way of the third. The initial high inflation had wiped out the savings of most Russians so there were not enough people in the country who had the money to buy the enterprises being privatized. Even if they could afford to buy the enterprises, it would be difficult to revitalize them, given the high interest rates and lack of financial institutions to provide capital.

Privatization was supposed to be the first step in the process of restructuring the economy. Not only did ownership have to change but so did management; and production had to be reoriented, from producing what firms were told to produce to producing what consumers wanted. This restructuring would, of course, require new investment, and in many cases job cuts. Job cuts help overall efficiency, of course, only if they result in workers moving from low-productivity jobs to high-productivity employment. Unfortunately, too little of this positive restructuring occurred, partly because the strategy put almost insurmountable obstacles in the way.

The radical reform strategy did not work: gross domestic product in post-1989 Russia fell, year after year. What had been envisioned as a short transition recession turned into one of a decade or more. The bottom seemed never in sight. The devastation—the loss in GDP—was greater than Russia had suffered in World War II. In the period 1940–46 the Soviet Union industrial production fell 24 percent. In the period 1990–99, Russian industrial production fell by almost 60 percent—even greater than the fall in GDP (54%). Those familiar with the history of the earlier transition in the Russian Revolution, *into* communism, could draw some comparisons between that socioeconomic trauma and the post-1989 transition: farm livestock decreased by half, investment in manufacturing came almost to a stop. Russia was able to attract some foreign investment in natural resources; Africa had shown long ago that if you price natural resources low enough, it is easy to attract foreign investment in them.

The stabilization/liberalization/privatization program was, of course, not a growth program. It was intended to set the preconditions for growth. Instead, it set the preconditions for decline. Not only was investment halted, but capital was used up—savings vaporized by inflation, the proceeds of privatization or foreign loans largely misappropriated. Privatization, accompanied by the opening of the capital markets, led not to wealth creation but to asset stripping. It was perfectly logical. An oligarch who has just been able to use political influence to garner assets worth billions, after paying only a pittance, would naturally want to get his money out of the country. Keeping money in Russia meant investing it in a country in deep depression, and risking not only low returns but having the assets seized by the next government, which would inevitably complain, quite rightly, about the "illegitimacy" of the privatization process. Anyone smart enough to be a winner in the privatization sweepstakes would be smart enough to put their money in the booming U.S. stock market, or into the safe haven of secretive offshore bank accounts. It was not even a close call; and not surprisingly, billions poured out of the country.

The IMF kept promising that recovery was around the corner. By 1997, it had reason for this optimism. With output having already fallen 41 percent since 1990, how much further down could it go? Besides, the country was doing much of what the Fund had stressed. It had liberalized, if not completely; it had stabilized, if not completely (inflation rates were brought down dramatically); and it had privatized. But of course it is easy to privatize quickly, if one does not pay any attention to *how* one privatizes: essentially give away valuable state property to one's friends. Indeed, it can be highly profitable for governments to do so—whether the kickbacks come back in the form of cash payments or in campaign contributions (or both).

But the glimpses of recovery seen in 1997 were not to last long. Indeed, the mistakes the IMF made in a distant part of the world were pivotal. In 1998, the fallout from the East Asian crisis hit. The crisis had led to a general skittishness about investing in emerging markets, and investors demanded higher returns to compensate them for lending capital to these countries. Mirroring the weaknesses in GDP and investment were weaknesses in public finance: the Russian government had been borrowing heavily. Though it had difficulty making budget ends meet, the government, pressured by the United

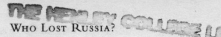

States, the World Bank, and the IMF to privatize rapidly, had turned over its state assets for a pittance, and done so before it had put in place an effective tax system. The government created a powerful class of oligarchs and businessmen who paid but a fraction of what they owed in taxes, much less what they would have paid in virtually any other country.

Thus, at the time of the East Asia crisis, Russia was in a peculiar position. It had an abundance of natural resources, but its government was poor. The government was virtually giving away its valuable state assets, yet it was unable to provide pensions for the elderly or welfare payments for the poor. The government was borrowing billions from the IMF, becoming increasingly indebted, while the oligarchs, who had received such largesse from the government, were taking billions out of the country. The IMF had encouraged the government to open up its capital accounts, allowing a free flow of capital. The policy was supposed to make the country more attractive for foreign investors; but it was virtually a one-way door that facilitated a rush of money out of the country.

The 1998 Crisis

The country was deeply in debt, and the higher interest rates that the East Asia crisis had provoked created an enormous additional strain. This rickety tower collapsed when oil prices fell. Due to recessions and depressions in Southeast Asia, which IMF policies had exacerbated, oil demand not only failed to expand as expected but actually contracted. The resulting imbalance between demand and supply of oil turned into a dramatic fall in crude oil prices (down over 40% in the first six months of 1998 compared to the average prices in 1997). Oil is both a major export commodity and a source of government tax revenue for Russia, and the drop in prices had a predictably devastating effect. At the World Bank, we became aware of the problem early in 1998, when prices looked ready to fall even below Russia's cost of extraction plus transportation. Given the exchange rate at the time, Russia's oil industry could cease being profitable. A devaluation would then be inevitable.

It was clear that the ruble was overvalued. Russia was flooded with imports, and domestic producers were having a hard time competing. The switch to a market economy and away from the military was supposed to allow a redeployment of resources to produce more consumer goods, or more machines to produce consumer goods. But investment had halted, and the country was not producing consumer goods. The overvalued exchange rate—combined with the other macroeconomic policies foisted on the country by the IMF—had crushed the economy, and while the official unemployment rate remained subdued, there was massive disguised unemployment. The managers of many firms were reluctant to fire workers, given the absence of an adequate safety net. Though unemployment was disguised, it was no less traumatic: while the workers only pretended to work, the firms only pretended to pay. Wage payments fell into massive arrears, and when workers were paid, it was often with bartered goods rather than rubles.

If for these people, and for the country as a whole, the overvalued exchange rate was a disaster, for the new class of businessmen the overvalued exchange rate was a boon. They needed fewer rubles to buy their Mercedes, their Chanel handbags, and imported Italian gourmet foods. For the oligarchs trying to get their money out of the country, too, the overvalued exchange rate was a boon—it meant that they could get more dollars for their rubles, as they squirreled away their profits in foreign bank accounts.

Despite this suffering on the part of the majority of Russians, the reformers and their advisers in the IMF feared a devaluation, believing that it would set off another round of hyperinflation. They strongly resisted any change in the exchange rate and were willing to pour billions of dollars into the country to avoid it. By May, and certainly by June of 1998, it was clear Russia would need outside assistance to maintain its exchange rate. Confidence in the currency had eroded. In the belief that a devaluation was inevitable, domestic interest rates soared and more money left the country as people converted their rubles for dollars. Because of this fear of holding rubles, and the lack of confidence in the government's ability to repay its debt, by June 1998 the government had to pay almost 60 percent interest rates on its ruble loans (GKOs, the Russian equivalent of U.S. Treasury bills). That figure soared to 150 percent in a matter of weeks. Even when the government promised to pay back in dollars, it faced high interest rates (yields on dollar-denominated debt issued by the Russian government rose from slightly over 10% to almost 50%, 45 percentage points higher than the interest rate the U.S. government had to pay on its Treasury bills at the time); the market thought there was a high probability of default, and the market was right. Even that rate was lower than it might otherwise have been because many investors believed that Russia was too big and too important to fail. As the New York investment banks pushed loans to Russia, they whispered about how big the IMF bailout would have to be.

The crisis mounted in the way that these crises so frequently do. Speculators could see how much in the way of reserves was left, and as reserves dwindled, betting on a devaluation became increasingly a one-way bet. They risked almost nothing betting on the ruble's crash. As expected, the IMF came to the rescue with $4.8 billion in July 1998.[4]

In the weeks preceding the crisis, the IMF pushed policies that made the crisis, when it occurred, even worse. The Fund pushed Russia into borrowing more in foreign currency and less in rubles. The argument was simple: The ruble interest rate was much higher than the dollar interest rate. By borrowing in dollars, the government could save money. But there was a fundamental flaw in this reasoning. Basic economic theory argues that the difference in the interest rate between dollar bonds and ruble bonds should reflect the expectation of a devaluation. Markets equilibrate so that the risk-adjusted cost of borrowing (or the return to lending) is the same. I have much less confidence in markets than does the IMF, so I have much less faith that in fact the risk-adjusted cost of borrowing is the same, regardless of currency. But I also have much less confidence than the Fund that the Fund's bureaucrats can predict exchange rate movements better than the market. In the case of Russia, the IMF bureaucrats believed that they were smarter than the market—they were willing to bet Russia's money that the market was wrong. This was a misjudgment that the Fund was to repeat, in varied forms, time and time again. Not only was the judgment flawed; it exposed the country to enormous risk: if the ruble did devalue, Russia would find it far more difficult to repay the dollar-denominated loans.[5] The IMF chose to ignore this risk. By inducing greater foreign borrowing, by making Russia's position once it devalued so much less tenable, the IMF was partly culpable for the eventual suspension of payments by Russia on its debts.

The Rescue

When the crisis hit, the IMF led the rescue efforts, but it wanted the World Bank to provide $6 billion of the rescue package. The total rescue package was for $22.6 billion. The IMF would provide $11.2 billion of this total, as I stated before; the World Bank would lend $6 billion, and the rest would be provided by the Japanese government.

This was hotly debated inside the World Bank. There were many of us who had been questioning lending to Russia all along. We questioned whether the benefits to possible future growth were large enough to justify loans that would leave a legacy of debt. Many thought that the IMF was making it easier for the government to put off meaningful reforms, such as collecting taxes from the oil companies. The evidence of corruption in Russia was clear. The Bank's own study of corruption had identified that region as among the most corrupt in the world. The West knew that much of those billions would be diverted from their intended purposes to the families and associates of corrupt officials and their oligarch friends. While the Bank and the IMF had seemingly taken a strong stance against lending to corrupt governments, it appeared that there were two standards. Small nonstrategic countries like Kenya were denied loans because of corruption while countries such as Russia where the corruption was on a far larger scale were continually lent money.

Apart from these moral issues, there were straightforward economic issues. The IMF's bailout money was supposed to be used to support the exchange rate. However, if a country's currency is overvalued and this causes the country's economy to suffer, maintaining the exchange rate makes little sense. If the exchange rate support works, the country suffers. But in the more likely case that the support does not work, the money is wasted, and the country is deeper in debt. Our calculations showed that Russia's exchange rate was overvalued, so providing money to maintain that exchange rate was simply bad economic policy. Moreover, calculations at the World Bank before the loan was made, based on estimates of government revenues and expenditures over time, strongly suggested that the July 1998 loan would not work. Unless a miracle brought interest rates down drastically, by the time autumn rolled around, Russia would be back in crisis.

There was another route by which I reached the conclusion that a further loan to Russia would be a great mistake. Russia was a naturally resource-rich country. If it got its act together, it didn't need money from the outside; and if it didn't get its act together, it wasn't clear that any money from the outside would make much difference. Under either scenario, the case against giving money seemed compelling.

In spite of strong opposition from its own staff, the Bank was under enormous political pressure from the Clinton administration to lend money to Russia. The Bank managed a compromise, publicly announcing a very large loan, but providing the loan in tranches— installments. A decision was taken to make $300 million available immediately, with the rest available only later, as we saw how Russia's reforms progressed. Most of us thought that the program would fail long before the additional money had to be forthcoming. Our predictions proved correct. Remarkably, the IMF seemed able to overlook the corruption, and the attendant risks with what would happen with the money. It actually thought that maintaining the exchange rate at an overvalued level was a good thing, and that the money would enable it to do this for more than a couple months. It provided billions to the country.

The Rescue Fails

Three weeks after the loan was made, Russia announced a unilateral suspension of payments and a devaluation of the ruble.[6] The ruble crashed. By January 1999, the ruble had declined in real effective terms by more than 45 percent from its July 1998 level.[7] The August 17 announcement precipitated a global financial crisis. Interest rates to emerging markets soared higher than they had been at the peak of the East Asian crisis. Even developing countries that had been pursuing sound economic policies found it impossible to raise funds.

Brazil's recession deepened, and eventually it too faced a currency crisis. Argentina and other Latin American countries only gradually recovering from previous crises were again pushed nearer the brink. Ecuador and Colombia went over the brink and into crisis. Even the United States did not remain untouched. The New York Federal Reserve Bank engineered a private bailout of one of the nation's largest hedge funds, Long Term Capital Management, since the Fed feared its failure could precipitate a global financial crisis.

The surprise about the collapse was not the collapse itself, but the fact that it really did take some of the IMF officials—including some of the most senior ones—by surprise. They had genuinely believed that their program would work.

Our own forecasts proved only partially correct: we thought that the money might sustain the exchange rate for three months; it lasted three weeks. We felt that it would take days or even weeks for the oligarchs to bleed the money out of the country; it took merely hours and days. The Russian government even "allowed" the exchange rate to appreciate. As we have seen, this meant the oligarchs would need to spend fewer rubles to purchase their dollars. A smiling Viktor Gerashchenko, the chairman of the Central Bank of Russia, told the president of the World Bank and me that it was simply "market forces at work." When the IMF was confronted with the facts—the billions of dollars that it had given (loaned) Russia was showing up in Cypriot and Swiss bank accounts just days after the loan was made—it claimed that these weren't *their* dollars. The argument demonstrated either a remarkable lack of understanding of economics or a level of disingenuousness that rivaled Gerashchenko's, or both. When money is sent to a country, it is not sent in the form of marked dollar bills. Thus, one cannot say it is "my" money that went anywhere. The IMF had lent Russia the dollars—funds that allowed Russia, in turn, to give its oligarchs the dollars to take out of the country. Some of us quipped that the IMF would have made life easier all around if it had simply sent the money directly into the Swiss and Cyprus bank accounts.

It was, of course, not just the oligarchs who benefited from the rescue. The Wall Street and other Western investment bankers, who had been among those pressing the hardest for a rescue package, knew it would not last: they too took the short respite provided by the rescue to rescue as much as they could, to flee the country with whatever they could salvage.

By lending Russia money for a doomed cause, IMF policies led Russia into deeper debt, with nothing to show for it. The cost of the mistake was not borne by the IMF officials who gave the loan, or America who had pushed for it, or the Western bankers and the oligarchs who benefited from the loan, but by the Russian taxpayer.

There was one positive aspect of the crisis: The devaluation spurred Russia's import competing sectors—goods actually produced in Russia finally took a growing share of the home market. This "unintended consequence" ultimately led to the long-awaited growth in Russia's real (as opposed to black) economy. There was a certain irony in this failure: macroeconomics was supposed to be the IMF's strength, and yet even here it had failed. These macroeconomic failures compounded the other failures, and contributed mightily to the enormity of the decline.

THE FAILED TRANSITIONS

Seldom has the gap between expectations and reality been greater than in the case of the transition from communism to the market. The combination of privatization, liberalization, and decentralization was supposed to lead quickly, after perhaps a short transition recession, to a vast increase in production. It was expected that the benefits from transition would be greater in the long run than in the short run, as old, inefficient machines were replaced, and a new generation of entrepreneurs was created. Full integration into the global economy, with all the benefits that that would bring, would also come quickly, if not immediately.

These expectations for economic growth were not realized, not only in Russia but in *most* of the economies in transition. Only a few of the former Communist countries—such as Poland, Hungary, Slovenia, and Slovakia—have a GDP equal to that of a decade ago. For the rest, the magnitudes of the declines in incomes are so large that they are hard to fathom. According to World Bank data, Russia today (2000) has a GDP that is less than two-thirds of what it was in 1989. Moldova's decline is the most dramatic, with output today less than a third of what it was a decade ago. Ukraine's 2000 GDP is just a third of what it was ten years ago.

Underlying the data were true symptoms of Russia's malady. Russia had quickly been transformed from an industrial giant—a country that had managed with Sputnik to put the first satellite into orbit—into a natural resource exporter; resources, and especially oil and gas, accounted for over half of all exports. While the Western reform advisers were writing books with titles like *The Coming Boom in Russia* or *How Russia Became a Market Economy,* the data itself was making it hard to take seriously the rosy pictures they were painting, and more dispassionate observers were writing books like *The Sale of the Century: Russia's Wild Ride from Communism to Capitalism.*[8]

The magnitude of GDP decline in Russia (not to mention other former Communist countries) is the subject of controversy, and some argue that because of the growing and critical informal sector—from street vendors to plumbers, painters, and other service providers, whose economic activities are typically hard to capture in national income statistics—the numbers represent an overestimate of the size of the decline. However, others argue that because so many of the transactions in Russia entail barter (over 50% of industrial sales),[9] and because the "market" prices are typically higher than these "barter" prices, the statistics actually underestimate the decline.

Taking all this into account, there is still a consensus that most individuals have experienced a marked deterioration in their basic standard of living, reflected in a host of social indicators. While in the rest of the world life spans were increasing markedly, in Russia they were over three years shorter, and in Ukraine almost three years shorter. Survey data of household consumption—what people eat, how much they spend on clothing, and what type of housing they live in—corroborates a marked decline in standards of living, on par with those suggested by the fall in GDP statistics. Given that the government was spending less on defense, standards of living should have increased even more than GDP. To put it another way, assume that somehow previous expenditures on consumption could have been preserved, and a third of the expenditures on military could have been shifted into new production of consumption goods, and that there had been no restructuring to increase efficiency or to take advantage of the new trade opportunities. Consumption—living standards—would then have increased by 4 percent, a small amount but far better than the actual decline.

Increased Poverty and Inequality

These statistics do not tell the whole story of the transition in Russia. They ignore one of the most important successes: How do you value the benefits of the new democracy, as imperfect as it might be? But they also ignore one of the most important failures: The increase in poverty and inequality.

While the size of the national economic pie was shrinking, it was being divided up more and more inequitably so the average Russian was getting a smaller and smaller slice. In 1989, only 2 percent of those living in Russia were in poverty. By late 1998, that number had soared to 23.8 percent, using the $2 a day standard. More than 40 percent of the country had less than $4 a day, according to a survey conducted by the World Bank. The statistics for children revealed an even deeper problem, with more than 50 percent living in families in poverty. Other post-Communist countries have seen comparable, if not worse, increases in poverty.[10]

Shortly after I arrived at the World Bank, I began taking a closer look at what was going on, and at the strategies that were being pursued. When I raised my concerns about these matters, an economist at the Bank who had played a key role in the privatizations responded heatedly. He cited the traffic jams of cars, many of them Mercedes, leaving Moscow on a summer weekend, and the stores filled with imported luxury goods. This was a far different picture from the empty and colorless retail establishments under the former regime. I did not disagree that a substantial number of people had been made wealthy enough to cause a traffic jam, or to create a demand for Gucci shoes and other imported luxury items sufficient for certain stores to prosper. At many European resorts, the wealthy Russian has replaced the wealthy Arab of two decades ago. In some, street signs are even given in Russian along with the native language.

But a traffic jam of Mercedes in a country with a per capita income of $4,730 (as it was in 1997) is a sign of a sickness, not health. It is a clear sign of a society that concentrates its wealth among the few, rather than distributing it among the many.

While the transition has greatly increased the number of those in poverty, and led a few at the top to prosper, the middle class in Russia has perhaps been the hardest hit. The inflation first wiped out their meager savings, as we have seen. With wages not keeping up with inflation, their real incomes fell. Cutbacks in expenditures on education and health further eroded their standards of living. Those who could, emigrated. (Some countries, like Bulgaria, lost 10% or more of their population, and an even larger fraction of their educated workforce.) The bright students in Russia and other countries of the former Soviet Union that I've met work hard, with one ambition in mind: to migrate to the West. These losses are important not just for what they imply today for those living in Russia, but for what they portend for the future: historically, the middle class has been central to creating a society based on the rule of law and democratic values.

The magnitude of the increase in inequality, like the magnitude and duration of the economic decline, came as a surprise. Experts did expect some increase in inequality, or at least measured inequality. Under the old regime, incomes were kept similar by suppressing wage differences. The Communist system, while it did not make for an easy life, avoided the extremes of poverty, and kept living standards relatively equal, by providing a high common denominator of quality for education, housing, health care and child care services. With a switch to a market economy, those who worked hard and produced well would reap the rewards for their efforts, so some increase in inequality was inevitable. However, it was expected that Russia would be spared the inequality arising from inherited wealth. Without this legacy of inherited inequality, there was the promise of a more egalitarian market economy. How differently matters have turned out! Russia today has a level of inequality comparable with the worst in the world, those Latin American societies which were based on a semifeudal heritage.[11]

Russia has gotten the worst of all possible worlds—an enormous decline in output and an enormous increase in inequality. And the prognosis for the future is bleak: extremes of inequality impede growth, particularly when they lead to social and political instability.

HOW MISGUIDED POLICIES LED TO THE FAILURES OF TRANSITION

We have already seen some of the ways that the Washington consensus policies contributed to the failures: privatization done the wrong way had not led to increased efficiency or growth but to asset stripping and decline. We have seen how the problems were compounded by interactions between reforms, as well as their pace and sequencing: capital market liberalization and privatization made it easier to take money out of the country; privatization before a legal infrastructure was in place enhanced the ability and incentive for asset stripping rather than reinvesting in the country's future. A full description of what went on, and a full analysis of the ways in which IMF programs contributed to the decline of the country, is a book in itself. Here, I want to sketch three examples. In each case, defenders of the IMF will say that things would have been worse, but for their programs. In some cases—such as the absence of competition policies—the IMF will insist that such policies were part of the program, but, alas, Russia did not implement them. Such a defense is ingenuous: with dozens of conditions, *everything* was in the IMF program. Russia knew, however, that when it came to the inevitable charade in which IMF would threaten to cut off aid, Russia would bargain hard, an agreement (not often fulfilled) would be reached, and the money spigot opened up again. What was important were the monetary targets, the budget deficits, and the pace of privatization—the number of firms that had been turned over to the private sector, never mind how. Almost everything else was secondary; much—like competition policy—was virtually window-dressing, a defense against critics who said they were leaving out important ingredients to a successful transition strategy. As I repeatedly pushed for stronger competition policies, those inside Russia who agreed with me, who were trying to establish a true market economy, who were trying to create an effective competition authority, repeatedly thanked me.

Deciding what to emphasize, establishing priorities, is not easy. Textbook economics often provides insufficient guidance. Economic theory says that for markets to work well, there must be both competition and private property. If reform was easy, one would wave a magic wand and have both. The IMF chose to emphasize privatization, giving short shrift to competition. The choice was perhaps not surprising: corporate and financial interests often oppose competition policies, for these policies restrict their ability to make profits. The consequences of IMF's mistake here were far more serious than just high prices: privatized firms sought to establish monopolies and cartels, to enhance their profits, undisciplined by effective antitrust policies. And as so often happens, the profits of monopoly prove especially alluring to those who are willing to resort to mafialike techniques either to obtain market dominance or to enforce collusion.

Inflation

Earlier we saw how the rapid liberalization at the beginning had led to the burst of inflation. The sad part of Russia's story was that each mistake was followed by another, which compounded the consequences.

Having set off the rapid inflation through abrupt price liberalization in 1992, it was necessary for the IMF and the Yeltsin regime to contain it. But balance has never been the strong suit of the IMF, and its excessive zeal led to excessively high interest rates. There is little evidence that lowering inflation below a moderate level increases growth. The most successful countries, like Poland, ignored the IMF's pressure and maintained inflation at around 20 percent through the critical years of adjustment. IMF's star pupils, like the Czech Republic, which pushed inflation down to 2 percent, saw their economy stagnate. There are some good reasons to believe that excessive zeal in fighting inflation can dampen real economic growth. The high interest rate clearly stifled new investment. Many of the new, privatized firms, even those who began without an eye to looting them, saw that they could not expand and switched to asset stripping. The IMF-driven high interest rates led to an overvaluation of the exchange rate, making imports cheap and exports difficult. No wonder then that any visitor to Moscow after 1992 could see the stores filled with imported clothing and other goods, but would be hard-pressed to find much with a "Made in Russia" label. And this was true even five years after the transition began.

The tight monetary policies also contributed to the use of barter. With a shortage of money, workers were paid in kind—with whatever it was that the factory produced or had available, from toilet paper to shoes. While the flea markets that were established everywhere throughout the country as workers tried to get cash to buy the bare necessities of life gave a semblance of entrepreneurial activity, they masked huge inefficiencies. High rates of inflation are costly to an economy because they interfere with the workings of the price system. But barter is every bit as destructive to the effective workings of the price system, and the excesses of monetary stringency simply substituted one set of inefficiencies for a possibly even worse set.

Privatization

The IMF told Russia to privatize as fast as possible; how privatization was done was viewed as secondary. Much of the failure of which I wrote earlier—both the decline in incomes and the increase in inequality—can be directly linked to this mistake. In a World Bank review of the ten-year history of transition economies, it became apparent that privatization, in the absence of the institutional infrastructure (like corporate governance), had no positive effect on growth.[12] The Washington Consensus had again just gotten it wrong. It is easy to see the links between the way privatization was done and the failures.

For instance, in Russia and other countries, the lack of laws ensuring good corporate governance meant that those who could get control of a corporation had an incentive to steal assets from the minority shareholders; and managers had similar incentives vis-à-vis shareholders. Why expend energy in creating wealth when it was so much easier to steal it? Other aspects of the privatization process, as we have seen, enhanced the incentives as well as opportunities for corporate theft. Privatization in Russia turned over large national enterprises, typically to their old managers. Those insiders knew how uncertain and difficult was the road ahead. Even if they were predisposed to do so, they dared not wait for the creation of capital markets and the hosts of other changes that would be required for them to reap the full value of any investments and restructuring. They focused on what they could get out of the firm in the next few years, and all too often, this was maximized by stripping assets.

Privatization was also supposed to eliminate the role of the state in the economy; but those who assumed that had a far too naive view of the role of the state in the modern economy. It exercises its influence in a myriad of ways at a myriad of levels. Privatization did reduce the power of the central government, but that devolution left the local and regional governments with far wider discretion. A city like, say, St. Petersburg, or an *oblast* (regional government) like Novgorod, could use a host of regulatory and tax measures to extort "rents" from firms that operated in their jurisdiction. In advanced industrial countries there is a rule of law which keeps local and state governments from abusing their potential powers; not so in Russia. In advanced industrial countries, competition among communities makes each try to make itself more attractive to investors. But in a world in which high interest rates and an overall depression make such investments unlikely in any case, local governments spent little time creating attractive "environments for investment" and focused instead on seeing how much they could extract from existing enterprises—just as the owners and managers of newly privatized firms themselves did. And when these privatized firms operated across many jurisdictions, authorities in one district reasoned that they had better take what they could grab before others took their own bites out of assets. And this only reinforced the incentive of managers to grab whatever they could as quickly as possible. After all, the firms would be left destitute in any case. It was a race to the bottom. There were incentives for asset stripping at every level.

Just as the radical "shock therapy" reformers claim that the problem with liberalization was not that it was too slow, but that it was not fast enough, so too with privatization. While the Czech Republic, for example, was praised by the IMF even as it faltered, it became clear that the country's rhetoric had outpaced its performance: it had left the banks in state hands. If a government privatizes corporations, but leaves banks in the state hands, or without effective regulation, that government does not create the hard budget constraints that lead to efficiency, but rather an alternative, less transparent way of subsidizing firms—and an open invitation to corruption. Critics of Czech privatization claim the problem was not that privatization was too rapid, but that it was too slow. But no country has succeeded in privatizing everything, overnight, well, and it is likely that were a government to try to do instantaneous privatization, there would be a mess. The task is too difficult, the incentives for malfeasance too high. The failures of the rapid privatization strategies were predictable—and predicted.

Not only did privatization, as it was imposed in Russia (as well as in far too many of its former Soviet bloc dependencies), not contribute to the economic success of the country; it undermined confidence in government, in democracy, and in reform. The result of giving away its rich natural resources before it had in place a system to collect natural resource taxes was that a few friends and associates of Yeltsin became billionaires, but the country was unable to pay pensioners their $15 a month pension.

The most egregious example of bad privatization was the loans-for-share program. In 1995, the government, instead of turning to the Central Bank for needed funds, turned to private banks. Many of these private banks belonged to friends of the government who had been given bank charters. In an environment with underregulated banks, the charters were effectively a license to print money, to make loans either to themselves or their friends or to the government. As a condition of the loan, the government put up shares of its own enterprises as collateral. Then—surprise!—the government defaulted on its loans; the private banks took over the companies in what might be viewed as a sham sale (though the government did go through a charade of having "auctions"); and a few oligarchs became instant billionaires. These privatizations had no political legitimacy. And, as noted previously, the fact that they had no legitimacy made it even more imperative that the oligarchs take their funds quickly out of the country—before a new government that might try to reverse the privatizations or undermine their position came to power.

Those who benefited from the largesse of the state, or more accurately from Yeltsin's largesse, worked hard to ensure Yeltsin's reelection. Ironically, while there was always a presumption that part of Yeltsin's giveaway went to finance his campaign, some critics think that the oligarchs were far too smart to use their money to pay for the election campaign; there was plenty of government slush funds that could be used. The oligarchs provided Yeltsin with something that was far more valuable—modern campaign management techniques and positive treatment by the TV networks they controlled.

The loans-for-share scheme constituted the final stage of the enrichment of the oligarchs, the small band of people (some of whom owed their origins, reportedly at least, partly to mafialike connections) who came to dominate not just the economic but the political life of the country. At one point, they claimed to control 50 percent of the country's wealth! Defenders of the oligarchs liken them to America's robber barons, the Harrimans and Rockefellers. But there is a big difference between the activities of such figures in nineteenth-century capitalism, even those carving out railway and mining baronies in America's Wild West, and the Russian oligarchy's exploitation of Russia, what has been called the Wild East. America's robber barons created wealth, even as they accumulated fortunes. They left a country much richer, even if they got a big slice of the larger pie. Russia's oligarchs stole assets, stripped them, leaving their country much poorer. The enterprises were left on the verge of bankruptcy, while the oligarch's bank accounts were enriched.

The Social Context

The officials who applied Washington Consensus policies failed to appreciate the social context of the transition economies. This was especially problematic, given what had happened during the years of communism.

Market economies entail a host of economic relationships—exchanges. Many of these exchanges involve matters of trust. An individual lends another money, trusting that he will be repaid. Backing up this trust is a legal system. If individuals do not live up to their contractual obligations, they can be forced to do so. If an individual steals property from another, he can be brought to court. But in countries with mature market economies and adequate institutional infrastructures, individuals and corporations resort only occasionally to litigation.

Economists often refer to the glue that holds society together as "social capital." Random violence and Mafia capitalism are often cited as reflections of the erosion of social capital, but in some of the countries of the former Soviet Union that I visited, one could see everywhere, in more subtle ways, direct manifestations of the erosion of social capital. It is not just a question of the misbehavior of a few managers; it is an almost anarchic theft by all from all. For instance, the landscape in Kazakhstan is dotted with greenhouses—missing their glass. Of course, without the glass, they fail to function. In the early days of the transition, there was so little confidence in the future that each individual took what he could: each believed that others would take the glass out of the greenhouse—in which case the greenhouse (and their livelihood) would be destroyed. But if the greenhouse was, in any case, fated to be destroyed, it made sense for each to take what he could—even if the value of the glass was small.

The way in which transition proceeded in Russia served to erode this social capital. One got wealthy not by working hard or by investing, but by using political connections to get state property on the cheap in privatizations. The social contract, which bound citizens together with their government, was broken, as pensioners saw the government giving away valuable state assets, but claiming that it had no money to pay their pensions.

The IMF's focus on macroeconomics—and in particular on inflation—led it to shunt aside issues of poverty, inequality, and social capital. When confronted about this myopia of focus, it would say, "Inflation is especially hard on the poor." But its policy framework was not designed to minimize the impact on the poor. And by ignoring the impacts of its policies on the poor and on social capital, the IMF actually impeded *macroeconomic* success. The erosion of social

capital created an environment that was not conducive to investment. The Russian government's (and the IMF's) lack of attention to
a minimal safety net slowed down the process of restructuring, as
even hardheaded plant managers often found it difficult to fire workers, knowing there was little standing between their fired workers
and extreme hardship, if not starvation.

Shock Therapy

The great debate over reform strategy in Russia centered on the pace
of reform. Who was right, in the end—the "shock therapists" or the
"gradualists"? Economic theory, which focuses on equilibrium and
idealized models, has less to say about dynamics, the order, timing,
and pacing of reforms, than one would like—though IMF economists often tried to convince client countries otherwise. The debaters
resorted to metaphors to convince others of the merits of their side.
The rapid reformers said, "You can't cross a chasm in two leaps,"
while the gradualists argued that it took nine months to make a baby,
and talked about crossing the river by feeling the stones. In some
cases, what separated the two views was more a difference in perspective than reality. I was present at a seminar in Hungary where
one participant said, "We must have rapid reform! It must be accomplished in five years." Another said, "We should have gradual reform.
It will take us five years." Much of the debate was more about the
manner of reform than the speed.

We have already encountered two of the essential critiques of the
gradualists: "Haste makes waste"—it is hard to design good reforms
well; and sequencing matters. There are, for instance, important prerequisites for a successful mass privatization, and creating these
prerequisites takes time.[13] Russia's peculiar pattern of reforms
demonstrates that incentives do matter, but that Russia's kind of
ersatz capitalism did not provide the incentives for wealth creation
and economic growth but rather for asset stripping. Instead of a
smoothly working market economy, the quick transition led to a dis-
orderly Wild East.

The Bolshevik Approach to Market Reform

Had the radical reformers looked beyond their narrow focus on economics, they would have found that history shows that most of the experiments in radical reform were beset by problems. This is true from the French Revolution in 1789, to the Paris Commune of 1871, to the Bolshevik Revolution in Russia in 1917, and to China's Cultural Revolution of the 1960s and 1970s. It is easy to understand the forces giving rise to each of these revolutions, but each produced its own Robespierre, its own political leaders who were either corrupted by the revolution or took it to extremes. By contrast, the successful American "Revolution" was not a true revolution in society; it was a *revolutionary* change in political structures, but it represented an *evolutionary* change in the structure of society. The radical reformers in Russia were trying simultaneously for a revolution in the economic regime and in the structure of society. The saddest commentary is that, in the end, they failed in both: a market economy in which many old party apparatchiks had simply been vested with enhanced powers to run and profit from the enterprises they formerly managed, in which former KGB officials still held the levers of power. There was one new dimension: a few new oligarchs, able and willing to exert immense political and economic power.

In effect, the radical reformers employed Bolshevik strategies—though they were reading from different texts. The Bolsheviks tried to impose communism on a reluctant country in the years following 1917. They argued that the way to build socialism was for an elite cadre to "lead" (often a euphemism for "force") the masses into the correct path, which was not necessarily the path the masses wanted or thought best. In the "new" post-Communist revolution in Russia, an elite, spearheaded by international bureaucrats, similarly attempted to force rapid change on a reluctant population.

Those who advocated the Bolshevik approach not only seemed to ignore the history of such radical reforms but also postulated that political processes would work in ways for which history provided no evidence. For instance, economists such as Andrei Shleifer, who recognized the importance of the institutional infrastructure for a market economy, believed that privatization, no matter how implemented, would lead to a political demand for the institutions that govern private property.

Shleifer's argument can be thought of as an (unwarranted) extension of Coase's theorem. The economist Ronald H. Coase, who was awarded a Nobel Prize for his work, argued that in order to achieve efficiency, well-defined property rights are essential. Even if one distributed assets to someone who did not know how to manage them well, in a society with well-defined property rights that person would have an incentive to sell to someone who could manage the assets efficiently. That is why, advocates of rapid privatization argued, one didn't really need to pay close attention to how privatization was accomplished. It is now recognized that the conditions under which Coase's conjecture is valid are highly restrictive[14]—and certainly weren't satisfied in Russia as it embarked on its transition.

Shleifer and company, however, took Coase's ideas further than Coase himself would have done. They believed that political processes were governed in the same way as economic processes. If a group with vested interests in property could be created, it would demand the establishment of an institutional infrastructure necessary to make a market economy work, and its demands would be reflected in the political process. Unfortunately, the long history of political reforms suggests that the distribution of income does matter. It has been the middle class that has demanded the reforms that are often referred to as "the rule of law." The very wealthy usually do far better for themselves behind closed doors, bargaining special favors and privileges. Certainly it has not been demands from the Rockefellers and the Bill Gates of the world that have led to strong competition policies. Today, in Russia, we do not see demands for strong competition policy forthcoming from the oligarchs, the new monopolists. Demands for the rule of law have come from these oligarchs, who obtained their wealth through behind-the-scenes special deals within the Kremlin, only as they have seen their special influence on Russia's rulers wane.

Demands for an open media, free from concentration in the hands of a few, came from the oligarchs, who sought to control the media in order to maintain their power—but only when the government sought to use its power to deprive them of theirs. In most democratic and developed countries such concentrations of economic power would not long be tolerated by a middle class forced to pay monopoly prices. Americans have long been concerned with the dangers of concentration of media power, and concentrations of power in the United States on a scale comparable to that in Russia today would be unacceptable. Yet U.S. and IMF officials paid little attention to the dangers posed by the concentration of media power; rather, they focused on the rapidity of privatization, a sign that the privatization process was proceeding apace. And they took comfort, indeed even pride, in the fact that the concentrated private media was being used, and used effectively, to keep their friends Boris Yeltsin and the so-called reformers in power.

One of the reasons that it is important to have an active and critical media is to ensure that the decisions that get made reflect not just the interests of a few but the general interest of society. It was essential for the continuation of the Communist system that there not be public scrutiny. One of the problems with the failure to create an effective, independent, and competitive media in Russia was that the policies—such as the loans-for-share scheme—were not subjected to the public critique that they deserved. Even in the West, however, the critical decisions about Russian policy, both at the international economic institutions and in the U.S. Treasury, went on largely behind closed doors. Neither the taxpayers in the West, to whom these institutions were supposed to be accountable, nor the Russian people, who paid the ultimate price, knew much about what was going on at the time. Only now are we wrestling with the question of "Who lost Russia?"—and why. The answers, as we are beginning to see, are not edifying.

CHAPTER 6

UNFAIR FAIR TRADE LAWS AND OTHER MISCHIEF

THE IMF IS a political institution. The 1998 bailout was dictated by a concern to maintain Boris Yeltsin in power, though on the basis of all the *principles* which should have guided lending, it made little sense. The quiet acquiescence, if not outright support, to the corrupt loans-for-share privatization was partially based on the fact that the corruption too was for good purpose—to get Yeltsin reelected.[1] IMF policies in these areas were inextricably linked to the political judgments of the Clinton administration's Treasury.

Within the administration as a whole, there were, in fact, misgivings about Treasury's strategy. After the defeat of the reformers in December 1993, Strobe Talbott, at the time in charge of Russia policy (later to become deputy secretary of state), expressed the widespread apprehensive view of the shock therapy strategy: Had there been too much shock and too little therapy? We at the Council of Economic Advisers felt strongly that the United States was giving bad advice to Russia and using taxpayers' money to induce them to accept it. But Treasury claimed Russian economic policy as its own turf; turned aside any attempts to have an open dialogue, either within government or outside; and stood stubbornly by its commitment to shock therapy and rapid privatization.

Political judgments as much as economics lay behind the stances of the people at the Treasury. They worried about the imminent danger of backsliding into communism. The gradualists worried that the real danger was the failure of shock therapy: increasing poverty and falling incomes would undermine support for market reforms. Again, the gradualists proved right. The Moldova elections in February 2000, in which the old Communists got 70 percent of the seats in the Duma, were perhaps the most extreme case, but disillusionment with radical reform and shock therapy is now common among the economies in transition.[2] Seeing the transition as the last round in the battle between good and evil, between markets and communism, led to one further problem: the IMF and U.S. Treasury treated most of the ex-Communists with disdain and distrust, except for a few chosen ones who became their allies. There were, of course, some die-hard Communists, but some, perhaps many of those who had served in the Communist governments, were far from true believers. Instead, they were pragmatists who wanted to get ahead in the system. If the system required that they join the Communist Party, that did not seem an overly excessive price to pay. Many were as happy as anyone else to see the end of the Communist domination and the restoration of democratic processes. If these people carried over anything from their Communist days, it was a belief that the state bore a responsibility for taking care of those in need, and a belief in a more egalitarian society.

In fact, many of these ex-Communists became what, in European terms, are called Social Democrats of various persuasions. In American political terms they might range anywhere from the old New Deal Democrats to the more recent New Democrats, though most would have been closer to the former than the latter. It was ironic that the Democratic Clinton administration, seemingly embracing views highly consonant with these Social Democrats, would so often ally itself in the economies in transition with reformers who leaned to the right, the disciples of Milton Friedman and of radical market reforms, who paid too little attention to the social and distributional consequences of policy.

In Russia, there was no one but ex-Communists to be dealt with.

Yeltsin himself was an ex-Communist—a candidate member of the Politburo. In Russia, the Communists were never really ousted from power. Almost all of Russia's reformers were well-connected ex-Communists. At one time, it seemed the fault line would lie between those who were closely connected to the KGB and Gosplan—the centers of political and economic control under the old regime—and everyone else. The "good guys" were the apparatchiks who had run businesses, like Viktor Chernomyrdin, the head of Gazprom, who succeeded Gaidar as prime minister, practical men with whom we could deal. While some of these "practical men" were ready to steal as much of the state's wealth for themselves and their friends as they could get away with, they were clearly no left-wing ideologues. While (mistaken or not) judgments about who would likely lead Russia into the promised land of free markets may have guided decisions about whom the United States (and the IMF) should ally itself with in the early days of the transition, by 2000 a hard pragmatism had set in. If there had been idealism in the beginning, the failings of Yeltsin and many of those around him had led to cynicism. Putin was embraced with seeming warmth by the Bush administration as someone we could work with, his KGB credentials of little moment. It had taken a long time for us finally to stop judging people by whether they were or were not Communists during the old regime—or even by what they did under the old regime. If mistaken ideology may have blinded us in dealing with emerging leaders and parties in Eastern Europe, as well as the design of economic policies, mistaken political judgments played no less a role in Russia. Many of those with whom we allied ourselves were less interested in creating the kind of market economy that has worked so well in the West than in enriching themselves.

As time went on, and the problems with the reform strategy and the Yeltsin government became clearer, the reactions of people both in the IMF and the U.S. Treasury proved not unlike those of officials earlier inside the U.S. government as the failures of the Vietnam War became clearer: to ignore the facts, to deny the reality, to suppress the discussion, to throw more and more good money after bad. Russia was about to "turn a corner"; growth was about to occur; the next loan would enable Russia finally to get going; Russia had now shown that it would live up to the conditions of the loan agreements; and so on and so forth. As the prospects of success looked increasingly bleak, as the crisis looked increasingly around still another corner, the rhetoric changed: the emphasis switched from confidence in Yeltsin to fearing the threat of the alternative.

The sense of anxiety was palpable. I received a call one day from the office of a very senior adviser to the Russian government. He wanted to organize a brainstorming session in Russia on what the country might do to get itself going. The best that the IMF had been able to provide in years of advice was stabilization; it had nothing to offer in the way of growth. And it was clear that stabilization—at least as presented by the IMF—did not lead to growth. When the IMF and the U.S. Treasury got wind of this, they leaped into action. Treasury (reportedly at the most senior level) called the president of the Bank and I was ordered not to go. But, while Treasury would like to think of the World Bank as its own property, other countries can, when carefully orchestrated, outflank even the U.S. Treasury secretary. And so it happened here: with the appropriate calls and letters from Russia, I proceeded to Russia to do what the Russians had asked—to open a discussion unfettered by either IMF ideology or U.S. Treasury's special interests.

My visit was fascinating. The breadth of the discussions was impressive. There were a number of bright people struggling to craft a strategy for economic growth. They knew the numbers—but to them the decline in Russia was not just a matter of statistics. Many people I talked to recognized the importance of what had been left out of, or given insufficient attention in, the IMF programs. They knew that growth requires more than stabilization, privatization, and liberalization. They worried that the pressure from the IMF for rapid privatization, which they were still feeling, would lead to still more problems. Some recognized the importance of creating strong competition policies, and bemoaned the lack of support that they were receiving. But what struck me most was the incongruity between the spirit in Washington and in Moscow. In Moscow, there was (at the time) a healthy policy debate. Many were concerned, for instance, that the high exchange rate was suppressing growth—and they were right. Others worried that a devaluation would set off inflation—and they too were right. These are complicated matters, and in democracies, they need to be debated and discussed. Russia was trying to do that, trying to open up the discussion to different voices. It was Washington—or more accurately, the IMF and the U. S. Treasury—that were afraid of democracy, that wanted to suppress debate. I could not but note, and feel sad about, the irony.

As the evidence of the failures mounted, and as it became increasingly clear that the United States had been backing a weak horse, the U.S. administration tried even harder to clamp down on criticisms and public discussion. Treasury tried to eliminate discussions from within the Bank with the press, to be sure that only their interpretations of what was going on would be heard. Yet it was remarkable how, even as evidence on possible corruption unfolded in U.S. newspapers, the Treasury Department hardly wavered in its strategy.

For many, the loans-for-share privatization scheme discussed in chapter 5 (in which a few oligarchs got control of a vast portion of the country's rich natural resources) became the critical point at which the United States should have spoken out. Within Russia, the United States was not unjustly perceived as having allied itself with corruption. In what would have been perceived as a public display of support, Deputy Treasury Secretary Lawrence Summers invited to his house Anatoly Chubais, who had been in charge of privatization, who was deeply involved in the loans-for-share scam, and who not surprisingly has become one of the least popular public officials in all Russia. The U.S. Treasury and the IMF entered into the political life of Russia. By siding so firmly for so long with those at the helm when the huge inequality was created through this corrupt privatization process, the U.S.A., the IMF, and the international community have indelibly associated themselves with policies that, at best, promoted the interests of the wealthy at the expense of the average Russian.

When U.S. and European newspapers finally exposed the corruption publicly, Treasury's condemnation had a hollow and disingenuous ring. The reality is that the Duma's inspector general brought these charges to Washington long before the news stories broke. Within the World Bank, I was urged not to meet with him, lest we give credence to his charges. If the extent of corruption was not known, it was because ears and eyes were covered.

WHAT SHOULD HAVE BEEN DONE

The West's long-term interests would have been far better served had we stayed out of close involvement with particular leaders, and provided broad-based support to democratic processes. This could have been done by supporting young and emerging leaders in Moscow and in the provinces who were against corruption and who were trying to create a true democracy.

I wish there had been an open debate about America's Russian strategy at the beginning of the Clinton administration, a debate more reflective of the discussion going on in the outside world. I believe that if Clinton had been confronted with the arguments, he would have adopted a more balanced approach. He would have been more sensitive to the concerns of the poor, and more aware of the importance of political processes than the people at Treasury. But as is so often the case, the president was never given a chance to hear the full range of issues and views. Treasury viewed the issue as too important to let the president have an important role in making the decisions. Perhaps because of the lack of interest from the American people, Clinton himself did not feel that this issue was important enough for him to demand an accounting in greater detail.

U.S. INTERESTS AND RUSSIAN REFORM

There are many in Russia (and elsewhere) who believe the failed policies were not just accidental: the failures were deliberate, intended to eviscerate Russia, to remove it as a threat for the indefinite future. This rather conspiratorial view credits those at the IMF and the U.S. Treasury with both greater malevolence and greater wisdom than I think they had. I believe that they actually thought the policies they were advocating would succeed. They believed that a strong Russian economy and a stable Russian reform-oriented government were in the interests of both the United States and global peace.

But the policies were not totally altruistic. U.S. economic interests—or more accurately, U.S. financial and commercial market interests—were reflected in the policies. For instance, the July 1998 bailout was just as much a bailout of Western banks that stood to lose billions of dollars (and eventually did lose billions) as it was a bailout of Russia. But it was not just Wall Street's direct interests that influenced policy; it was the ideology that prevailed in the financial community. For instance, Wall Street regards inflation as the worst thing in the world: it erodes the real value of what is owed to creditors, which leads to increases in interest rates, which in turn lead to declines in bond prices. To financiers, unemployment is far less of a concern. For Wall Street, nothing could be more sacrosanct than private property; no wonder then the emphasis on privatization. Their commitment to competition is far less passionate—after all, it is the current U.S. secretary of the Treasury, Paul O'Neill, who engineered the global aluminum cartel and has worked to suppress competition with the global steel market. And notions of social capital and political participation may not even appear on their radar screen; they feel far more comfortable with an independent central bank than one whose actions are more directly under the control of political processes. (In the case of Russia, there was a certain irony in this stance; in the aftermath of the 1998 crisis, it was Russia's independent central banker that threatened to push a more inflationary policy than the IMF—and some members of the government—wanted, and it was the independence of the Central Bank that partly accounted for its ability to ignore charges of corruption.)

Broader special economic interests in the United States affected policies in ways that conflicted with broader national interests and made the country look more than a little hypocritical. The United States supports free trade, but all too often, when a poor country does manage to find a commodity it can export to the United States, domestic American protectionist interests are galvanized. This mix of labor and business interests uses the many trade laws—officially referred to as "fair trade laws," but known outside the United States as "unfair fair trade laws"—to construct barbed-wire barriers to imports. These laws allow a company that believes a foreign rival is selling a product below cost to request that the government impose special tariffs to protect it. Selling products below cost is called dumping, and the duties are called dumping duties. Often, however, the U.S. government determines costs on the basis of little evidence, and in ways which make little sense. To most economists, the dumping duties are simply naked protectionism. Why, they ask, would a rational firm sell goods below cost?

The Aluminum Case

During my term in government, perhaps the most grievous instance of U.S. special interests interfering in trade—and the reform process—occurred in early 1994, just after the price of aluminum plummeted. In response to the fall in price, U.S. aluminum producers accused Russia of dumping aluminum. Any economic analysis of the situation showed clearly that Russia was not dumping. Russia was simply selling aluminum at the international price, which was lowered both because of a global slowdown in demand occasioned by slower global growth and because of the cutback in Russian aluminum use for military planes. Moreover, new soda can designs used substantially less aluminum than before, and this also led to a decline in the demand. As I saw the price of aluminum plummet, I knew the industry would soon be appealing to the government for some form of relief, either new subsidies or new protection from foreign competition. But even I was surprised at the proposal made by the head of Alcoa, Paul O'Neill: a global aluminum cartel. Cartels work by restricting output, thereby raising prices. O'Neill's interest was no surprise to me; what did surprise me was the idea that the U.S. government would not only condone a cartel but actually play a pivotal role in setting one up. He also raised the specter of using the antidumping laws if the cartel was not created. These laws allow the United States to impose special duties on goods that are sold at below a "fair market value," and particularly when they are sold below the cost of production. The issue, of course, was not whether Russia was or was not dumping. Russia was selling its aluminum at international prices. Given the excess capacity in its industry and the low price of Russian electricity, much if not all of what it was selling on international markets was being sold above its costs of production. However, the way the dumping laws are typically implemented, countries can be charged with dumping even when they were— from an economic point of view—not dumping. The U.S. estimates costs of production using a peculiar methodology, which, if applied to American firms, would probably conclude that most American firms were dumping as well; but worse, the Department of Commerce, which acts simultaneously as judge, jury, and prosecutor, estimates costs based on what it calls BIA, best information available, which is typically that provided by the American firms trying to keep out the foreign competition. In the case of Russia and the other former Communist countries, it often estimates costs by looking at costs in a comparable country. In one case, Poland was charged with dumping golf carts: the supposedly "comparable" country was Canada. In the case of aluminum, had dumping charges been brought, there was a reasonable chance that sufficiently high duties would be imposed so that Russia would not be able to sell its aluminum in the United States. It might be able to sell its aluminum elsewhere (unless other countries followed the U.S. lead), in which case international aluminum prices would have continued to have been depressed. For Alcoa, a global cartel was thus preferable: it offered a better chance of getting the high prices that Alcoa wanted.

I opposed the cartel. What makes market economies work is competition. Cartels are illegal inside the United States, and they should be illegal globally. The Council of Economic Advisers had become a strong ally of the Antitrust Division of the U.S. Justice Department in pushing for strong enforcement of competition laws. For the United States now to help create a global cartel was a violation of every principle. Here, however, more was at stake. Russia was struggling to create a market economy. The cartel would hurt Russia, by restricting its sales of one of the few goods that it could market internationally. And creating the cartel would be teaching Russia the wrong lesson about how market economies work.

On a quick trip to Russia, I talked to Gaidar, then the first deputy prime minister in charge of economics; he and I both knew that Russia was not dumping—in the sense in which that word would be used by economists—but we both knew how the U.S. laws work. Were dumping charges brought, there was a good chance that dumping duties would be levied. Nonetheless, he knew how bad a cartel would be for Russia, both economically and in terms of the impact on the reforms he was trying to put into place. He agreed that we should resist as strongly as we could. He was willing to face the risk of the imposition of dumping duties.[3]

I worked hard to convince those in the National Economic Council that it would be a mistake to support O'Neill's idea, and I made great progress. But in a heated subcabinet meeting, a decision was made to support the creation of an international cartel. People in the Council of Economic Advisers and the Department of Justice were livid. Ann Bingaman, the assistant attorney general for antitrust, put the cabinet on notice that there might have been a violation of the antitrust laws in the presence of the subcabinet. Reformers within the Russian government were adamantly opposed to the establishment of the cartel and had communicated their feelings directly to me. They knew that the quantitative restrictions that the cartel would impose would give more power back to the old-line ministries. With a cartel, each country would be given certain quotas, amounts of aluminum they could produce or export. The ministries would control who got the quotas. This was the kind of system with which they were familiar, the kind of system that they loved. I worried that the excess profits generated by the trade restrictions would give rise to a further source of corruption. We did not fully grasp that in the new Mafiaized Russia, it would also give rise to a bloodbath in the struggle over who got the quotas.

While I had managed to convince almost everyone of the dangers of the cartel solution, two voices dominated. The State Department, with its close connections to the old-line state ministries, supported the establishment of a cartel. The State Department prized order above all else, and cartels do provide order. The old-line ministries, of course, were never convinced that this movement to prices and markets made sense in the first place, and the experience with aluminum simply served to confirm their views. Rubin, at that time head of the National Economic Council, played a decisive role, siding with State. At least for a while, the cartel did work. Prices were raised. The profits of Alcoa and other producers were enhanced. The American consumers—and consumers throughout the world—lost, and indeed, the basic principles of economics, which teach the value of competitive markets, show that the losses to consumers outweigh the gains to producers. But in the case at point, more was at issue: we were trying to teach Russia about market economics. They learned a lesson, but it was the wrong lesson, a lesson that was to cost them dearly over the succeeding years: the way to do well in market economics was to go to the government! We did not intend to teach crony-capitalism 101, and they probably did not need to take crony-capitalism 101 from us; they probably could have learned all that was required on their own. But we unwittingly provided them with a bad example.[4]

National Security for Sale

The aluminum case was not the first, nor would it be the last instance, where special interests dominated over the national and global goal of a successful transition. At the end of the Bush administration and the beginning of the Clinton administration, a historical "swords to plowshares" agreement was made between Russia and the United States. A U.S. government enterprise called the United States Enrichment Corporation (USEC) would buy Russian uranium from deactivated nuclear warheads and bring it to the United States. The uranium would be de-enriched so that it could no longer be used for nuclear weapons, and would then be used in nuclear power plants. The sale would provide Russia with needed cash, which it could use to better keep its nuclear material under control.

Unbelievable as it may seem, the fair trade laws were again invoked, to impede this transfer. The American uranium producers argued that Russia was dumping uranium on U.S. markets. Just as in the case of aluminum, there was no economic validity to this charge. However, the U.S. unfair fair trade laws are not written on the basis of economic principles. They exist solely to protect American industries adversely affected by imports.

When the U.S. government's import of uranium for purposes of disarmament was challenged by American uranium producers under the fair trade laws, it became clear that a change in these laws was needed. The Department of Commerce and the U.S. Trade Representative were—with high-level coaxing—finally persuaded to propose changes in the laws to Congress. Congress turned the proposals down. It has remained unclear to me whether Commerce and the

U.S. Trade Representative sabotaged efforts at getting a change in the laws by presenting the proposal to Congress in a way that made the outcome inevitable, or whether they fought against a Congress which always has taken a strong protectionist stand.

Equally striking was what happened next, in the mid-1990s. Much to the embarrassment of the Reagan and Bush administrations, the United States was far behind in the sweepstakes on privatization in the 1980s. Margaret Thatcher had privatized billions, while the United States had privatized only a $2 million helium plant in Texas. The difference, of course, was that Thatcher had far more and far larger nationalized industries that she could privatize. At last privatization advocates in the United States thought of something that few others would, or could, privatize: USEC, which not only enriches uranium for nuclear reactors but also for atomic bombs. The privatization was beset by problems. USEC had been entrusted with bringing in the enriched uranium from Russia; as a private firm, this was a kind of monopoly power that would not have passed scrutiny of the antitrust authorities. Worse still, we at the Council of Economic Advisers had analyzed the incentives of a privatized USEC, and had shown convincingly that it had every incentive to keep the Russian uranium out of the United States. This was a real concern: there were major worries about nuclear proliferation—about nuclear material getting into the hands of a rogue state or a terrorist organization—and having a weakened Russia with enriched uranium to sell to anyone willing to pay was hardly a pretty picture. USEC adamantly denied that it would ever act counter to broader U.S. interests, and affirmed that it would always bring in Russian uranium as fast as the Russians were willing to sell; but the very week that it made these protestations, I got hold of a secret agreement between USEC and the Russian agency. The Russians had offered to triple their deliveries, and USEC had not only turned them down but paid a handsome amount in what could only be termed "hush money" to keep the offer (and USEC's refusal) secret. One might have thought that this itself would have been enough to stop the privatization, but not so: the U.S. Treasury was as adamant about privatization at home as it was in Russia.

Interestingly, this, America's only major privatization of the decade, has been beset with problems almost as bad as those that have befallen privatization elsewhere, so much so that bipartisan bills have been introduced into Congress to renationalize the enterprise. Our forecasts that the privatization would interfere with the importation of the enriched uranium from Russia proved all too prescient. Indeed, at one point, it looked as if all exports to the United States might be held up. In the end, USEC asked for huge subsidies to continue with the importation. The rosy economic picture painted by USEC (and the U.S. Treasury) proved false, and investors became angry as they saw share prices plummet. There was nervousness about a firm with bare financial viability in charge of our nation's production of enriched uranium. Within a couple of years of privatization, questions were being raised about whether Treasury could, with a straight face, give the financial certification required by the law for USEC to continue to operate.

LESSONS FOR RUSSIA

Russia had a crash course in market economics, and we were the teachers. And what a peculiar course it was. On the one hand, they were given large doses of free market, textbook economics. On the other hand, what they saw *in practice* from their teachers departed markedly from this ideal. They were told that trade liberalization was necessary for a successful market economy, yet when they tried to export aluminum and uranium (and other commodities as well) to the United States, they found the door shut. Evidently, America had succeeded without trade liberalization; or, as it is sometimes put, "trade is good, but imports are bad." They were told that competition is vital (though not much emphasis was put on this), yet the U.S. government was at the center of creating a global cartel in aluminum, and gave the monopoly rights to import enriched uranium to the U.S. monopoly producer. They were told to privatize rapidly and honestly, yet the one attempt at privatization by the United States took years and years, and in the end its integrity was questioned. The United States lectured everyone, especially in the aftermath of the East Asia crisis, about crony capitalism and its dangers. Yet issues of the use of influence appeared front and center not only in the instances described in this chapter but in the bailout of Long Term Capital Management described in the last.

If the West's preaching is not taken seriously everywhere, we should understand why. It is not just past injuries, such as the unfair trade treaties referred to in earlier chapters. It is what we are doing today. Others look not only at what we say, but also at what we do. It is not always a pretty picture.

CHAPTER 7

BETTER ROADS
TO THE MARKET

A<small>S THE FAILURES</small> of the radical reform strategies in Russia and elsewhere have become increasingly evident, those who pushed them claim that they had no choices. But there were alternative strategies available. This was brought home forcefully at a meeting in Prague in September 2000, when former government officials from a number of the Eastern European countries—both those that were experiencing success and those whose performance was disappointing—reappraised their experiences. The government of the Czech Republic headed by Vaclav Klaus initially got high marks from the IMF because of its policy of rapid privatization; but its management of the overall transition process resulted in a GDP that, by the end of the 1990s, was lower than the country's 1989 level. Officials in his government said they had no choice in the policies adopted. But this contention was challenged by speakers from the Czech Republic and those from the other countries. There were alternatives; other countries made different choices—and there is a clear link between the different choices and the different outcomes.

Poland and China employed alternative strategies to those advocated by the Washington Consensus. Poland is the most successful of the Eastern European countries; China has experienced the fastest rate of growth of any major economy in the world over the past twenty years. Poland started with "shock therapy" to bring hyperinflation down to more moderate levels, and its initial and limited use of this measure has led many to think that this was one of the shock therapy transitions. But that is totally wrong. Poland quickly realized that shock therapy was appropriate for bringing down hyperinflation, but was inappropriate for societal change. It pursued a gradualist policy of privatization, while simultaneously building up the basic institutions of a market economy, such as banks that actually lend, and a legal system that could enforce contracts and process bankruptcies fairly. It recognized that without those institutions, a market economy cannot function. (In contrast to Poland, the Czech Republic privatized corporations before it privatized the banks. The state banks continued to lend to the privatized corporations; easy money flowed to those favored by the state, and privatized entities were not subjected to rigorous budgetary constraint, which allowed them to put off real restructuring.) Poland's former deputy premier and finance minister, Grzegorz W. Kolodko, has argued that the success of his nation was due to its explicit rejection of the doctrines of the Washington Consensus.[1] The country did not do what the IMF recommended—it did not engage in rapid privatization, and it did not put reducing inflation to lower and lower levels over all other macroeconomic concerns. But it did emphasize some things to which the IMF had paid insufficient attention—such as the importance of democratic support for the reforms, which entailed trying to keep unemployment low, providing benefits for those who were unemployed and adjusting pensions for inflation, and creating the institutional infrastructure required to make a market economy function.

The gradual process of privatization allowed restructuring to take place prior to privatization, and the large firms could be reorganized into smaller units. A new, vibrant small enterprise sector was thus created, headed by young managers willing to invest for their future.[2]

Similarly, China's success over the past decade stands in marked contrast to Russia's failure. While China grew at an average rate of over 10 percent in the 1990s, Russia declined at an average annual rate of 5.6 percent. By the end of the decade, real incomes (so-called purchasing power) in China were comparable to those in Russia. Whereas China's transition has entailed the largest reduction in poverty in history in such a short time span (from 358 million in

1990 to 208 million in 1997, using China's admittedly lower poverty standard of $1 a day), Russia's transition has entailed one of the largest increases in poverty in history in such a short span of time (outside of war and famine).

The contrast between China's strategy and that of Russia could not be clearer, and it began from the very first moves along the path to transition. China's reforms began in agriculture, with the movement from the commune (collective) system of production in agriculture to the "individual responsibility" system—effectively, *partial* privatization. It was not complete privatization: individuals could not buy and sell land freely; but the gains in output showed how much could be gained from even partial and limited reforms. This was an enormous achievement, involving hundreds of millions of workers, accomplished in a few years. But it was done in a way that engendered widespread support: a successful trial in one province, followed by trials in several others, equally successful. The evidence was so compelling that the central government did not have to *force* this change; it was willingly accepted. But the Chinese leadership recognized that they could not rest on their laurels, and the reforms had to extend to the entire economy.

At this juncture, they called upon several American advisers, including Kenneth Arrow and myself. Arrow had been awarded the Nobel Prize partly for his work on the foundations of a market economy; he had provided the mathematic underpinnings that explained why, *and when*, market economies work. He had also done path-breaking work on dynamics, on how economies changed. But unlike those transition gurus who marched into Russia armed with textbook economics, Arrow recognized the limitations of these textbook models. He and I each stressed the importance of competition, of creating the institutional infrastructure for a market economy. Privatization was secondary. The most challenging questions that were posed by the Chinese were questions of dynamics, and especially how to move from distorted prices to market prices. The Chinese came up with an ingenious solution: a two-tier price system in which what a firm produced under the old quotas (what it was required to produce under the old command-and-control system) is priced using old prices, but anything produced in excess of the old quota is priced using free market prices. The system allowed full incentives *at the margin*—which, as economists are well aware, is where they matter—but avoided the huge redistributions that would have occurred if the new prices were instantaneously to prevail over the entire output. It allowed the market to "grope" for the undistorted prices, a process that is not always smooth, with minimal disturbance. Most important, the Chinese gradualist approach avoided the pitfall of rampant inflation that had marked the shock therapies of Russia and the other countries under IMF tutelage, and all the dire consequences that followed, including the wiping out of savings accounts. As soon as it had accomplished its purpose, the two-tier price system was abandoned.

In the meanwhile, China unleashed a process of *creative* destruction: of eliminating the old economy by creating a new one. Millions of new enterprises were created by the townships and villages, which had been freed from the responsibility of managing agriculture and could turn their attention elsewhere. At the same time, the Chinese government invited foreign firms into the country, to participate in joint ventures. And foreign firms came in droves—China became the largest recipient of foreign direct investment among the emerging markets, and number eight in the world, below only the United States, Belgium, United Kingdom, Sweden, Germany, the Netherlands, and France.[3] By the end of the decade, its ranking was even higher. It set out, simultaneously, to create the "institutional infrastructure"—an effective securities and exchange commission, bank regulations, and safety nets. As safety nets were put into place and new jobs were created, it began the task of restructuring the old state-owned enterprises, downsizing them as well as the government bureaucracies. In a short span of a couple of years, it privatized much of the housing stock. The tasks are far from over, the future far from clear, but this much is undisputed: the vast majority of Chinese live far better today than they did twenty years ago.

The "transition" from the authoritarianism of the ruling Communist Party in China, however, is a more difficult problem. Economic growth and development do not automatically confer personal freedom and civil rights. The interplay between politics and economics is complex. Fifty years ago, there was a widespread view that there was a trade-off between growth and democracy. Russia, it was thought, might be able to grow faster than America, but it paid a high price. We now know that the Russians gave up their freedom but did not gain economically. There are cases of successful reforms done under dictatorship—Pinochet in Chile is one example. But the cases of dictatorships destroying their economies are even more common.

Stability is important for growth and anyone familiar with China's history realizes that the fear of instability runs deep in this nation of over 1 billion people. Ultimately, growth and prosperity, widely shared, are necessary, if not sufficient, for long-run stability. The democracies of the West have, in turn, shown that free markets (often disciplined by governments) succeed in bringing growth and prosperity in a climate of individual freedom. As valid as these precepts are for the past, they are likely to be even more so for the New Economies of the future.

In its quest for both stability and growth, China put creating competition, new enterprises and jobs, before privatization and restructuring existing enterprises. While China recognized the importance of macrostabilization, it never confused ends with means, and it never took fighting inflation to an extreme. It recognized that if it was to maintain social stability, it had to avoid massive unemployment. Job creation had to go in tandem with restructuring. Many of its policies can be interpreted in this light. While China liberalized, it did so gradually and in ways which ensured that resources that were displaced were redeployed to more efficient uses, not left in fruitless unemployment. Monetary policy and financial institutions facilitated the creation of new enterprises and jobs. Some money did go to support inefficient state enterprises, but China thought that it was more important, not only politically but also economically, to maintain social stability, which would be undermined by high unemployment. Although China did not rapidly privatize its state enterprises, as new enterprises were created the state ones dwindled in importance, so much so that twenty years after the transition began, they accounted for only 28.2 percent of industrial production. It recognized the dangers of full capital market liberalization, while it opened itself up to foreign direct investment.

The contrast between what happened in China and what has happened in countries like Russia, which bowed to IMF ideology, could not be starker. In case after case, it seemed that China, a newcomer to market economies, was more sensitive to the incentive effects of each of its policy decisions than the IMF was to its.

Township and village public enterprises were central in the early years of transition. IMF ideology said that because these were *public* enterprises, they could not have succeeded. But the IMF was wrong. The township and village enterprises solved the governance problem, a problem to which the IMF gave scant attention, but which underlay many of the failures elsewhere. The townships and villages channeled their precious funds into wealth creation, and there was strong competition for success. Those in the townships and villages could see what was happening to their funds; they knew whether jobs were being created and incomes increased. Although there may not have been democracy, there was accountability. New industries in China were sited in rural areas. This helped to reduce the social upheaval that inevitably accompanies industrialization. Thus China built the foundation of a New Economy on existing institutions, maintaining and enhancing its social capital, while in Russia it eroded.

The ultimate irony is that many of the countries that have taken a more gradualist policy have succeeded in making deeper reforms more rapidly. China's stock market is larger than Russia's. Much of Russia's agriculture today is managed little differently than it was a decade ago, while China managed the transition to the "individual responsibility system" in less than five years. The contrasts I have depicted between Russia on the one hand and China and Poland on the other could be repeated elsewhere in the economies in transition. The Czech Republic received accolades early on from the IMF and the World Bank for its rapid reforms; it later became apparent that it had created a capital market which did not raise money for new investment, but allowed a few smart money managers (more accurately, white-collar criminals—if they did what they did in the

Czech Republic in the United States, they would be behind bars) to walk off with millions of dollars of others' money. As a result of these and other mistakes in its transition, *relative to where it was in 1989*, the republic has fallen behind—in spite of its huge advantages in location and the high level of education of its populace. In contrast, Hungary's privatization may have gotten off to a slow start, but its firms have been restructured, and are now becoming internationally competitive.

Poland and China show that there were alternative strategies. The political, social, and historical context of each country differs; one cannot be sure that what worked in these countries would have worked in Russia, and would have been politically feasible there. By the same token, some argue that comparing the successes is unfair, given the markedly different circumstances. Poland began with a stronger market tradition than Russia; it even had a private sector during the Communist era. But China began from a less advanced position. The presence of entrepreneurs in Poland prior to the transition might have enabled Poland to undertake a more rapid privatization strategy; yet Poland as well as China chose a more gradualist approach.

Poland is alleged to have had an advantage because it was more industrialized, China because it was less so. China, according to these critics, was still in the midst of industrialization and urbanization; Russia faced the more delicate task of reorienting an already industrialized but moribund economy. But one could argue just the converse: development is not easy, as the rarity of successes clearly demonstrates. If transition is difficult, and development is difficult, it is not obvious why doing both simultaneously should be easy. The difference between China's success and Russia's failure in reforming agriculture was, if anything, even greater than the two countries' success in reforming industry.

One attribute of the success cases is that they are "homegrown," designed by people within each country, sensitive to the needs and concerns of their country. There was no cookie-cutter approach in China or Poland or Hungary. These and all the other successful transitioning countries were pragmatic—they never let ideology and simple textbook models determine policy.

Science, even an imprecise science like economics, is concerned with predictions and analyzing *causal* links. The predictions of the gradualists were borne out—both in the countries that followed their strategies, and in the shock therapy countries that followed the alternative course. By contrast, the predictions of the shock therapists were not.

In my judgment, the successes in countries that did not follow IMF prescriptions were no accident. There was a clear link between the policies pursued and the outcomes, between the successes in China and Poland and what they did, and the failure in Russia, and what it did. The outcomes in Russia were, as we have noted, what the critics of shock therapy predicted—only worse. The outcomes in China were precisely the opposite of what the IMF would have predicted—but were totally consonant with what the gradualists had suggested, only better.

The excuse of the shock therapists that measures called for by their prescription were never fully implemented is not convincing. In economics, no prescription is followed precisely, and policies (and advice) must be predicated on the fact that fallible individuals working within complex political processes will implement them. If the IMF failed to recognize this, that itself is a serious indictment. What is worse is that many of the failures were foreseen by independent observers and experts—and ignored.

The criticism of the IMF is not just that its predictions were not borne out. After all, no one, not even the IMF, could be sure of the consequences of the far-ranging changes that were entailed by the transition from communism to a market economy. The criticism is that the Fund's vision was too narrow—it focused only on the economics—and that it employed a particularly limited economic model.

We now have far more evidence about the reform process than we did five years ago when the IMF and the World Bank rushed to the judgment that their strategies were working.[4] Just as matters look strikingly different today than they did in the mid-1990s, so too in another decade, we may, given outcomes of reforms now underway, have to revise our judgments. From the current vantage point, however, some things seem clear. The IMF said that those who engaged in shock therapy, while they might feel more pain in the short run, would be more successful in the long. Hungary, Slovenia, and Poland have shown that gradualist policies lead to less pain in the short run, greater social and political stability, and faster growth in the long. In the race between the tortoise and the hare, it appears that the tortoise has won again. The radical reformers, whether the star pupils like the Czech Republic or the slightly unruly ones like Russia, have lost.[5]

THE ROAD TO THE FUTURE

Those who are responsible for the mistakes of the past have had scant advice for where Russia should go in the future. They repeat the same mantras—the need to continue with stabilization, privatization, and liberalization. The problems caused by the past now have forced them to recognize the need for strong institutions, but they have little advice to offer on what that means or how it is to be achieved. At meeting after meeting on Russian policy, I was struck by the absence of a strategy either for attacking poverty or enhancing growth. Indeed, the World Bank discussed scaling back on its programs in the rural sector. This made sense for the Bank, given the problems that its previous programs in this area had caused, but it made no sense for Russia, given that this was where much of the country's poverty lay. The only "growth" strategy proposed was that the country had to adopt policies that would repatriate the capital that had fled the country. Those who held this position overlooked that this recommendation could mean making a permanent fixture of the oligarchs, and the kleptocracy and crony/Mafia capitalism that they represented. There was no other reason for them to bring their capital back, when they could earn good returns in the West. Moreover, the IMF and U.S. Treasury never addressed the fact that they were supporting a system that lacked political legitimacy, where many of those with wealth had obtained their money by stealth and political connections with a leader—Boris Yeltsin—who too had lost all credibility and legitimacy. Sadly, for the most part, Russia must treat what has happened as pillage of national assets, a theft for which the nation can never be recompensed. Russia's objective in the future must be to try to stop further pillage, to attract legitimate investors by creating a rule of law and, more broadly, an attractive business climate.

The 1998 crisis had one benefit, to which I referred earlier: the devaluation of the ruble spurred growth, not so much in exports, but in import substitutes; it showed that the IMF policies had indeed been stifling the economy, keeping it below its potential. The devaluation, combined with a stroke of luck—the enormous increase in oil prices in the late 1990s—fueled a recovery, from an admittedly low base. There are lasting benefits from this growth spurt; some of the enterprises that took advantage of the favorable circumstances seem on the road to new opportunities and continued growth. There are other positive signs: some of those who took advantage of the system of ersatz capitalism to become very wealthy are working for a change in the rules, to make sure that what they did to others cannot be done to them. There are moves in some quarters for better corporate governance—some of the oligarchs, while they are not willing to risk all of their money in Russia, would like to entice others to risk more of theirs, and know that to do so they have to behave better than they have in the past. But there are other, less positive signs. Even in the heyday of very high oil prices, Russia was barely able to make its budget balance; it should have been putting money aside for the likelihood of a "rainy day" when oil prices come down. As this book goes to press, the recovery is uncertain. Oil prices have come down from their peak, and as usual, the impacts of devaluation are mostly felt in the first two years. But at the lower growth rates that are now emerging, Russia will need another decade or two, or more, just to catch up to where it was in 1990—unless there are some marked changes.

Russia has learned many lessons. In the aftermath of communism, many of its people swung from the old religion of Marx to the new religion of free markets. The sheen has been taken off this new religion, and a new pragmatism has settled in.

There are some policies that might make a difference. In cataloging what was to be done, it is natural to begin by thinking about the mistakes of the past: the lack of attention to the underpinnings of a market economy—from financial institutions that lend to new enterprises, to laws that enforce contracts and promote competition, to an independent and honest judiciary.

Russia must go beyond its focus on macrostabilization and encourage economic growth. Throughout the 1990s, the IMF focused on making countries work on getting budgets in order and controlling the growth of money supplies. Although when conducted in *moderation*, this stabilization may be a prerequisite to growth, it is hardly a growth strategy. In fact, the stabilization strategy has contracted aggregate demand. This decrease in aggregate demand has interacted with misguided restructuring strategies, to contract aggregate supply. In 1998, there was an active debate about the role of demand and supply. The IMF argued that any increase in aggregate demand would be inflationary. If this is true, it is a terrible admission of failure. In six years, Russia's productive capacity had been cut by more than 40 percent—far deeper than the reduction in defense, a far greater loss in capacity than occurs in any but the worst wars. I knew that the IMF policies had contributed greatly to the reduction in productive capacity, but I believed that lack of aggregate demand still remained a problem. As it turned out, the IMF again proved to be wrong: when the devaluation occurred, at last domestic producers could compete with foreign imports, and they were able to meet the new demands. Production increased. There had indeed been excess capacity, which IMF policies had left idle for years.

Growth will only succeed if Russia creates an investment-friendly environment. This entails actions at all levels of government. Good policies at the national level can be undone by bad policies at the local and regional level. Regulations at all levels can make it difficult to establish new businesses. Unavailability of land can be an impediment just as lack of availability of capital can be. Privatization does little good if local government officials squeeze firms so hard that they have no incentive to invest. This implies that issues of federalism have to be attacked head-on. A federalist structure that provides compatible incentives at all levels has to be put into place. This will be difficult. Policies aimed at curtailing abuses at lower levels of government can themselves be abused, to give excessive power to the center, and deprive local and regional authorities of the capacity to devise creative and entrepreneurial growth strategies. Although Russia has stagnated overall, there has been progress in a few localities—and there is concern that the Kremlin's recent attempts at reining in local authorities will in fact stifle these local initiatives.

But there is one factor essential to establishing a good business climate, something which will prove particularly difficult to achieve given what has happened over the past decade: political and social stability. The huge inequality, the enormous poverty, which has been created over the past decades provides fertile ground for a variety of movements, from nationalism to populism, some of which may not only be a threat to Russia's economic future but to global peace. It will be difficult—and likely take considerable time—to reverse the inequality that was created so quickly.

Finally, Russia must collect taxes. Collections should be least difficult in Russia's dominant natural resource businesses, since revenues and output in the natural resources sector are *in principle* easily monitored, so taxes should be easy to collect. Russia must put firms on notice that if taxes are not paid in, say, sixty days, their property will be seized. If taxes are not paid and the government does seize the property, it can reprivatize it in a way that has more legitimacy than the discredited loans-for-share privatization under Yeltsin. On the other hand, if the businesses do pay their taxes, Russia, the Russian government, will have the resources to attack some of the important outstanding problems.

And just as those who owe taxes must pay what they owe, those who owe money to banks—especially the banks that are now in the hands of the government as a result of defaults—must be made to pay those debts. Again, this may entail an effective renationalization of the enterprise, a renationalization to be followed by a more legitimate privatization than had occurred previously.

The success of this agenda is predicated on there being a relatively honest government interested in improving the common weal. We in the West should realize this: there is relatively little that we can do to bring that about. The hubris of those in the Clinton administration and the IMF, that they could "pick" those to support, push reform programs that worked, and usher in a new day for Russia, has been shown for what it was: the arrogant attempt by those who knew little of the country, using a narrow set of economic conceptions, to change the course of history, an attempt that was doomed to failure. We can help support the kinds of institutions that are the underpinnings of democracies—building up think tanks, creating space for public dialogue, supporting independent media, helping to educate a new generation that understands how democracies work. At the national, regional, and provincial level there are many young officials who would like to see their country take a different course, and broad-based support—intellectual as much as financial—could make a difference. If the devastation of its middle class represents the longest-term threat to Russia, then while we cannot fully reverse the damage that has been done, at least we can work to stop its further erosion.

George Soros has shown that the assistance provided by a single individual can make a difference; surely the concerted efforts of the West, if well directed, could do even more. As we forge broader democratic interactions, we should distance ourselves from those that are allied to the power structures of the past as well as the newly emerging power structures of the oligarchs—at least as far as *realpolitik* will allow. This above all else: We should do no harm. IMF loans to Russia were harmful. It is not only that these loans and the policy decisions behind them have left the country more indebted and impoverished, and maintained exchange rates at high levels that squelched the economy; they were also intended to maintain the existing groups in power, as corrupt as it was clear they were, so to the extent that they succeeded in this deliberate intervention in the political life of the country, they arguably set back a deeper reform agenda that went beyond creating a particular, narrow vision of a market economy to the creation of a vibrant democracy. My conclusion as I sat in the meetings debating the 1998 loan remains as true today as it was then: If Russia, an oil- and natural resource–rich country, is able to get its act together, it will not need these loans; and if it does not, the loans will be of little benefit. It is not money that Russia needs. It is something else, something the rest of the world can give; but it will require a very different kind of program.

DEMOCRATIC ACCOUNTABILITY
AND THE FAILURES

I have painted a bleak picture of Russia in transition: massive poverty, a few oligarchs, a devastated middle class, a declining population, and disillusionment with market processes. This indictment should be balanced with a recognition of the achievements. Russia now has a fragile democracy, far better than the totalitarian regime of the past. It suffers from a largely captive media—formerly, too much under the control of a few oligarchs, now too much under the control of the state—but a media that still presents a diversity of viewpoints far wider than under the state control system of the past. Young, well-educated, dynamic entrepreneurs, while they too often seek to migrate to the West rather than face the difficulties of doing business in Russia or the other former Soviet republics, represent the promise of a more vibrant private sector in the future.

In the end, Russia and its leaders must be held accountable for Russia's recent history and its fate. To a large extent, Russians, at least a small elite, created their country's predicament. Russians made the key decisions—like the loans-for-share privatization. Arguably, the Russians were far better at manipulating Western institutions than the Westerners were at understanding Russia. Senior government officials, like Anatoly Chubais, have openly admitted how they misled (or worse, lied to) the IMF.* They felt they had to, to get the money they needed.

But we in the West, and our leaders, have played a far from neutral and not insignificant role. The IMF let itself be misled, because it wanted to believe that its programs were working, because it wanted to continue lending, because it wanted to believe that it was reshaping Russia. And we surely did have some influence on the course of the country: we gave our imprimatur to those who were in power.

---

*When Chubais was asked if the Russian government has the right to lie to the IMF about the true fiscal situation, he literally said: "In such situations, the authorities have to do it. We ought to. The financial institutions understand, despite the fact that we conned them out of $20 billion, that we had no other way out." See R. C. Paddock, "Russia Lied to Get Loans, Says Aide to Yeltsin," *Los Angeles Times*, September 9, 1998.

That the West seemed willing to deal with them—big time with billions of dollars—gave them credibility; the fact that others might not be able to elicit such support clearly counted against them. Our tacit support for the loans-for-share program may have quieted criticisms; after all, the IMF was the expert on transition; it had urged privatization as rapidly as possible and the loans-for-share was, if nothing else, rapid. That it was corrupt was evidently not a source of concern. The support, the policies—and the billions of dollars of IMF money— may not just have enabled the corrupt government with its corrupt policies to remain in power; they may even have reduced pressure for more meaningful reforms.

We have placed our bets on favored leaders and pushed particular strategies of transition. Some of those leaders have turned out to be incompetent, others to have been corrupt, and some both. Some of those policies have turned out to be wrong, others to have been corrupt, and some both. It makes no sense to say that the policies were right, and simply not implemented well. Economic policy must be predicated not on an ideal world but on the world as it is. Policies must be designed not for how they might be implemented in an ideal world but for how they will be implemented in the world in which we live. Judgment calls were made not to investigate more promising alternative strategies. Today, just as Russia begins to hold its leaders accountable for the consequences of their decisions, we too should hold our leaders accountable.

CHAPTER 8

THE IMF'S
OTHER AGENDA

THE INTERNATIONAL MONETARY Fund's less than successful efforts in the 1980s and 1990s raise troubling questions about the way the Fund sees the process of globalization—how it sees its objectives and how it seeks to accomplish these objectives as part of its role and mission.

The Fund believes it is fulfilling the tasks assigned to it: promoting global stability, helping developing countries in transition achieve not only stability but also growth. Until recently it debated whether it should be concerned with poverty—that was the responsibility of the World Bank—but today it has even taken that on board as well, at least rhetorically. I believe, however, that it has failed in its mission, that the failures are not just accidental but the consequences of how it has understood its mission.

Many years ago former president of General Motors and secretary of defense Charles E. Wilson's famous remark to the effect that "What's good for General Motors is good for the country" became the symbol of a particular view of American capitalism. The IMF often seems to have a similar view—"what the financial community views as good for the global economy is good for the global economy and should be done." In some instances, this is true; in many, it is not. In some instances, what the financial community may think is in its interests is actually not, because the prevalent free market ideology blurs clear thinking about how best to address an economy's ills.

Losing Intellectual Coherency: From Keynes's IMF to Today's IMF

There was a certain coherency in Keynes's (the intellectual godfather of the IMF) conception of the Fund and its role. Keynes identified a market failure—a reason why markets could not be left to themselves—that might benefit from collective action. He was concerned that markets might generate persistent unemployment. He went further. He showed why there was a need for *global* collective action, because the actions of one country spilled over to others. One country's imports are another country's exports. Cutbacks in imports by one country, for whatever reason, hurt other countries' economies.

There was another market failure: he worried that in a severe downturn, monetary policy might be ineffective, but that some countries might not be able to borrow to finance the expenditure increases or compensate for tax cuts needed to stimulate the economy. Even if a country was seemingly creditworthy, it might not be able to get money. Keynes not only identified a set of market failures; he explained why an institution like the IMF could improve matters: by putting pressure on countries to maintain their economy at full employment, and by providing liquidity for those countries facing downturns that could not afford an expansionary increase in government expenditures, *global* aggregate demand could be sustained.

Today, however, market fundamentalists dominate the IMF; they believe that markets by and large work well and that governments by and large work badly. We have an obvious problem: a public institution created to address certain failures in the market but currently run by economists who have both a high level of confidence in markets and little confidence in public institutions. The inconsistencies at the IMF appear particularly troubling when viewed from the perspective of the advances in economic theory in the last three decades.

The economics profession has developed a systematic approach to *the market failure theory of governmental action*, which attempts to identify why markets might not work well and why collective action is necessary. At the international level, the theory identifies why individual governments might fail to serve global economic welfare, and how global collective action, concerted action by governments working together, often through international institutions, would improve things. Developing an intellectually coherent view of international policy for an international agency such as the IMF thus requires identifying important instances in which markets might fail to work, and analyzing how particular policies might avert or minimize the damage done by these failures. It should go further, showing how the particular interventions are the *best* way to attack the market failures, to address problems *before* they occur, and to remedy them when they do.

As we have noted, Keynes provided such an analysis, explaining why countries might not pursue sufficiently expansionary policies on their own—they would not take into account the benefits it would bring to other countries. That was why the Fund, in its original conception, was intended to put international pressure on countries to have more expansionary policies than they would choose of their own accord. Today, the Fund has reversed course, putting pressure on countries, particularly developing ones, to implement more contractionary policies than these countries would choose of their own accord. But while seemingly rejecting Keynes's views, today's IMF has, in my judgment, not articulated a coherent theory of market failure that would justify its own existence and provide a rationale for its particular interventions in the market. As a result, as we have seen, all too often the IMF forged policies which, in addition to exacerbating the very problems they sought to address, allowed these problems to play out over and over again.

A New Role for a New Exchange Rate Regime?

Some thirty years ago, the world switched to a system of flexible exchange rates. There was a coherent theory behind the switch: exchange rates, like other prices, should be determined by market forces. Attempts by government to intervene in the determination of this price are no more successful than attempts to intervene in the determination of any other price. Yet, as we have seen, the IMF has recently undertaken massive interventions. Billions of dollars were spent trying to sustain the exchange rates of Brazil and Russia at unsustainable levels. The IMF justifies these interventions on the grounds that *sometimes* markets exhibit excessive pessimism—they "overshoot"—and the calmer hand of the international bureaucrat can then help stabilize markets. It struck me as curious that an institution committed to the doctrine that markets work well, if not perfectly, should decide that this one market—the exchange rate market—requires such massive intervention. The IMF has never put forward a good explanation either for why this expensive intervention is desirable in this particular market—or for why it is undesirable in other markets.

I agree with the IMF that markets may exhibit excessive pessimism. But I also believe that markets may exhibit excessive optimism, and that it is not just in the exchange rate market that these problems occur. There is a wider set of imperfections in markets, and especially capital markets, requiring a wider set of interventions.

For instance, it was excessive exuberance that led to Thailand's real estate and stock market bubble, a bubble reinforced, if not created, by hot speculative money flowing into the country. The exuberance was followed by excessive pessimism when the flow abruptly reversed. In fact, this change in the direction of speculative capital was the root cause of the excessive volatility in exchange rates. If this is a phenomenon comparable to a *disease*, it makes sense to treat the disease rather than just its manifestation, exchange rate volatility. But IMF free market ideology led the Fund to make it easier for speculative hot money to flow into and out of a country. In treating the symptoms directly, by pouring billions of dollars into the market, the IMF actually made the underlying disease worse. If speculators only made money off each other, it would be an unattractive game—a highly risky activity, which *on average* made a zero return, as the gains by some were matched by equal losses from others. What makes speculation profitable is the money coming from governments, supported by the IMF. When the IMF and the Brazilian government, for instance, spent some $50 billion maintaining the exchange rate at an overvalued level in late 1998, where did the money go? The money doesn't disappear into thin air. It goes into somebody's pocket—much of it into the pockets of the speculators. Some speculators may win, some may lose, but speculators as a whole make an amount equal to what the government loses. In a sense, it is the IMF that keeps the speculators in business.

Contagion

There is another, equally striking example of how the IMF's lack of a coherent and reasonably complete theory can lead to policies which exacerbate the very problems the IMF is supposed to solve. Consider what happens when the Fund attempts to quarantine "contagion." In essence, the Fund argues that it must intervene, and quickly, if it determines that an ongoing crisis in one country will spill over to others, that is, the crisis will spread like an infectious, contagious disease.

If contagion is a problem, it is important to understanding the workings of the mechanism through which it occurs, just as epidemiologists, in trying hard to contain an infectious disease, work hard to understand its transmission mechanism. Keynes had a coherent theory; the downturn in one country leads that country to import less, and this hurts its neighbors. We saw in chapter 4 how the IMF, while talking about contagion, took actions in the Asian financial crisis that actually accelerated transmission of the disease, as it forced country after country to tighten their belts. The reductions in incomes led quickly to large reductions in imports, and in the closely integrated economies of the region, these led to the successive weakening of neighboring countries. As the region imploded, the declining demand for oil and other commodities led to the collapse of commodity prices, which wrought havoc in other countries, thousands of miles away, whose economies depended on the export of those commodities.

Meanwhile the IMF clung to fiscal austerity as the antidote, claiming that was essential to restore investor confidence. The East Asian crisis spread from there to Russia through the collapse of oil prices, not through any mysterious connection between "confidence" on the part of investors, foreign and domestic, in the East Asia Miracle economies and the Mafia capitalism of Russia. Because of the lack of coherent and persuasive theory of contagion, the IMF had spread the disease rather than contained it.

When Is a Trade Deficit a Problem?

Problems of coherence plague not only the IMF's remedies but also its diagnoses. IMF economists worry a lot about balance of payments deficits; such deficits are, in their calculus, a sure sign of a problem in the offing. But in railing against such deficits, they often pay little attention to what the money is actually being used for. If a government has a fiscal surplus (as Thailand did in the years before the 1997 crisis), then the balance of payments deficit essentially arises from *private* investment exceeding private savings. If a firm in the private sector borrows a million dollars at 5 percent interest and invests it in something that yields a 20 percent return, then it's not a problem for it to have borrowed the million dollars. The investment will more than pay back the borrowing. Of course, even if the firm makes a mistake in judgment, and the returns are 3 percent, or even zero, there is no problem. The borrower then goes into bankruptcy, and the creditor loses part or all of his loan. This may be a problem for the creditor, but it is not a problem that the country's government—or the IMF—need worry about.

A *coherent approach* would have recognized this. It would have also recognized that if some country imports more than it exports (i.e., it has a trade deficit), another country must be exporting more than it imports (it has a trade surplus). It is an unbreakable law of international accounting that the sum of all deficits in the world must add up to the sum of all surpluses. This means that if China and Japan insist on having a trade surplus, then some countries must have deficits. One cannot just inveigh against the deficit countries; the surplus countries are equally at fault. If Japan and China maintain their surpluses, and Korea converts its deficit into a surplus, the problem of deficit *must* appear on somebody else's doorstep.

Still, large trade deficits can be a problem. They can be a problem because they imply a country has to borrow year after year. And if those who are providing the capital change their minds and stop

making loans, the country can be in big trouble—a crisis. It is spending more to buy goods from abroad than it gets from selling its goods
abroad. When others refuse to continue to finance the trade gap, the
country will have to adjust quickly. In a few cases, the adjustment can
be made easily: if a country is borrowing heavily to finance a binge
of car buying (as was the case recently in Iceland), then if foreigners
refuse to provide the financing for the cars, the binge stops, and the
trade gap closes. But more typically the adjustment does not work so
smoothly. And problems are even worse if the country has borrowed
short term, so that creditors can demand back *now* what they have
lent to finance previous years' deficits, whether they were used to
finance consumption splurges or long-term investments.

Bankruptcy and Moral Hazard

Such crises occur, for instance, when a real estate bubble bursts, as it
did in Thailand. Those who borrowed from abroad to finance their
real estate ventures could not repay their loans. Bankruptcy became
widespread. How the IMF handles bankruptcy represents still
another arena where the Fund's approach is plagued with intellectual
inconsistencies.

In standard market economics, if a lender makes a bad loan, he
bears the consequence. The borrower may well go into bankruptcy,
and countries have laws on how such bankruptcies should be worked
out. This is the way market economies are supposed to work. Instead,
repeatedly, the IMF programs provide funds for governments to bail
out Western creditors. The creditors, anticipating an IMF bailout,
have weakened incentives to ensure that the borrowers will be able
to repay. This is the infamous moral hazard problem well known in
the insurance industry and, now, in economics. Insurance reduces
your incentive to take care, to be prudent. A bailout in the event of a
crisis is like "free" insurance. If you are a lender, you take less care in
screening your applicants—when you know you will be bailed out if
the loans go sour. Meanwhile prudent firms that face foreign
exchange volatility can insure against it in complicated but readily
accessible ways. But—as we saw earlier—if borrowers in a country
don't buy insurance to minimize their risk, or exposure, but they

know or believe that an IMF bailout is likely, then borrowers are being encouraged to incur excess risk—and not worry about it. This is what happened in the lead-up to the ruble crisis in Russia in 1998. In that instance, even as the Wall Street creditors were making loans to Russia, they were letting it be known how large a bailout they thought was needed and, given Russia's nuclear status, they believed would get.

The IMF, focusing on the symptoms, tries to defend its interventions by saying that without them, the country will default, and as a result it will not be able to get credit in the future. A coherent approach would have recognized the fallacy in this argument. *If* capital markets work well—certainly, if they worked anywhere near as well as the IMF market fundamentalists seem to argue—then they are forward-looking; in assessing what interest rates to charge, they look at the risk *going forward*. A country that has discharged a heavy overhang of debt, even by defaulting, is in better shape to grow, and thus *more* able to repay any additional borrowing. That is part of the rationale for bankruptcy in the first place: the discharge or restructuring of debt allows firms—and countries—to move forward and grow. Eighteenth-century debtor prisons may have provided strong incentives for individuals not to go into bankruptcy, but they did not help debtors get reestablished. Not only were they inhumane, but they did not enhance overall economic efficiency.

History supports this theoretical analysis. In the most recent instance, Russia, which had a massive debt default in 1998 and was widely criticized for not even consulting creditors, was able to borrow from the market by 2001 and capital began to flow back to the country. Likewise, capital started flowing back to South Korea, even though the nation effectively forced a restructuring of its debt, giving foreign creditors a choice of rolling over loans or not being repaid.

Consider how the IMF, if it had developed a coherent model, might have approached one of the most difficult problems in East Asia: whether or not to raise interest rates in the midst of the crisis. Raising them, of course, would force thousands of firms into bankruptcy. The contention of the IMF was that failing to raise rates would lead to a collapse of the exchange rate, and the collapse of the exchange rate would lead to even more bankruptcy. Put aside, for the moment, the question of whether raising interest rates (with the resulting exacerbation of the recession) would lead to a stronger exchange rate (in real life it did not). Put aside, too, the empirical question of whether more firms would be hurt by raising interest rates or the fall in the exchange rate (at least in Thailand, the evidence strongly suggested that the damage from a further fall in the exchange rate would be smaller). The *problem* of economic disruption caused by exchange rate devaluations is *caused* by the firms that choose not to buy insurance against the collapse of the exchange rate. A coherent analysis of the problem would have begun by asking why the seeming market failure—why do firms not buy the insurance? And any analysis would have suggested that the IMF itself was a big part of the problem: IMF interventions to support the exchange rate, as noted above, make it less necessary for firms to buy insurance, exacerbating in the future the very problem the intervention was supposed to address.

From Bailout to Bail-In

As the IMF's failures became increasingly evident, it sought new strategies, but the lack of coherency ensured that its quest for viable alternatives had little chance of success. The extensive criticism of its bailout strategy induced it to try what some have called a "bail-in" strategy. The IMF wanted the private sector institutions to be "in" on any bailouts. It began to insist that before it lent money to a country in a bailout, there had to be extensive "participation" by the private sector lenders; they would have to take a "haircut," forgiving a substantial part of the debt that was owed. Not surprisingly, this new strategy was first tried not on major countries like Brazil and Russia, but on powerless countries like Ecuador and Romania, too weak to resist the IMF. The strategy quickly proved to be both problematic in conception and flawed in implementation, with highly negative consequences for the countries targeted for the experiment.

Romania was a particularly mystifying example. It was not threatening a default; it only wanted new money from the IMF to signal that it was creditworthy, which would help to lower the interest rates it paid. But new lenders will only lend if they get an interest rate commensurate with the risk they face. New lenders cannot be forced to take a "haircut." If the IMF had based its policies on a coherent theory of well-functioning capital markets, it would have realized this.

But there was a more serious problem, which goes to the IMF's core mission. The Fund was created to deal with the liquidity crises caused by the credit market's occasional irrationality, its refusal to lend to countries that were in fact creditworthy. Now the IMF was handing power over its lending policies to the same individuals and institutions that precipitated crises. Only if they were willing to lend could it be willing to lend. These lenders quickly saw the profound implications of the change, even if the IMF did not. If creditors refuse to lend the client country money, or to go along with a settlement, the borrowing country will not be able to get funds—not just from the IMF but from the World Bank and other institutions which made their lending contingent on IMF approval. The creditors suddenly had enormous leverage. A twenty-eight-year-old man in the Bucharest branch of an international private bank, by making a loan of a few million dollars, had the power to decide whether or not the IMF, the World Bank, and the EU would provide Romania with more than a billion dollars of money. In effect, the Fund had delegated its responsibility for assessing whether to lend to the country to this twenty-eight-year-old. Not surprisingly, the twenty-eight-year-old, and other thirty- and thirty-five-year-old bankers in the branches of the other international banks in Bucharest, quickly grasped their newly granted bargaining powers. Each time the Fund lowered the amount of money it demanded that the private banks put up, the private banks lowered the amount that they were willing to offer. At one point, Romania appeared to be only $36 million of private sector loans short to receive the billion-dollar aid package. The private banks assembling the money required by the IMF demanded not only top dollar (high interest rates) but, at least in one case, some discreet relaxation of Romania's regulatory rules. This "regulatory forbearance" would allow the creditor to do things he might otherwise not be able to do—to lend more, or to make riskier, higher interest rate loans—increasing his profits, but increasing the riskiness of the banking system, and undermining the very reason for regulation. Less competent or more corrupt governments might have been tempted, but Romania did not accept the offer, partly because it was not really that desperate for money in the first place.

The issue can be seen another way. The IMF's decision to make a loan is supposed to be based on how a country is addressing its fundamental macroeconomic problems. Under the "participatory" strategy, a country could have a perfectly satisfactory set of macropolicies, but if it could not raise the amount that the IMF said it had to raise from the private banks, it might not be able to receive funds from any of the sources. The IMF is supposed to have the expertise on these questions, not the twenty-eight-year-old bank officer in Bucharest.

Eventually, at least in the case of Romania, the failings of the strategy became evident even to the IMF, and it proceeded to provide funds to the country even though the private sector had not provided the amounts the IMF had "insisted" upon.

The Best Defense Is an Offense: Expanding the Role of the IMF as "Lender of Last Resort"

In the light of increasing perceptions of the Fund's failures and growing demands that its scope be cut back, in 1999 the IMF's first deputy manager, Stanley Fischer, proposed that the Fund expand its role to make it a lender of last resort. Given that the IMF had failed to use the powers it had well, the proposal to increase its power was quite bold. It was based on an appealing analogy: Inside countries, central banks act as a lender of last resort, lending money to banks which are "solvent but not liquid," that is, which have a positive net worth, but which cannot obtain funds from elsewhere. The IMF would perform the same role for countries. Had the IMF had a coherent view of the capital market, it would have quickly seen the flaw in the idea.[1] Under the perfect market theory, if a business is solvent, it should be able to borrow money from the market; any firm that is solvent *is* liquid. Just as IMF economists, who normally seem to have such faith in markets, believe that they can judge better than the market what the exchange rate should be, so too do they seem to think that they can judge better than the market whether the borrowing country is creditworthy.

I don't believe capital markets work perfectly. Ironically, while I think they work far less well than IMF economists typically suggest, I think that they are somewhat more "rational" than the IMF seems to believe when it intervenes. There are advantages to IMF lending; often the Fund lends when the capital markets simply refuse to do so. But at the same time, I recognize that the country pays dearly for the "cheap" money it gets from the IMF. If a national economy goes sour and default looms, the IMF is the preferred creditor. It gets paid back first—even if others, such as foreign creditors, do not. These get what's left over. They might get nothing. So a rational private sector financial institution is going to insist on a risk premium—a higher interest rate to cover the higher likelihood of not getting paid back. If more of a country's money goes to the IMF, there is less to go to private sector foreign lenders, and these lenders will insist on a commensurately higher interest rate. A coherent theory of the capital market would have made the IMF more aware of this—and made it more reluctant to lend the billions and billions it has provided in bailout packages. A more coherent theory of markets would have had the IMF, in times of crisis, looking harder for alternatives, like those we discussed in chapter 4.

THE IMF'S NEW AGENDA?

The fact that a lack of coherence has led to a multitude of problems is perhaps not surprising. The question is, why the lack of coherence? Why does it persist, on issue after issue, even after the problems are pointed out? Part of the explanation is that the problems that the IMF has to confront are difficult; the world is complex; the Fund's economists are practical men striving to make hard decisions quickly, rather than academics calmly striving for intellectual coherence and consistency. But I think that there is a more fundamental reason: The IMF is pursuing not just the objectives set out in its original mandate, of enhancing global stability and ensuring that there are funds for countries facing a threat of recession to pursue expansionary policies. It is also pursuing the interests of the financial community.

This means the IMF has objectives that are often in conflict with each other.

The tension is all the greater because this conflict can't be brought out into the open: if the new role of the IMF were publicly acknowledged, support for that institution might weaken, and those who have succeeded in changing the mandate almost surely knew this. Thus the new mandate had to be clothed in ways that *seemed* at least superficially consistent with the old. Simplistic free market ideology provided the curtain behind which the real business of the "new" mandate could be transacted.

The change in mandate and objectives, while it may have been quiet, was hardly subtle: from serving global *economic* interests to serving the interests of global *finance*. Capital market liberalization may not have contributed to global economic stability, but it did open up vast new markets for Wall Street.

I should be clear: the IMF never *officially* changed its mandate, nor did it ever formally set out to put the interests of the financial community over the stability of the global economy or the welfare of the poor countries they were supposed to be helping. We cannot talk meaningfully about the motivations and intentions of any institution, only of those who constitute and govern it. Even then, we often cannot ascertain true motivations—there may be a gap between what they say are their intentions and their true motivations. As social scientists, we can, however, attempt to describe the behavior of an institution in terms of what it *appears* to be doing. Looking at the IMF *as if* it were pursuing the interests of the financial community provides a way of making sense of what might otherwise seem to be contradictory and intellectually incoherent behaviors.

Moreover, the IMF's behavior should come as no surprise: it approached the problems from the perspectives and ideology of the financial community, and these naturally were closely (though not perfectly) aligned with its interests. As we have noted before, many of its key personnel came from the financial community, and many of its key personnel, having served these interests well, left to well-paying jobs in the financial community. Stan Fischer, the deputy managing director who played such a role in the episodes described in this book, went directly from the IMF to become a vice chairman at Citigroup, the vast financial firm that includes Citibank. A chairman of Citigroup (chairman of the Executive Committee) was Robert Rubin, who, as secretary of Treasury, had had a central role in IMF policies. One could only ask, Was Fischer being richly rewarded for having faithfully executed what he was told to do?

But one does not need to look for venality. The IMF (or at least many of its senior officials and staff members) believed that capital market liberalization would lead to faster growth for the developing countries, believed it so strongly that it did not need to look at any evidence and gave little credence to any evidence that suggested otherwise. The IMF never wanted to harm the poor and believed that the policies it advocated would eventually benefit them; it believed in trickle-down economics and, again, did not want to look too closely at evidence that might suggest otherwise. It believed that the discipline of the capital markets would help poor countries grow, and therefore it believed that keeping in good stead with the capital markets was of first-order importance.

LOOKING AT THE IMF policies this way, its emphasis on getting foreign creditors repaid rather than helping domestic businesses remain open becomes more understandable. The IMF may not have become the bill collector of the G-7, but it clearly worked hard (though not always successfully) to make sure that the G-7 lenders got repaid. There was an alternative to its massive interventions, as we saw in chapter 4, an alternative that would have been better for the developing nations, and in the longer run, better for global stability. The IMF could have facilitated the workout process; it could have tried to engineer a standstill (the temporary interruption of payments) that would have given the countries—and their firms—time to recoup, to restart their stalled economies. It could have tried to create an accelerated bankruptcy process.[2] But bankruptcy and standstills were not (and are still not) welcome options, for they meant that the creditors would not be repaid. Many of the loans were uncollateralized, so in the event of bankruptcy, little might be recovered.

The IMF worried that a default, by breaking the sanctity of contracts, would undermine capitalism. In this, they were wrong in several respects. Bankruptcy is an unwritten part of every credit contract; the law provides for what will happen if the debtor cannot pay the creditor. Because bankruptcy is an implicit part of the credit contract, bankruptcy does not violate the "sanctity" of the credit contract. But there is another, equally important, *unwritten* contract, that between citizens and their society and government, what is sometimes called "the social contract." This contract requires the provision of basic social and economic protections, including reasonable opportunities for employment. While misguidingly working to preserve what it saw as the sanctity of the credit contract, the IMF was willing to tear apart the even more important social contract. In the end, it was the IMF policies which undermined the market as well as the long-run stability of the economy and society.

IT IS UNDERSTANDABLE then why the IMF and the strategies it foists on countries around the world are greeted with such hostility. The billions of dollars which it provides are used to maintain exchange rates at unsustainable levels for a short period, during which the foreigners and the rich are able to get their money out of the country at more favorable terms (through the open capital markets that the IMF has pushed on the countries). For each ruble, for each rupiah, for each cruzeiro, those in the country get more dollars as long as the exchange rates are sustained. The billions too are often used to pay back foreign creditors, even when the debt was private. What had been private liabilities were in effect in many instances nationalized.

In the Asian financial crisis, this was great for the American and European creditors, who were glad to get back the money they had lent to Thai or Korean banks and businesses or at least more of it than they otherwise would have. But it was not so great for the workers and other taxpayers of Thailand and Korea, whose tax money is used to repay the IMF loans, whether or not they got much benefit from the money. But adding insult to injury, after the billions are spent to maintain the exchange rate at an unsustainable level and to bail out the foreign creditors, after their governments have knuckled under to the pressure of the IMF to cut back on expenditures, so that the countries face a recession in which millions of workers lose their jobs, there seems to be no money around when it comes to finding the far more modest sums to pay subsidies for food or fuel for the poor. No wonder that there is such anger against the IMF.

If one sees the IMF as an institution pursuing policies that are in the interests of creditors, other IMF policies also become more understandable. We noted earlier the focus on the trade deficit. After the crisis, the massive contractionary policies imposed on the East Asian countries led to quick reductions in imports and a massive rebuilding of reserves. From the perspective of an institution worried about the ability to repay creditors, this made sense: without reserves, the countries would not be able to repay the dollar loans that they and the firms in their country owed. But if one had focused more on the issue of global stability and the economic recovery of the countries and the region, one would have taken a more lax approach to the rebuilding of reserves, and at the same time instituted other policies to insulate the countries from the effects of the vagaries of international speculators. Thailand had run out of reserves because they had been used in 1997 to fight off speculators. Once it was decided that Thailand needed quickly to rebuild reserves, it was inevitable that it would have a deep recession. The IMF's beggar-thyself policies, which, as we saw in chapter 4, have replaced the beggar-thy-neighbor policies of the Great Depression, were even worse in spreading the global crisis. From the perspective of the creditors, the policies sometimes worked, and remarkably quickly: In Korea, reserves went from essentially zero to almost $97 billion by July 2001; in Thailand, from essentially negative to more than $31 billion by July 2001. For the creditors, of course, all of this was good news; they could now rest assured that Korea had the dollars to repay any loans, should the creditors demand it.

I would have taken a strategy that was sympathetic to the concerns of the debtors, less focused on the interests of the creditors. I would have said that it was more important to keep the economy going and to postpone building up reserves for a couple of years until the economy was back on track. I would have explored other ways of providing short-term stability—not only the standstills or bankruptcies to which I referred earlier, but short-term capital controls and "exit taxes" of the kind that Malaysia used. There are ways of protecting a country against the ravages of speculators, or even of short-term lenders or investors who have suddenly changed their sentiments. No policy comes without its risks or price; but these alternatives would almost surely have imposed lower costs and risks on those *inside* the crisis countries, even if they had imposed higher costs on the creditors.

Defenders of the IMF's policies point to the fact that the creditors did have to bear some of the costs. Many were not fully repaid. But this misses the point on two counts: The creditor-friendly policies attempted to *reduce* the losses from what they otherwise have been. They did not engineer a full bailout, but a partial one; they did not stop the exchange rate from falling, but they worked to prevent it from falling further. Secondly, the IMF did not always succeed in doing what it set out to do. The IMF pushed contractionary policies in Indonesia too far, so that in the end, the interests of the creditors were not well served. More broadly, global financial stability was arguably not only in the interests of the global economy but also in the interests of the financial markets; yet many of its policies—from the capital market liberalization to the massive bailouts—almost surely contributed to global instability.

The fact that the IMF was concerned about and reflected the perspectives of the financial community also helps explain some of its defensive rhetoric. In the East Asia crisis, the IMF and the U.S. Treasury quickly sought to blame the problems on the borrowing countries, and in particular on their lack of transparency. Even then, it was clear that lack of transparency does not cause crises nor can transparency inoculate a country against crises. Prior to the East Asian crisis, the most recent financial crisis was the real estate crash in the late 1980s and early 1990s in Sweden, Norway, and Finland, some of the most transparent nations in the world. There were many countries that were far less transparent than Korea, Malaysia, and Indonesia— and they did not have a crisis. If transparency is the key to the economic riddle, then the countries of East Asia should have had *more* crises earlier, since the data showed that they were becoming more, not less, transparent. Despite its alleged failures on the transparency front, East Asia had not only shown remarkable growth but also remarkable stability. If the East Asian countries were as "highly vulnerable" as the IMF and the Treasury claimed, it was a newfound vulnerability based not on an increased lack of transparency but on another familiar factor: the premature capital and financial market liberalization that the IMF had pushed on these countries

In retrospect, there was a "transparent" reason for this focus on transparency:[3] it was important for the financial community, the IMF, and the U.S. Treasury to shift blame. The policies that the Fund and Treasury had pushed in East Asia, Russia, and elsewhere were to blame: capital market liberalization had led to destabilizing speculation, financial market liberalization to bad lending practices. As their recovery programs failed to work as they said they would, they had further incentive to try to say the real problem lay not with their programs but elsewhere, with the afflicted countries.

Closer scrutiny, however, showed that the industrialized nations were at fault in many other ways; weak banking regulation in Japan, for instance, might have provided an incentive for banks to lend to Thailand at such attractive rates that the borrowers could not resist borrowing more than was prudent. Liberalized banking regulatory policies in the United States and other major industrialized countries also encouraged unwise lending—banks were allowed to treat short-term foreign lending as safer than long-term. This encouraged short-term lending, and the short-term loans were among the important sources of instability in East Asia.

The major investment firms also wanted to exculpate their advisers, who had encouraged their clients to put their money into these countries. Fully backed up by the governments in the United States and the other major industrialized nations, investment advisers from Frankfurt to London to Milan could claim that there was no way they could have been expected to know how bad things really were, given the lack of transparency in East Asian countries. These experts quietly slid over the fact that in a fully open and transparent market, one with perfect information, returns are low. Asia had been an attractive investment—it produced high returns—precisely because it was more risky. The advisers' belief that they had *better* information—and their clients' thirst for high returns—drove funds to the region. The key problems—South Korea's high indebtedness, Thailand's huge trade deficits and real estate boom that inevitably would bust,

Suharto's corruption—were well known, and the risks these posed should have been disclosed to investors.

The international banks too found it convenient to shift blame. They wanted to blame the borrowers and bad lending practices of the Thai and South Korean banks, which, they alleged, were making bad loans with the connivance of the corrupt governments in their countries—and the IMF and the U.S. Treasury again joined them in the attack. From the start, one should have been suspicious of the IMF/Treasury arguments. Despite their attempt to get the major international lenders off the hook, the hard truth is that every loan has both a borrower and a lender. If the loan is inherently bad, the lender is as much at fault as the borrower. Moreover, banks in the Western developed countries were lending to the large Korean firms, knowing full well how leveraged many Korean firms were. The bad loans were a result of bad judgment, not of any pressure from the United States or other Western governments, and were made in spite of the Western banks' allegedly good risk management tools. No wonder, then, that these big banks wanted to shift the scrutiny away from themselves. The IMF had good reason for supporting them, for the Fund itself shared in the culpability. Repeated IMF bailouts elsewhere had contributed to lack of due diligence on the part of the lenders.

There was an even more profound issue at stake. The U.S. Treasury had during the early 1990s heralded the global triumph of capitalism. Together with the IMF, it had told countries that followed the "right policies"—the Washington Consensus policies—they would be assured of growth. The East Asia crisis cast doubt on this new worldview *unless it could be shown that the problem was not with capitalism, but with the Asian countries and their bad policies.* The IMF and the U.S. Treasury had to argue that the problem was not with the reforms—implementing liberalization of capital markets, above all, that sacred article of faith—but with the fact that the reforms had not been carried far enough. By focusing on the weaknesses of the crisis countries, they not only shifted blame away from their own failures—both the failures of policy and the failures in lending—but they attempted to use the experience to push their agenda still further.

CHAPTER 9

THE WAY AHEAD

GLOBALIZATION TODAY IS not working for many of the world's poor. It is not working for much of the environment. It is not working for the stability of the global economy. The transition from communism to a market economy has been so badly managed that, with the exception of China, Vietnam, and a few Eastern European countries, poverty has soared as incomes have plummeted.

To some, there is an easy answer: Abandon globalization. That is neither feasible nor desirable. As I noted in chapter 1, globalization has also brought huge benefits—East Asia's success was based on globalization, especially on the opportunities for trade, and increased access to markets and technology. Globalization has brought better health, as well as an active global civil society fighting for more democracy and greater social justice. The problem is not with globalization, but with how it has been managed. Part of the problem lies with the international economic institutions, with the IMF, World Bank, and WTO, which help set the rules of the game. They have done so in ways that, all too often, have served the interests of the more advanced industrialized countries—and particular interests within those countries—rather than those of the developing world.

But it is not just that they have served those interests; too often, they have approached globalization from particular narrow mind-sets, shaped by a particular vision of the economy and society.

The demand for reform is palpable—from congressionally appointed commissions and foundation-supported groups of eminent economists writing reports on changes in the global financial architecture to the protests that mark almost every international meeting. In response, there has already been some change. The new round of trade negotiations that was agreed to in November 2001 at Doha, Qatar, has been characterized as the "development round," intended not just to open up markets further but to rectify some of the imbalances of the past, and the debate at Doha was far more open than in the past. The IMF and the World Bank have changed their rhetoric— there is much more talk about poverty, and at least at the World Bank, there is a sincere attempt to live up to its commitment to "put the country in the driver's seat" in its programs in many countries. But many of the critics of the international institutions are skeptical. They see the changes as simply the institutions facing the political reality that they *must* change their rhetoric if they are to survive. These critics doubt that there is real commitment. They were not reassured when, in 2000, the IMF appointed to its number two position someone who had been chief economist at the World Bank during the period when it took on market fundamentalist ideology. Some critics are so doubtful about these reforms that they continue to call for more drastic actions such as the abolition of the IMF, but I believe this is pointless. Were the Fund to be abolished, it would most likely be recreated in some other form. In times of international crises, government leaders like to feel there is someone in charge, that an international agency is doing something. Today, the IMF fills that role.

I believe that globalization can be reshaped to realize its potential for good and I believe that the international economic institutions can be reshaped in ways that will help ensure that this is accomplished. But to understand how these institutions should be reshaped, we need to understand better why they have failed, and failed so miserably.

Interests and Ideology

In the last chapter we saw how, by looking at the policies of the IMF *as if* the organization was pursuing the interests of the financial markets, rather than simply fulfilling its original mission of helping countries in crises and furthering global economic stability, one could make sense of what otherwise seemed to be a set of intellectually incoherent and inconsistent policies.

If financial interests have dominated thinking at the International Monetary Fund, commercial interests have had an equally dominant role at the World Trade Organization. Just as the IMF gives short shrift to the concerns of the poor—there are billions available to bail out banks, but not the paltry sums to provide food subsidies for those thrown out of work as a result of IMF programs—the WTO puts trade over all else. Those who seek to prohibit the use of nets that harvest shrimp but also catch and endanger turtles are told by the WTO that such regulation would be an unwarranted intrusion on free trade. They discover that trade considerations trump all others, including the environment!

While the institutions seem to pursue commercial and financial interests above all else, they do not see matters that way. They genuinely believe the agenda that they are pursuing is in the *general interest*. In spite of the evidence to the contrary, many trade and finance ministers, and even some political leaders, believe that everyone will eventually benefit from trade and capital market liberalization. Many believe this so strongly that they support forcing countries to accept these "reforms," through whatever means they can, even if there is little popular support for such measures.

The greatest challenge is not just in the institutions themselves but in mind-sets: Caring about the environment, making sure the poor have a say in decisions that affect them, promoting democracy and fair trade are necessary if the potential benefits of globalization are to be achieved. The problem is that the institutions have come to reflect the mind-sets of those to whom they are accountable. The typical central bank governor begins his day worrying about inflation statistics, not poverty statistics; the trade minister worries about export numbers, not pollution indices.

The world is a complicated place. Each group in society focuses
on a part of the reality that affects it the most. Workers worry about
jobs and wages, financiers about interest rates and being repaid. A
high interest rate is good for a creditor—provided he or she gets paid
back. But workers see high interest rates as inducing an economic
slowdown; for them, this means unemployment. No wonder that
they see the danger in high interest rates. For the financier who has
lent his money out long term, the real danger is inflation. Inflation
may mean that the dollars he gets repaid will be worth less than the
dollars he lent.

In public policy debates, few argue openly in terms of their own
self-interest. Everything is couched in terms of *general interest*. Assessing how a particular policy is likely to affect the general interest
requires a model, a view of how the entire system works. Adam
Smith provided one such model, arguing in favor of markets; Karl
Marx, aware of the adverse effects that capitalism seemed to be having on workers of his time, provided an alternative model. Despite its
many well-documented flaws, Marx's model has had enormous
influence, especially in developing countries where for the billions of
poor capitalism seemed not to be delivering on its promises. But
with the collapse of the Soviet empire, its weaknesses have become
all too evident. And with that collapse, and the global economic
dominance of the United States, the market model has prevailed.

But there is not just *one* market model. There are striking differences between the Japanese version of the market system and the
German, Swedish, and American versions. There are several countries
with per capita income comparable to that of the United States, but
where inequality is lower, poverty is less, and health and other aspects
of living standards higher (at least in the judgment of those living
there). While the market is at the center of both the Swedish and
American versions of capitalism, government takes on quite different
roles. In Sweden, the government takes on far greater responsibilities
promoting social welfare; it continues to provide far better public
health, far better unemployment insurance, and far better retirement
benefits than does the United States. Yet it has been every bit as successful, even in terms of the innovations associated with the "New
Economy." For many Americans, but not all, the American model has

worked well; for most Swedes, the American model is viewed as unacceptable—they believe their model has served them well. For Asians, a variety of Asian models has worked well, and this is true for Malaysia and Korea as well as China and Taiwan, even taking into account the global financial crisis.

Over the past fifty years, economic science has explained why, and the conditions under which, markets work well *and when they do not*. It has shown why markets may lead to the underproduction of some things—like basic research—and the overproduction of others—like pollution. The most dramatic market failures are the periodic slumps, the recessions and depressions, that have marred capitalism over the past two hundred years, that leave large numbers of workers unemployed and a large fraction of the capital stock underutilized. But while these are the most obvious examples of market failures, there are a myriad of more subtle failures, instances where markets failed to produce efficient outcomes.

Government can, and has, played an essential role not only in mitigating these market failures but also in ensuring *social justice*. Market processes may, by themselves, leave many people with too few resources to survive. In countries that have been most successful, in the United States and in East Asia, government has performed these roles and performed them, for the most part, reasonably well. Governments provided a high-quality education to all and furnished much of the infrastructure—including the institutional infrastructure, such as the legal system, which is required for markets to work effectively. They regulated the financial sector, ensuring that capital markets worked more in the way that they were supposed to—they provided a safety net for the poor. And they promoted technology, from telecommunications to agriculture to jet engines and radar. While there is a vigorous debate in the United States and elsewhere about what the *precise* role of government should be, there is broad agreement that government has a role in making any society, any economy, function efficiently—and humanely.

There are important disagreements about economic and social policy in our democracies. Some of these disagreements are about values—how concerned should we be about our environment (how much environmental degradation should we tolerate, if it allows us to have a higher GDP); how concerned should we be about the poor (how much sacrifice in our total income should we be willing to make, it if allows some of the poor to move out of poverty, or to be slightly better off); or how concerned should we be about democracy (are we willing to compromise on basic rights, such as the rights to association, if we believe that as a result, the economy will grow faster). Some of these disagreements are about how the economy functions. The *analytic propositions* are clear: whenever there is imperfect information or markets (that is always), there are, in principle, interventions by the government—even a government that suffers from the same imperfections of information—which can increase the markets' efficiency. As we saw in chapter 3, the assumptions underlying market fundamentalism do not hold in developed economies, let alone in developing countries. But the advocates of market fundamentalism still argue that the inefficiencies of markets are relatively small and the inefficiencies of government are relatively large. They see government more as part of the problem than the solution; unemployment is blamed on government setting too-high wages, or allowing unions too much power.

Adam Smith was far more aware of the limitations of the market, including the threats posed by imperfections of competition, than those who claim to be his latterday followers. Smith too was more aware of the social and political context in which all economies must function. Social cohesion is important if an economy is to function: urban violence in Latin America and civil strife in Africa create environments that are hostile to investment and growth. But while social cohesion can affect economic performance, the converse is also true: excessively austere policies—whether they be contractionary monetary, or fiscal policies in Argentina, or cutting off food subsidies to the poor in Indonesia—predictably give rise to turmoil. This is especially the case when it is believed that there are massive inequities—such as billions going to corporate and financial bailouts in Indonesia, leaving nothing left for those forced into unemployment.

In my own work—both in my writings and in my role as the president's economic adviser and chief economist of the World Bank—I have advocated a balanced view of the role of government, one which recognizes both the limitations and failures of markets *and*

government, but which sees the two as working together, in partnership, with the precise nature of that partnership differing among
countries, depending on their stages of both political and economic
development.

But at whatever stage of political and economic development a
country is, government makes a difference. Weak governments and
too-intrusive governments have both hurt stability and growth. The
Asia financial crisis was brought on by a lack of adequate regulation
of the financial sector, Mafia capitalism in Russia by a failure to
enforce the basics of law and order. Privatization without the necessary institutional infrastructure in the transition countries led to asset
stripping rather than wealth creation. In other countries, privatized
monopolies, without regulation, were more capable of exploiting
consumers than the state monopolies. By contrast, privatization
accompanied by regulation, corporate restructuring, and strong corporate governance[1] has led to higher growth.

My point here, however, is not to resolve these controversies, or to
push for my particular conception of the role of government and
markets, but to emphasize that there are real disagreements about
these issues among even well-trained economists. Some critics of
economics and economists jump to the conclusion that economists
always disagree, and therefore try to dismiss *whatever* economists say.
That is wrong. On some issues—like the necessity of countries living
within their means, and the dangers of hyperinflation—there is
widespread agreement.

The problem is that the IMF (and sometimes the other international economic organizations) presents as received doctrine propositions and policy recommendations for which there is not widespread
agreement; indeed, in the case of capital market liberalization, there
was scant evidence in support and a massive amount of evidence
against. While there is agreement that no economy can succeed
under hyperinflation, there is no consensus about the gains from
lowering inflation to lower and lower levels; there is little evidence
that pushing inflation to lower and lower levels yields gains commensurate with the costs, and some economists even think that there are
negative benefits from pushing inflation too low.[2]

The discontent with globalization arises not just from economics seeming to be pushed over everything else, but because a particular view of economics—market fundamentalism—is pushed over all other views. Opposition to globalization in many parts of the world is not to globalization per se—to the new sources of funds for growth or to the new export markets—but to the particular set of doctrines, the Washington Consensus policies that the international financial institutions have imposed. And it is not just opposition to the policies themselves, but to the notion that there is a single set of policies that is right. This notion flies in the face both of economics, which emphasizes the importance of trade-offs, and of ordinary common sense. In our own democracies we have active debates on every aspect of economic policy; not just on macroeconomics, but on matters like the appropriate structure of bankruptcy laws or the privatization of Social Security. Much of the rest of the world feels as if it is being deprived of making its own choices, and even forced to make choices that countries like the United States have rejected.

But while the commitment to a particular ideology deprived countries of the choices that should have been theirs, it also contributed strongly to their failures. The economic structures in each of the regions of the world differ markedly; for instance, East Asian firms had high levels of debt, those in Latin America relatively little. Unions are strong in Latin America, relatively weak in much of Asia. Economic structures also change over time—a point emphasized by the New Economy discussions of recent years. The advances in economics of the past thirty years have focused on the role of financial institutions, on information, on changing patterns of global competition. I have noted how these changes altered views concerning the efficiency of the market economy. They also altered views concerning the appropriate responses to crises.

At the World Bank and the IMF, these new insights—and more important, their implications for economic policy—were resisted, just as these institutions had resisted looking at the experiences of East Asia, which had *not* followed the Washington Consensus policies and had grown faster than any other region of the world. This failure to take on board the lessons of modern economic science left these institutions ill-prepared to deal with the East Asia crisis when it occurred, and less able to promote growth around the world.

The IMF felt it had little need to take these lessons on board because it knew the answers; if economic science did not provide them, ideology—the simple belief in free markets—did. Ideology provides a lens through which one sees the world, a set of beliefs that are held so firmly that one hardly needs empirical confirmation. Evidence that contradicts those beliefs is summarily dismissed. For the believers in free and unfettered markets, capital market liberalization was *obviously* desirable; one didn't need evidence that it promoted growth. Evidence that it caused instability would be dismissed as merely one of the adjustment costs, part of the pain that had to be accepted in the transition to a market economy.

The Need for International Public Institutions

We cannot go back on globalization; it is here to stay. The issue is how can we make it work. And if it is to work, there have to be global public institutions to help set the rules.

These international institutions should, of course, focus on issues where global collective action is desirable, or even necessary. Over the past three decades there has been an increased understanding of the circumstances under which collective action, at whatever level, is required. Earlier, I discussed how collective action is required when markets by themselves do not result in efficient outcomes. When there are externalities—when the actions of individuals have effects on others for which they neither pay nor are compensated—the market will typically result in the overproduction of some goods and the underproduction of others. Markets cannot be relied upon to produce goods that are essentially public in nature, like defense.[3] In some areas, markets fail to exist;[4] governments have provided student loans, for instance, because the market, on its own, failed to provide funding for investments in human capital. And for a variety of reasons, markets are often not self-regulating—there are booms and busts—so the government has an important role in promoting economic stability.

Over the past decade, there has been an increased understanding of the appropriate level—local, national, or global—at which collective action is desirable. Actions the benefits of which accrue largely locally (such as actions related to local pollution) should be conducted at the local level; while those that benefit the citizens of an entire country should be undertaken at the national level. Globalization has meant that there is increasing recognition of arenas where impacts are global. It is in these arenas where global collective action is required—and systems of global governance are essential. The recognition of these areas has been paralleled by the creation of global institutions to address such concerns. The United Nations can be thought of as focusing upon issues of global political security, while the international financial institutions, and in particular the IMF, are supposed to focus on global economic stability. Both can be thought of as dealing with externalities that can take on global dimensions. Local wars, unless contained and defused, can draw in others, until they become global conflagrations. An economic downturn in one country can lead to slowdowns elsewhere. In 1998 the great concern was that a crisis in emerging markets might lead to a global economic meltdown.

But these are not the only arenas in which global collective action is essential. There are global environmental issues, especially those that concern the oceans and atmosphere. Global warming caused by the industrial countries' use of fossil fuels, leading to concentrations of greenhouse gasses (CO_2), affects those living in preindustrial economies, whether in a South Sea island or in the heart of Africa. The hole in the ozone layer caused by the use of chlorofluorocarbons (CFCs) similarly affects everyone—not just those who made use of these chemicals. As the importance of these international environmental issues has grown, international conventions have been signed. Some have worked remarkably well, such as the one directed at the ozone problem (the Montreal Protocol of 1987); while others, such as those that address global warming, have yet to make a significant dent in the problem.

There are also global health issues like the spread of highly contagious diseases such as AIDS, which respect no boundaries. The World Health Organization has succeeded in eradicating a few diseases, notably river blindness and smallpox, but in many areas of global public health the challenges ahead are enormous. Knowledge itself is an important global public good: the fruits of research can be of benefit to anyone, anywhere, at essentially no additional cost.

International humanitarian assistance is a form of collective action that springs from a shared compassion for others. As efficient as markets may be, they do not ensure that individuals have enough food, clothes to wear, or shelter. The World Bank's main mission is to eradicate poverty, not so much by providing humanitarian assistance at the time of crisis as by enabling countries to grow, to stand on their own.

Although specialized institutions in most of these areas have evolved in response to specific needs, the problems they face are often interrelated. Poverty can lead to environmental degradation, and environmental degradation can contribute to poverty. People in poor countries like Nepal with little in the way of heat and energy resources are reduced to deforestation, stripping the land of trees and brush to obtain fuel for heating and cooking, which leads to soil erosion, and thus to further impoverishment.

Globalization, by increasing the interdependence among the people of the world, has enhanced the need for global collective action and the importance of global public goods. That the global institutions which have been created in response have not worked perfectly is not a surprise: the problems are complex and collective action at any level is difficult. But in previous chapters we have documented complaints that go well beyond the charge that they have not worked perfectly. In some cases their failures have been grave; in other cases they have pursued an agenda that is unbalanced—with some benefiting from globalization much more than others, and some actually being hurt.

Governance

So far, we have traced the failures of globalization to the fact that in setting the rules of the game, commercial and financial interests and mind-sets have seemingly prevailed within the international economic institutions. A particular view of the role of government and markets has come to prevail—a view which is not universally accepted within the developed countries, but which is being forced upon the developing countries and the economies in transition.

The question is, why has this come about? And the answer is not hard to find: It is the finance ministers and central bank governors who sit around the table at the IMF making decisions, the trade ministers at the WTO. Even when they stretch, to push policies that are in their countries' broader national interests (or occasionally, stretching further, to push policies that are in a broader global interest), they see the world through particular, inevitably more parochial, perspectives.

I have argued that there needs to be a change in mind-set. But the mind-set of an institution is inevitably linked to whom it is *directly* accountable. Voting rights matter, and who has a seat at the table—even with limited voting rights—matters. It determines whose voices get heard. The IMF is not just concerned with technical arrangements among bankers, such as how to make bank check-clearing systems more efficient. The IMF's actions affect the lives and livelihoods of billions throughout the developing world; yet they have little say in its actions. The workers who are thrown out of jobs as a result of the IMF programs have no seat at the table; while the bankers, who insist on getting repaid, are well represented through the finance ministers and central bank governors. The consequences for policy have been predictable: bailout packages which pay more attention to getting creditors repaid than to maintaining the economy at full employment. The consequences for the choice of the institution's management have equally been predictable: there has been more of a concern with finding a leader whose views are congruent with the dominant "shareholders" than with finding one that has expertise in the problems of the developing countries, the mainstay of the Fund's business today.

Governance at the WTO is more complicated. As at the IMF, it is the voices of trade ministers that are heard. No wonder, then, that little attention is often paid to concerns about the environment. Yet while the voting arrangements at the IMF ensure that the rich countries predominate, at the WTO each country has a single vote, and decisions are largely by consensus. But in practice, the United States, Europe, and Japan have dominated in the past. This may now be changing. At the last meeting at Doha, the developing countries insisted that if another round of trade negotiations was to be initiated, their concerns had to be heard—and they achieved some notable concessions. With China's joining the WTO, the developing countries have a powerful voice on their side—though the interests of China and those of many of the other developing countries do not fully coincide.

The most fundamental change that is required to make globalization work in the way that it should is a change in governance. This entails, at the IMF and the World Bank, a change in voting rights, and in all of the international economic institutions changes to ensure that it is not just the voices of trade ministers that are heard in the WTO or the voices of the finance ministries and treasuries that are heard at the IMF and World Bank.

Such changes are not going to be easy. The United States is unlikely to give up its effective veto at the IMF. The advanced industrial countries are not likely to give up their votes so that the developing countries can have more votes. They will even put up specious arguments: voting rights, as in any corporation, are assigned on the basis of capital contributions. China would long ago have been willing to increase its capital contribution, if that was required to give it more voting rights. U.S. Treasury Secretary Paul O'Neill has tried to give the impression that it is the American taxpayers, its plumbers and carpenters, who pay for the multi-billion-dollar bailouts—and because they pay the costs, they ought to have the vote. But that is wrong. The money comes ultimately from the workers and other taxpayers in the developing countries, for the IMF almost always gets repaid.

But although change is not easy, it is possible. The changes that the developing countries wrenched from the developed countries in November 2001 as the price for beginning another round of trade negotiations show that, at least in the WTO, there has been a change in bargaining power.

Still, I am not sanguine that fundamental reforms in the *formal* governance of the IMF and World Bank will come soon. Yet in the short run, there are changes in *practices* and *procedures* that can have significant effects. At the World Bank and the IMF there are twenty-four seats at the table. Each seat speaks for several countries. In the present configuration, Africa has very few seats simply because it has so few votes, and it has so few votes because, as we noted, votes are allocated on the basis of economic power. Even without changing the voting arrangements, one could have more African seats; their voice would be heard even if their votes were not counted.

Effective participation requires that the representatives of the developing countries be well informed. Because the countries are poor, they simply cannot afford the kinds of staff that the United States, for instance, can muster to support its positions at all the international economic institutions. If the developed countries were serious about paying more attention to the voices of the developing countries, they could help fund a think tank—independent from the international economic organizations—that would help them formulate strategies and positions.

Transparency

Short of a fundamental change in their governance, the most important way to ensure that the international economic institutions are more responsive to the poor, to the environment, to the broader political and social concerns that I have emphasized is to increase openness and transparency. We have come to take for granted the important role that an informed and free press has in reining in even our democratically elected governments: any mischief, any minor indiscretion, any favoritism, is subject to scrutiny, and public pressure works powerfully. Transparency is even more important in public institutions like the IMF, the World Bank, and the WTO, because their leaders are not elected directly. Though they are public, there is no *direct* accountability to the public. But while this should imply that these institutions be even more open, in fact, they are even less transparent.

The problem of lack of transparency affects each of the international institutions, though in slightly different ways. At the WTO, the negotiations that lead up to agreements are all done behind closed doors, making it difficult—until it is too late—to see the influence of corporate and other special interests. The deliberations of the WTO panels that rule on whether there has been a violation of the WTO agreements occur in secret. It is perhaps not surprising that the trade lawyers and ex-trade officials who often comprise such panels pay, for instance, little attention to the environment; but by bringing the deliberations more out into the open, public scrutiny would either make the panels more sensitive to public concerns or force a reform in the adjudication process.

The IMF comes by its penchant for secrecy naturally: central banks, though public institutions, have traditionally been secretive. Within the financial community, secrecy is viewed as natural—in contrast to academia, where openness is the accepted norm. Before September 11, 2001, the secretary of treasury even defended the secrecy of the offshore banking centers. The billions of dollars in the Cayman Islands and other such centers are not there because those islands provide better banking services than Wall Street, London, or Frankfurt; they are there because the secrecy allows them to engage in tax evasion, money laundering, and other nefarious activities. Only after September 11 was it recognized that among those other nefarious activities was the financing of terrorism.

But the IMF is not a private bank; it is a public institution.

The absence of open discourse means that models and policies are not subjected to timely criticism. Had the actions and policies of the IMF during the 1997 crisis been subject to conventional democratic processes, and there had been a full and open debate in the crisis countries about the proffered IMF policies, it is possible that they would never have been adopted, and that far saner policies would have emerged. That discourse might not only have exposed the faulty economic assumptions on which the policy prescriptions were based but also revealed that the interests of the creditors were being placed ahead of those of workers and small businesses. There were alternative courses of actions, where less of the risk was borne by these less powerful parties, and these alternative courses of actions might have been given the serious consideration that they deserved.

Earlier, in my days at the Council of Economic Advisers, I had seen and come to understand the strong forces that drove secrecy. Secrecy allows government officials the kind of discretion that they would not have if their actions were subject to public scrutiny.

Secrecy not only makes their life easy but allows special interests full sway. Secrecy also serves to hide the mistakes, whether innocent or not, whether the result of a failure to think matters through or not. As it is sometimes put, "Sunshine is the strongest antiseptic."

Even when policies are not driven by special interests, secrecy engenders suspicions—whose interests are really being served?—and such suspicions, even when groundless, undermine the political sustainability of the policies. It is this secrecy, and the suspicions it gives rise to, that has helped sustain the protest movement. One of the demands of the protestors has been for greater openness and transparency.

These demands had a special resonance because the IMF itself emphasized the importance of transparency during the East Asia crisis. One of the clearly *unintended* consequences of the IMF's rhetorical emphasis on transparency was that eventually, when the transparency spotlight was turned around to shine on the IMF itself, it was found wanting.[5]

Secrecy also undermines democracy. There can be democratic accountability only if those to whom these public institutions are supposed to be accountable are well informed about what they are doing—including what choices they confronted and how those decisions were made. We saw in chapter 2 how modern democracies had come to recognize the citizens' basic *right to know*, implemented through laws such as America's Freedom of Information Act. We saw also, however, that while nominally espousing transparency and openness, the IMF and the World Bank have not yet embraced these ideas. They must.

REFORMING THE IMF AND THE GLOBAL FINANCIAL SYSTEM

There are some common themes facing reform in all of the international economic institutions, but each institution has a set of problems of its own. I begin with the IMF, partly because it brings out more clearly some problems that are present to a lesser extent in other institutions.

I began the previous chapter by asking, How could an organization with such talented (and high paid) government bureaucrats make so many mistakes? I suggested that *part* of its problems arose from the dissonance between its supposed objective, the objective for which it was originally created, promoting global economic stability, and the newer objectives—such as capital market liberalization— which did more to serve the interests of the financial community than of global stability. This dissonance led to intellectual incoherency and inconsistencies that were more than just matters of academic interest. No wonder, then, that it was hard to derive coherent policies. Economic science was too often replaced by ideology, an ideology that gave clear directions, if not always guidance that worked, and an ideology that was broadly consonant with the interests of the financial community, even if, when it failed to work, those interests themselves were not well served.

One of the important distinctions between *ideology* and *science* is that science recognizes the limitations on what one knows. There is always uncertainty. By contrast, the IMF never likes to discuss the uncertainties associated with the policies that it recommends, but rather, likes to project an image of being infallible. This posture and mind-set makes it difficult for it to learn from past mistakes—how can it learn from those mistakes if it can't admit them? While many organizations would like outsiders to believe that they are indeed infallible, the problem with the IMF is that it often acts as if it *almost* believes in its infallibility.

The IMF has admitted to mistakes in the East Asia crisis, acknowledging that the contractionary fiscal policies exacerbated the downturn, and that the strategy for restructuring the financial system in Indonesia led to a bank run, which only made matters worse. But, not surprisingly, the Fund—and the U.S. Treasury, which was responsible for pushing many of the policies—has tried to limit the criticisms and their discussion. Both were furious when a World Bank report touched on these and other mistakes and got front-page coverage in the *New York Times*. Orders to muzzle the critics were issued. More tellingly, the IMF never pursued the issues further. It never asked why the mistakes had occurred, what was wrong with the models, or what could be done to prevent a recurrence in the next crisis—and there surely will be another crisis in the future. (As of January 2002, Argentina is going through a crisis. Once again, the IMF bailout policies failed to work; the contractionary fiscal policies that it insisted upon pushed the economy into an ever deeper recession.) The IMF never asked why its models *systematically* underestimated the depth of recessions—or why its policies are *systematically* excessively contractionary.

The Fund tries to defend its stance of institutional infallibility, saying that if it showed it was wavering in its conviction that its policies were correct, it would lose credibility—and the success of its policies requires that markets give it credibility. Here again, there is real irony. Does the IMF, always praising the "perfection and rationality" of the market, really believe that it enhances its credibility by making overly confident forecasts? Predictions that repeatedly don't pan out make the Fund look rather less than infallible, especially if the markets are as rational as it claims. Today, the IMF has lost much of its credibility, not only in developing countries but also with its cherished constituency, the financial community. Had the IMF been more honest, more forthright, more modest, it would arguably be in a better standing today.

Sometimes, IMF officials give another reason for their failure to discuss alternative policies and the risks associated with each. They say that it would simply confuse the developing countries—a patronizing attitude that reflects a deep skepticism about democratic processes.

It would be nice if the IMF, having had these problems pointed out, would change its mind-set and its modes of behavior. But this is not likely to be the case. Indeed, the Fund has been remarkably slow in learning from its mistakes—partly, as we have seen, because of the strong role of ideology and its belief in institutional infallibility, partly because its hierarchical organizational structure is used to ensure its prevailing worldviews dominate throughout the institution. The IMF is not, in the jargon of modern business schools, a "learning organization," and like other organizations that find it difficult to learn and adapt, it finds itself in difficulties when the environment around it changes.

Earlier in this chapter, I argued that a fundamental change in mind-set is likely to occur only with a change in governance, but that such changes are unlikely in the near term. Increased transparency would help; but even there, meaningful reforms were being resisted.

A broad consensus—outside the IMF—has developed that the IMF should limit itself to its core area, managing crises; that it should no longer be involved (outside crises) in development or the economies of transition. I strongly concur—partly because the other reforms that would enable it to promote democratic, equitable, and sustainable development and transition are simply not forthcoming.

There are other dimensions to narrowing the focus. The IMF currently is responsible for the collection of valuable economic statistics, and though by and large it does a good job, the data it reports are compromised by its operating responsibilities; to make its programs *seem* to work, to make the numbers "add up," economic forecasts have to be adjusted. Many users of these numbers do not realize that they are not like ordinary forecasts; in these instances, GDP forecasts are not based on a sophisticated statistical model, or even on the best estimates of those who know the economy well, but are merely the numbers that have been *negotiated* as part of an IMF program. Such conflicts of interest invariably arise when the operating agency is also responsible for statistics, and many governments have responded by creating an independent statistical agency.

Another activity of the Fund is surveillance, reviewing a country's economic performance, under the Article 4 consultations discussed in chapter 2. This is the mechanism through which the IMF pushes its particular perspectives on developing countries that are not dependent on its aid. Because an economic slowdown in one country can have adverse effects on others, it does make sense for countries to put pressure on each other to maintain their economic strength; there is a global public good. The problem is the report card itself. The IMF emphasizes inflation; but unemployment and growth are equally important. And its policy recommendations too reflect its particular perspectives on the balance of government and markets. My direct experience with these Article 4 consultations in the United States convinces me that this too is a task that should be taken over by others. Because the most direct impact of one country's slowdown is on its neighbors, and the neighbors are much more attuned to the circumstances in the country, regional surveillance is a viable alternative.

Forcing the IMF to return to its original mission—narrowing its focus—enables greater accountability. We can attempt to ascertain whether it has prevented crises from happening, creating a more stable global environment, and whether it has resolved them well. But clearly, narrowing focus does not solve the institution's problem: part of the complaint is that it has pushed policies, such as capital market liberalization, which have increased global instability, and that its big bailout policies, whether in East Asia, or Russia, or Latin America, have failed.

Reform Efforts

In the aftermath of the East Asian crisis, and the failures of the IMF policies, there was a general consensus that something was wrong with the international economic system, something needed to be done to make the global economy more stable. However, many of those at the U.S. Treasury and IMF felt that only minor changes were needed. To compensate for the lack of grandness in the changes, they conceived a grandiose title for the reform initiative, *reform of the global financial architecture.* The term was intended to suggest a major change in the rules of the game that would prevent another crisis.

Underneath the rhetoric, there were some real issues. But just as those in charge at the IMF did everything to shift the blame away from their mistakes and away from the systemic problems, they did everything they could to curtail the reforms, except to the extent that they result in *more* power and money to the IMF and *more obligations* (such as compliance with new standards set by the advanced industrial countries) on the emerging markets.

These doubts are reinforced by the way discussions of reform have proceeded. The "official" reform debate has been centered in the same institutions and dominated by the same governments that have effectively "run" globalization for over fifty years. Around the world today, there is a great deal of cynicism about the reform debate. Faced with the same people at the table who had been responsible for the system all along, the developing countries wondered if it was likely that real change would occur. As far as these "client countries" were concerned, it was a charade in which the politicians pretended to do something to redress the problems while financial interests worked to preserve as much of the status quo as they could. The cynics were partly right, but only partly so. The crisis brought to the fore the sense that something was wrong with the process of globalization, and this perception mobilized critics across a wide landscape of issues, from transparency to poverty to the environment to labor rights.

· Inside the organizations themselves, among many influential members there is a sense of complacency. The institutions have altered their rhetoric. They talk about "transparency," about "poverty," about "participation." Even if there is a gap between the rhetoric and the reality, the rhetoric has an effect on the institutions' behavior, on transparency, on the concern for poverty. They have better Web sites and there is more openness. The participatory poverty assessments have generated more involvement and a greater awareness of the poverty impacts of programs. But these changes, as profound as they seem to those inside the institutions, appear superficial to outsiders. The IMF and World Bank still have disclosure standards far weaker than those of governments in democracies like the United States, or Sweden, or Canada. They attempt to hide critical reports; it is only their inability to prevent leaks that often forces the eventual disclosure. There is mounting unhappiness in developing countries with the new programs involving participatory poverty assessments, as those participating are told that important matters, such as the macroeconomic framework, are off limits.[6]

There are other instances where there has been more change in what is said than in what is done. Today, the dangers of short-term capital flows and premature capital and financial market liberalization are occasionally acknowledged even by senior officials at the IMF. This constitutes a major change in the official stance of the Fund— though it is still too soon to see whether, or how, the change in rhetoric will be reflected in policies implemented within countries.[7] So far, the evidence does not look promising, as one simple episode illustrates. Shortly after the new managing director Horst Köhler took office, he undertook a tour of some member countries. In a visit to Thailand at the end of May 2000, he noted what had by then become conventional wisdom outside the IMF, and was beginning to seep into the IMF itself: the dangers of capital market liberalization. Neighboring Indonesia quickly picked up on the opening, and by the time he visited there in June, its government had announced plans to explore interventions into the capital market. But quickly, the Indonesians—and Köhler—were set straight by the IMF staff. The bureaucracy won again: capital market liberalization might, in theory, be problematic; but capital market interventions (controls) evidently were not to be on the table for those seeking IMF assistance.

There were other gestures to reform, halfhearted or half-baked.[8] As criticism of the large bailouts in the 1990s mounted, there was a succession of failed reforms. First came the precautionary lending package—lending before a crisis actually had occurred—to Brazil, which forestalled that country's crisis but for a few months, and at great cost. Then there was the contingent credit line, another measure designed to have money ready when a crisis erupted.[9] That too didn't work, mainly because no one seemed interested in it on the proposed terms.[10] It was recognized that the bailouts may have contributed to moral hazard, to weak lending practices, and so a bail-in strategy whereby creditors would have to bear part of the costs was put into place, though not for major countries like Russia, but rather for the weak and powerless, like Ecuador, Ukraine, Romania, and Pakistan. As I explained in chapter 8, by and large the bail-in strategies were a failure. In some cases, such as Romania, they were abandoned, though not after considerable damage to that country's economy; in other cases, like Ecuador, they were enforced, with even more devastating effects. The new U.S. Treasury secretary and the IMF's new managing director both expressed reservations about the overall effectiveness of the large bailout strategy, but then went ahead with more of the same—$11 billion and $21.6 billion lent to Turkey and Argentina in 2000 and 2001, respectively. The eventual failure of the Argentine bailout seems to have finally forced the *beginning* of a rethinking of strategy.

Even when there was widespread, but not universal, consensus on reforms, resistance arose from those in financial centers, sometimes supported by the U.S. Treasury. In the East Asia crisis, as attention was focused on transparency, it became clear that to know what was going on in emerging markets, one had to know what hedge funds and off-shore banking centers were doing. Indeed, there was a worry that more transparency elsewhere would lead to more transactions going through these channels, and there would overall be less information about what was going on. Secretary Summers took the side of the hedge funds and the offshore banking centers, resisting calls for increased transparency, arguing that excessive transparency might reduce incentives for gathering information, the "price discovery" function in the technical jargon. Reforms in the offshore banking centers, established as tax and regulatory avoidance havens, only took on momentum after September 11. This should not come as a surprise; these facilities exist as a result of deliberate policies in the advanced industrial countries, pushed by financial markets and the wealthy.

Other, even seemingly minor reforms faced strong resistance, sometimes from the developing as well as developed countries. As it became clear that short-term indebtedness played a key role in the crisis, attention focused on bond provisions that allowed what seemed to be a long-term bond to be converted into a short-term indebtedness overnight.[11] And as demands for bail-in of creditors grew, so too did demands for provisions in bonds that would facilitate their "forced" participation in workouts, so-called collective action clauses. The bond markets have, so far successfully, resisted both reforms—even as these reforms have seemingly received some support from the IMF. The critics of these reforms argued that such provisions might make credit more costly to the borrowing country; but they miss the central point. Today, there are huge costs to borrowing, especially when things go badly, but only a fraction of those costs are borne by the borrower.

What Is Needed

The recognition of the problems has come a long way. But the reforms of the international financial system have only just begun. In my mind, among the key reforms required are the following:

1. Acceptance of the dangers of capital market liberalization, and

that short-term capital flows ("hot money") impose huge externalities, costs borne by those not directly party to the transaction (the lenders and borrowers). Whenever there are such large externalities, interventions—including those done through the banking and tax systems[12]—are desirable. Rather than resisting these interventions, the international financial institutions should be directing their efforts to making them work better.

2. Bankruptcy reforms and standstills. The appropriate way of addressing problems when private borrowers cannot repay creditors, whether domestic or foreign, is through bankruptcy, not through an IMF-financed bailout of creditors. What is required is bankruptcy reform that recognizes the special nature of bankruptcies that arise out of macroeconomic disturbances; what is needed is a super-Chapter 11, a bankruptcy provision that expedites restructuring and gives greater presumption for the continuation of existing management. Such a reform will have the further advantage of inducing more due diligence on the part of creditors, rather than encouraging the kind of reckless lending that has been so common in the past.[13] Trying to impose more creditor-friendly bankruptcy reforms, taking no note of the special features of macro-induced bankruptcies, is not the answer. Not only does this fail to address the problems of countries in crises; it is a medicine which likely will not take hold—as we have seen so graphically in East Asia, one cannot simply graft the laws of one country onto the customs and norms of another. The problems of defaults on *public* indebtedness (as in Argentina) are more complicated, but again there needs to be more reliance on bankruptcies and standstills, a point that the IMF too seems belatedly to have accepted. But the IMF cannot play the central role. The IMF is a major creditor, and it is dominated by the creditor countries. A bankruptcy system in which the creditor or his representative is also the bankruptcy judgment will never be accepted as fair.

3. Less reliance on bailouts. With increased use of bankruptcies and standstills, there will be less need for the big bailouts, which failed so frequently, with the money either going to ensure that Western creditors got paid back more than they otherwise would, or

that exchange rates were maintained at overvalued levels longer than they otherwise would have been (allowing the rich inside the country to get more of their money out at more favorable terms, but leaving the country more indebted). As we have seen, the bailouts have not just failed to work; they have contributed to the problem, by reducing incentives for care in lending, and for covering of exchange risks.

4. Improved banking regulation—both design and implementation—in the developed and the less developed countries alike. Weak bank regulation in developed countries can lead to bad lending practices, an export of instability. While there may be some debate whether the design of the risk-based capital adequacy standards adds to the stability of the financial systems in the developed countries, there is little doubt that it has contributed to global instability, by encouraging short-term lending. Financial sector deregulation and the excessive reliance on capital adequacy standards has been misguided and destabilizing; what is required is a broader, less ideological approach to regulation, adapted to the capacities and circumstances of each country. Thailand was right to have restricted speculative real estate lending in the 1980s. It was wrong to encourage the Thais to eliminate these restrictions. There are a number of other restrictions such as speed limits (restrictions on the rate of increase of banks' assets), which are likely to enhance stability. Yet the reforms cannot, at the same time, lose sight of the broader goals: a safe and sound banking system is important, but it must also be one that supplies capital to finance enterprise and job creation.[14]

5. Improved risk management. Today, countries around the world face enormous risk from the volatility of exchange rates. While the problem is clear, the solution is not. Experts—including those at the IMF—have vacillated in the kinds of exchange-rate systems that they have advocated. They encouraged Argentina to peg its currency to the dollar. After the East Asia crisis, they argued that countries should either have a freely floating exchange rate or a fixed peg. With the disaster in Argentina, this advice is likely to change again. No matter what reforms occur to the exchange rate mechanism, countries will still face enor-

mous risks. Small countries like Thailand buying and selling goods to many countries face a difficult problem, as the exchange rates among the major currencies vary by 50 percent or more. Fixing their exchange rate to one currency will not resolve the problems; it can actually exacerbate fluctuations with respect to other currencies. But there are other dimensions to risk. The Latin American debt crisis in the 1980s[15] was brought about by the huge increase in interest rates, a result of Federal Reserve Chairman Paul Volcker's tight money policy in the United States. Developing countries have to learn to manage these risks, probably by buying insurance against these fluctuations in the international capital markets. Unfortunately, today the countries can only buy insurance for short-run fluctuations. Surely the developed countries are much better able to handle these risks than the less developed countries, and they should help develop these insurance markets. It would therefore make sense for the developed countries and the international financial institutions to provide loans to the developing countries in forms that mitigate the risks, e.g., by having the creditors absorb the risks of large real interest fluctuations.

6. Improved safety nets. Part of the task of risk management is enhancing the capabilities of the vulnerable within the country to absorb risks. Most developing countries have weak safety nets, including a lack of unemployment insurance programs. Even in more developed countries, safety nets are weak and inadequate in the two sectors that predominate in developing countries, agriculture and small businesses, so international assistance will be essential if the developing countries are to make substantial strides in improving their safety nets.

7. Improved response to crises. We have seen the failure of the crisis responses in the 1997–98 crisis. The assistance given was badly designed and poorly implemented. The programs did not take sufficiently into account the lack of safety nets, that maintaining credit flows was of vital importance, and that collapse in trade between countries would spread the crisis. The policies were based not only on bad forecasts but on a failure to recognize that it is easier to destroy firms than to recreate them, that the damage

caused by high interest rates will not be reversed when they are lowered. There needs to be a restoration of balance: the concerns of workers and small businesses have to be balanced with the concerns of creditors; the impacts of policies on domestic capital flight have to balance the seemingly excessive attention currently paid to outside investors. Responses to future financial crises will have to be placed within a social and political context. Apart from the devastation of the riots that happen when crises are mismanaged, capital will not be attracted to countries facing social and political turmoil, and no government, except the most repressive, can control such turmoil, especially when policies are perceived to have been imposed from the outside.

Most important, there needs to be a return to basic economic principles; rather than focusing on ephemeral investor psychology, on the unpredictability of confidence, the IMF needs to return to its original mandate of providing funds to restore aggregate demand in countries facing an economic recession. Countries in the developing world repeatedly ask why, when the United States faces a downturn, does it argue for expansionary fiscal and monetary policy, and yet when they face a downturn, just the opposite is insisted upon. As the United States went into a recession in 2001, the debate was not whether there should be a stimulus package, but its design. By now, the lessons of Argentina and East Asia should be clear: confidence will never be restored to economies that remain mired in deep recessions. The conditions that the IMF imposes on countries in return for money need not only to be far more narrowly circumscribed but also to reflect this perspective.

There are other changes that would be desirable: forcing the IMF to disclose the expected "poverty" and unemployment impact of its programs would direct its attention to these dimensions. Countries should know the likely consequences of what it recommends. If the Fund systematically errs in its analyses—if, for instance, the increases in poverty are greater than it predicted—it should be held accountable. Questions can be asked: Is there something systematically wrong with its models? Or is it trying to deliberately mislead policy making?

REFORMING THE WORLD BANK
AND DEVELOPMENT ASSISTANCE

Part of the reason that I remain hopeful about the possibility of reforming the international economic institutions is that I have seen change occur at the World Bank. It has not been easy, nor has it gone as far as I would have liked. But the changes have been significant.

By the time I arrived, the new president, James Wolfensohn, was well on his way to trying to make the Bank more responsive to the concerns of developing countries. Though the new direction was not always clear, the intellectual foundations not always firm, and support within the Bank far from universal, the Bank had begun seriously to address the fundamental criticisms levied at it. Reforms involved changes in philosophy in three areas: development; aid in general and the Bank's aid in particular; and relationships between the Bank and the developing countries.

In reassessing its course, the Bank examined how successful development has occurred.[16] Some of the lessons that emerged from this reassessment were ones that the World Bank had long recognized: the importance of living within one's budget constraints, the importance of education, including female education, and of macroeconomic stability. However, some new themes also emerged. Success came not just from promoting primary education but also from establishing a strong technological basis, which included support for advanced training. It is possible to promote equality and rapid growth *at the same time*; in fact, more egalitarian policies appear to help growth. Support for trade and openness is important,[17] but it was the jobs created by export expansion, not the job losses from increased imports, that gave rise to growth. When governments took actions to promote exports and new enterprises, liberalization worked; otherwise, it often failed. In East Asia, government played a pivotal role in successful development by helping create institutions that promote savings and the efficient allocation of investment. Successful countries also emphasized competition and enterprise creation over privatization and the restructuring of existing enterprises.

Overall, the successful countries have pursued a comprehensive approach to development. Thirty years ago, economists of the left and the right often seemed to agree that the improvement in the efficiency of resource allocation and the increase in the supply of capital were at the heart of development. They differed only as to whether those changes should be obtained through government-led planning or unfettered markets. In the end, neither worked. Development encompasses not just resources and capital but a transformation of society.[18] Clearly, the international financial institutions cannot be held responsible for this transformation, but they can play an important role. And at the very least, they should not become impediments to a successful transformation.

Assistance

But the way assistance is often given may do exactly that—create impediments to effective transitions. We saw in chapter 2 that *conditionality*—the imposition of a myriad of conditions, some often political in nature—as a precondition for assistance did not work; it did not lead to better policies, to faster growth, to better outcomes. Countries that think reforms have been imposed on them do not really feel invested in and committed to such reforms. Yet their participation is essential if real societal change is to happen. Even worse, the conditionality has undermined democratic processes. At last, there is a glimmering of recognition, even by the IMF, that conditionality has gone too far, that the dozens of conditions make it difficult for developing countries to focus on priorities. But while there has, accordingly, been an attempt to refine conditionality, within the World Bank the discussion of reform has been taken further. Some argue that conditionality should be replaced by *selectivity*, giving aid to countries with a proven track record, allowing them to choose for themselves their own development strategies, ending the micromanagement that has been such a feature of the past. The evidence is that aid given selectively can have significant impacts both in promoting growth and in reducing poverty.

Debt Forgiveness

The developing countries require not only that aid be given in a way that helps their development but also that there be more aid. Relatively small amounts of money could make enormous differences in promoting health and literacy. In real terms, adjusted for inflation, the amounts of development assistance have actually been declining, and even more so either as a percentage of developed country income or on a per capita basis for those in the developing countries. There needs to be a basis for funding this assistance (and other global public goods) on a more sustained level, free from the vagaries of domestic politics in the United States or elsewhere. Several proposals have been put forward. When the IMF was established, it was given the right to create Special Drawing Rights (SDR's), a kind of international money. With countries today wisely putting aside billions of dollars into reserves every year to protect themselves against the vicissitudes of international markets, some income is not being translated into aggregate demand. The global economic slowdown of 2001–02 brought these concerns to the fore. Issuing SDRs to finance global public goods—including financing development assistance—could help maintain the strength of the global economy at the same time that it helped some of the poorest countries in the world. A second proposal entails using the revenues from global economic resources—the minerals in the seabed and fishing rights in the oceans—to help finance development assistance.

Recently, attention has focused on debt forgiveness, and for good reason. Without the forgiveness of debt, many of the developing countries simply cannot grow. Huge proportions of their current exports go to repaying loans to the developed countries.[19] The Jubilee 2000 movement mobilized enormous international support for debt forgiveness. The movement gained the backing of churches throughout the developed world. To them, it seemed a moral imperative, a reflection of basic principles of economic justice.

The issue of the moral responsibility of the creditors was particularly apparent in the case of cold war loans.[20] When the IMF and World Bank lent money to the Democratic Republic of Congo's notorious ruler Mobutu, they knew (or should have known) that most of the money would not go to help that country's poor people, but rather would be used to enrich Mobutu. It was money paid to ensure that this corrupt leader would keep his country aligned with the West. To many, it doesn't seem fair for ordinary taxpayers in countries with corrupt governments to have to repay loans that were made to leaders who did not represent them.

The Jubilee movement was successful in getting much larger commitments to debt forgiveness. Whereas before 2000 there had been a debt relief program for the highly indebted countries, few met the criteria that the IMF had erected. By the end of 2000, as a result of international pressure, twenty-four countries had passed the threshold.

But debt relief needs to go further: as it stands now, the agreements touch only the poorest of the countries. Countries like Indonesia, devastated by the East Asian crisis and the failures of the IMF policies there, are still too well off to be brought in under the umbrella.

REFORMING THE WTO AND
BALANCING THE TRADE AGENDA

The global protests over globalization began at the WTO meetings in Seattle, Washington, because it was the most obvious symbol of the global inequities and the hypocrisy of the advanced industrial countries. While these countries had preached—and forced—the opening of the markets in the developing countries to their industrial products, they had continued to keep their markets closed to the products of the developing countries, such as textiles and agriculture. While they preached that developing countries should not subsidize their industries, they continued to provide billions in subsidies to their own farmers, making it impossible for the developing countries to compete. While they preached the virtues of competitive markets, the United States was quick to push for global cartels in steel and aluminum when its domestic industries seemed threatened by imports. The United States pushed for liberalization of financial services, but resisted liberalization of the service sectors in which the developing countries have strength, construction and maritime services. As we have noted, so unfair has the trade agenda been that not only have the poorer countries not received a fair share of the benefits; the poorest region in the world, Sub-Saharan Africa, was actually made worse off as a result of the last round of trade negotiations.

These inequities have increasingly been recognized, and that, combined with the resolve of some of the developing countries, resulted in the Doha "development" round of trade negotiations (November 2001), which put on its agenda the redressing of some of these past imbalances. But there is a long way to go: the United States and the other advanced industrial countries only agreed to discussions; just to discuss redressing some of these imbalances was viewed as a concession!

One of the areas that was of particular concern at Doha was intellectual property rights. These are important, if innovators are to have incentives to innovate—though much of the most crucial research, such as that in basic science and mathematics, is not patentable. No one denies the importance of intellectual property rights. But these rights need to balance out the rights and interests of producers with those of users—not only users in developing countries but researchers in developed countries. In the final stages of the Uruguay negotiations, both the Office of Science and Technology and the Council of Economic Advisers worried that we had not got the balance right— the agreement put producers interests over users. We worried that in doing so, the rate of progress and innovation might actually be impeded; after all, knowledge is the most important input into research, and stronger intellectual property rights can increase the price of this input. We were also concerned about the consequences of the denial of life-saving medicines to the poor. This issue subsequently gained international attention in the context of the provision of AIDS medicines in South Africa. The international outrage forced the drug companies to back down—and it appears that, going forward, the most adverse consequences will be circumscribed. But it is worth noting that initially even the Democratic U.S. administration supported the pharmaceutical companies. What we were not fully aware of was another danger, what has come to be termed *bio-piracy*, international companies patenting traditional medicines or foods; it is not only that they seek to make money from "resources" and knowledge that rightfully belongs to the developing countries, but in so doing, they squelch domestic firms that have long provided the products. While it is not clear whether these patents would hold up in court if they were effectively challenged, it is clear that the less developed countries may not have the legal and financial resources required to challenge the patent. This issue has become a source of enormous emotional, and potentially economic, concern all around the developing world. I was recently in an Andean village in Ecuador, where the indigenous mayor railed against how globalization had led to bio-piracy.

Reforming the WTO will require thinking further about a more balanced trade agenda—more balanced in treating the interests of the developing countries, more balanced in treating concerns, like environment, that go beyond trade.

But redressing the current imbalances does not require that the world wait until the end of a new round of trade negotiations. International economic justice requires that the developed countries take actions to open themselves up to fair trade and equitable relationships with developing countries without recourse to the bargaining table or attempts to extract concessions in exchange for doing so. The European Union has already taken steps in this direction, with its "everything but Arms" initiative to allow the free importing of all goods, other than arms, from the poorest countries into Europe. It does not solve all the complaints of the developing countries: they still will not be able to compete against highly subsidized European agriculture. But it is a big step in the right direction. The challenge now is to get the United States and Japan to participate. Such a move would be of enormous benefit to the developing world and would even benefit the developed countries, whose consumers would be able to obtain goods at lower prices.

TOWARD A GLOBALIZATION WITH A
MORE HUMAN FACE

The reforms I have outlined would help make globalization fairer, and more effective in raising living standards, especially of the poor. It is not just a question of changing institutional structures. The mindset around globalization itself must change. Finance and trade ministers view globalization as largely an economic phenomenon; but to many in the developing world, it is far more than that.

One of the reasons globalization is being attacked is that it seems to undermine traditional values. The conflicts are real, and to some extent unavoidable. Economic growth—including that induced by globalization—will result in urbanization, undermining traditional rural societies. Unfortunately, so far, those responsible for managing globalization, while praising these positive benefits, all too often have shown an insufficient appreciation of this adverse side, the threat to cultural identity and values.[21] This is surprising, given the awareness of the issues within the developed countries themselves: Europe defends its agricultural policies not just in terms of those special interests, but to preserve rural traditions. People in small towns everywhere complain that large national retailers and shopping malls have killed their small businesses and their communities.

The pace of global integration matters: a more gradual process means that traditional institutions and norms, rather than being overwhelmed, can adapt and respond to the new challenges.

Of equal concern is what globalization does to democracy. Globalization, as it has been advocated, often seems to replace the old dictatorships of national elites with new dictatorships of international finance. Countries are effectively told that if they don't follow certain conditions, the capital markets or the IMF will refuse to lend them money. They are basically forced to give up part of their sovereignty, to let capricious capital markets, including the speculators whose only concerns are short-term rather than the long-term growth of the country and the improvement of living standards, "discipline" them, telling them what they should and should not do.

But countries do have choices, and among those choices is the extent to which they wish to subject themselves to international capital markets. Those, such as in East Asia, that have avoided the strictures of the IMF have grown faster, with greater equality and poverty reduction, than those who have obeyed its commandments. Because alternative policies affect different groups differently, it is the role of the political process—not international bureaucrats—to sort out the choices. Even if growth *were* adversely affected, it is a cost many developing countries may be willing to pay to achieve a more democratic and equitable society, just as many societies today are saying it is worth sacrificing some growth for a better environment. So long as globalization is presented in the way that it has been, it represents a disenfranchisement. No wonder then that it will be resisted, especially by those who are being disenfranchised.

TODAY, GLOBALIZATION IS being challenged around the world. There is discontent with globalization, and rightfully so. Globalization can be a force for good: the globalization of ideas about democracy and of civil society have changed the way people think, while global political movements have led to debt relief and the treaty on land mines. Globalization has helped hundreds of millions of people attain higher standards of living, beyond what they, or most economists, thought imaginable but a short while ago. The globalization of the economy has benefited countries that took advantage of it by seeking new markets for their exports and by welcoming foreign investment. Even so, the countries that have benefited the most have been those that took charge of their own destiny and recognized the role government can play in development rather than relying on the notion of a self-regulated market that would fix its own problems.

But for millions of people globalization has not worked. Many have actually been made worse off, as they have seen their jobs destroyed and their lives become more insecure. They have felt increasingly powerless against forces beyond their control. They have seen their democracies undermined, their cultures eroded.

If globalization continues to be conducted in the way that it has been in the past, if we continue to fail to learn from our mistakes, globalization will not only not succeed in promoting development but will continue to create poverty and instability. Without reform, the backlash that has already started will mount and discontent with globalization will grow.

This will be a tragedy for all of us, and especially for the billions who might otherwise have benefited. While those in the developing world stand to lose the most economically, there will be broader political ramifications that will affect the developed world too.

If the reforms outlined in this last chapter are taken seriously, then there is hope that a more humane process of globalization can be a powerful force for the good, with the vast majority of those living in the developing countries benefiting from it and welcoming it. If this is done, the discontent with globalization would have served us all well.

The current situation reminds me of the world some seventy years ago. As the world plummeted into the Great Depression, advocates of the free market said, "Not to worry; markets are self-regulating, and given time, economic prosperity will resume." Never mind the misery of those whose lives are destroyed waiting for this so-called eventuality. Keynes argued that markets were not self-correcting, or not at least in a relevant time frame. (As he famously put it, "In the long run, we are all dead.")* Unemployment could persist for years, and government intervention was required. Keynes was pilloried— attacked as a Socialist, a critic of the market. Yet in a sense, Keynes was intensely conservative. He had a fundamental belief in the markets: if only government could correct this one failure, the economy would be able to function reasonably efficiently. He did not want a wholesale replacement of the market system; but he knew that unless these fundamental problems were addressed, there would be enormous popular pressures. And Keynes's medicine worked: since World War II, countries like the United States, following Keynesian prescriptions, have had fewer and shorter-lived downturns, and longer expansions than previously.

Today, the system of capitalism is at a crossroads just as it was during the Great Depression. In the 1930s, capitalism was saved by Keynes, who thought of policies to create jobs and rescue those suf-

---

*J. M. Keynes, *A Tract on Monetary Reform* (London: Macmillan, 1924).

fering from the collapse of the global economy. Now, millions of people around the world are waiting to see whether globalization can be reformed so that its benefits can be more widely shared.

Thankfully, there is a growing recognition of these problems and increasing political will to do something. Almost everyone involved in development, even those in the Washington establishment, now agrees that rapid capital market liberalization without accompanying regulation can be dangerous. They agree too that the excessive tightness in fiscal policy in the Asian crisis of 1997 was a mistake. As Bolivia moved into a recession in 2001, caused in part by the global economic slowdown, there were some intimations that that country would not be forced to follow the traditional path of austerity and have to cut governmental spending. Instead, as of January 2002, it looks like Bolivia will be allowed to stimulate its economy, helping it to overcome the recession, using revenues that it is about to receive from its newly discovered natural gas reserves to tide it over until the economy starts to grow again. In the aftermath of the Argentina debacle, the IMF has recognized the failings of the big-bailout strategy and is beginning to discuss the use of standstills and restructuring through bankruptcy, the kinds of alternatives that I and others have been advocating for years. Debt forgiveness brought about by the work of the Jubilee movement and the concessions made to initiate a new development round of trade negotiations at Doha represent two more victories.

Despite these gains, there is still more to be done to bridge the gap between rhetoric and reality. At Doha, the developing countries only agreed to begin discussing a fairer trade agenda; the imbalances of the past have yet to be redressed. Bankruptcy and standstills are now on the agenda; but there is no assurance that there will be an appropriate balance of creditor and debtor interests. There is a lot more participation by those in developing countries in discussions concerning economic strategy, but there is little evidence yet of changes in policies that reflect greater participation. There need to be changes in institutions and in mind-sets. The free market ideology should be replaced with analyses based on economic science, with a more balanced view of the role of government drawn from an understanding of both market and government failures. There should be more sensitivity

about the role of outside advisers, so they support democratic decision making by clarifying the consequences of different policies,
including impacts on different groups, especially the poor, rather than
undermining it by pushing particular policies on reluctant countries.

It is clear that there must be a *multipronged* strategy of reform. One
should be concerned with reform of the international economic
arrangements. But such reforms will be a long time coming. Thus,
the second prong should be directed at encouraging reforms that
each country can take upon itself. The developed countries have a
special responsibility, for instance, to eliminate their trade barriers, to
practice what they preach. But while the developed countries'
responsibility may be great, their incentives are weak: after all, offshore banking centers and hedge funds serve interests in the developed countries, and the developed countries can withstand well the
instability that a failure to reform might bring to the developing
world. Indeed, the United States arguably benefited in several ways
from the East Asia crisis.

Hence, the developing countries must assume responsibility for
their well-being themselves. They can manage their budgets so that
they live within their means, meager though that might be, and eliminate the protectionist barriers which, while they may generate large
profits for a few, force consumers to pay higher prices. They can put
in place strong regulations to protect themselves from speculators
from the outside or corporate misbehavior from the inside. Most
important, developing countries need effective governments, with
strong and independent judiciaries, democratic accountability, openness and transparency and freedom from the corruption that has stifled the effectiveness of the public sector and the growth of the private.

What they should ask of the international community is only this:
the acceptance of their need, and right, to make their own choices, in
ways which reflect their own political judgments about who, for
instance, should bear what risks. They should be encouraged to adopt
bankruptcy laws and regulatory structures adapted to their own situation, not to accept templates designed by and for the more developed countries.[22]

What is needed are policies for sustainable, equitable, and democratic growth. This is the reason for development. Development is not

about helping a few people get rich or creating a handful of pointless protected industries that only benefit the country's elite; it is not about bringing in Prada and Benetton, Ralph Lauren or Louis Vuitton, for the urban rich and leaving the rural poor in their misery. Being able to buy Gucci handbags in Moscow department stores did not mean that country had become a market economy. Development is about transforming societies, improving the lives of the poor, enabling everyone to have a chance at success and access to health care and education.

This sort of development won't happen if only a few people dictate the policies a country must follow. Making sure that democratic decisions are made means ensuring that a broad range of economists, officials, and experts from developing countries are actively involved in the debate. It also means that there must be broad participation that goes well beyond the experts and politicians. Developing countries must take charge of their own futures. But we in the West cannot escape our responsibilities.

It's not easy to change how things are done. Bureaucracies, like people, fall into bad habits, and adapting to change can be painful. But the international institutions must undertake the perhaps painful changes that will enable them to play the role they *should* be playing to make globalization work, and work not just for the well off and the industrial countries, but for the poor and the developing nations.

The developed world needs to do its part to reform the international institutions that govern globalization. We set up these institutions and we need to work to fix them. If we are to address the legitimate concerns of those who have expressed a discontent with globalization, if we are to make globalization work for the billions of people for whom it has not, if we are to make globalization with a human face succeed, then our voices must be raised. We cannot, we should not, stand idly by.

NOTES

CHAPTER 1

1. J. Chirac, "The Economy Must Be Made to Serve People," address at the International Labour Conference, June 1996.
2. In 1990, 2.718 billion people were living on less than $2 a day. In 1998, the number of poor living on less than $2 a day is estimated at 2.801 billion—World Bank, *Global Economic Prospects and the Developing Countries 2000* (Washington, DC: World Bank, 2000), p. 29. For additional data, see *World Development Report* and *World Economic Indicators,* annual publications of the World Bank. Health data can be found in UNAIDS/WHO, *Report on the HIV/AIDS Epidemic 1998.*
3. See Gerard Caprio, Jr., et al., eds., *Preventing Bank Crises: Lessons from Recent Global Bank Failures. Proceedings of a Conference Co-Sponsored by the Federal Reserve Bank of Chicago and the Economic Development Institute of the World Bank.* EDI Development Studies (Washington, DC: World Bank, 1998).
4. While there have been a host of critiques of the structural adjustment program, even the IMF's review of the program noted its many faults. This review includes three parts: internal review by the IMF staff (IMF Staff, *The ESAF at Ten Years: Economic Adjustment and Reform in Low-Income Countries.* Occasional Papers #156, February 12, 1998); external review by an independent reviewer (K. Botchwey, et al., *Report by a Group of Independent Experts Review: External Evaluation of the ESAF* [Washington, DC: IMF, 1998]); and a report from IMF staff to the Board of Directors of the IMF, distilling the lessons from the two reviews (IMF Staff, *Distilling the Lessons from the ESAF Reviews* [Washington, DC: IMF, July 1998]).

CHAPTER 2

1. Mengistu's regime is blamed for killing at least 200,000 persons, according to Human Rights Watch, and for forcing about 750,000 citizens to become refugees.

2. T. Lane, A. Ghosh, J. Hamann, S. Phillips, M. Schulze-Ghattas, and T. Tsikata, "IMF-Supported Programs in Indonesia, Korea, and Thailand: A Preliminary Assessment," Occasional Paper 178, International Monetary Fund, January 1999.

3. There is considerable controversy about whether central banks should or should not be more independent. There is some evidence (based on cross-country regressions) that inflation rates may be lower, but there is little evidence that *real variables*, like growth or unemployment, are improved. My point here is not to resolve these disputes, but to emphasize that, given that there is such controversy, a particular view should not be imposed on the country.

CHAPTER 3

1. To take one example, see P. Waldman, "How U.S. Companies and Suharto's Cycle Electrified Indonesia," *Wall Street Journal*, December 23, 1998.

2. Adam Smith put forward the idea that markets by themselves lead to efficient outcomes in his classic book, *The Wealth of Nations*, written in 1776, the same year as the Declaration of Independence. The formal mathematical proof—specifying the conditions under which it was true—was provided by two Nobel Prize winners, Gerard Debreu of the University of California at Berkeley (Nobel laureate in 1983) and Kenneth Arrow of Stanford University (Nobel laureate in 1972). The basic result, showing that when information is imperfect or markets are incomplete, competitive equilibrium is not (constrained Pareto) efficient, is due to B. Greenwald and J. E. Stiglitz, "Externalities in Economies with Imperfect Information and Incomplete Markets," *Quarterly Journal of Economics* 101 (2) (May 1986), pp. 229–64.

3. See W. A. Lewis, "Economic Development with Unlimited Supplies of Labor," *Manchester School* 22 (1954), pp. 139–91, and S. Kuznets, "Economic Growth and Income Inequality," *American Economic Review* 45(1) (1955), pp. 1–28.

CHAPTER 4

1. For some contrasting views, see Paul Krugman, "The Myth of Asia's Miracle: A Cautionary Fable," *Foreign Affairs* (November 1994), and J. E. Stiglitz, "From Miracle to Crisis to Recovery: Lessons from Four Decades of East Asian Experience," in J. E. Stiglitz and S. Yusuf, eds., *Rethinking the East Asian Miracle* (Washington, DC, and New York: World Bank and Oxford University Press, 2001), pp. 509–26. See also World Bank, *The East Asian Miracle: Economic Growth and Public Policy* (New York: Oxford University Press, 1993); Alice Amsden, *The Rise of "the Rest": Challenges to the West from Late-Industrialization Economies* (New York: Oxford University Press, 2001); and, Masahiko Aoki, Hyung-Ki Kim, Okuno Okuno-Fujiwara, and Masahjiro Okuno-Fjujiwara, eds., *The Role of Government in East Asian Economic Development: Comparative Institutional Analysis* (New York: Oxford University Press, 1998). For an extremely readable account of the East Asia crisis, see Paul Blustein, *The Chastening: Inside the Crisis that Rocked the Global Financial System and Humbled the IMF* (New York: Public Affairs, 2001). More technical discussions are provided, e.g., in Morris Goldstein, *The Asian Financial Crisis: Causes, Cures, and Systemic Implications* (Washington, DC: International Institute for Economics, 1998), and Jason Furman and Joseph E. Stiglitz, *Brookings Papers on Economic Activity*, presented at Brookings Panel on Economic Activity, Washington, DC, September 3, 1998, vol. 2, pp. 1–114.

2. Since the U.S. economy was not affected, the United States did not offer any assistance, in marked contrast to the generous treatment it had given Mexico in its last crisis. This gave rise to enormous resentment in Thailand. Especially after the strong support it had provided the United States during the Vietnam War, Thailand thought it deserved better treatment.

3. See E. Kaplan and D. Rodrik, "Did the Malaysian Capital Controls Work?," working paper no. W8142 National Bureau of Economic Research, Cambridge, Mass., February 2001. It is possible to find this paper at Professor Rodrik's Web site, http://ksghome.harvard.edu/~.drodrik.academic.ksg/papers.html).

4. Korea received $55 billion, Indonesia $33 billion, and Thailand $17 billion.

5. See J. Sachs, "The Wrong Medicine for Asia," *New York Times*, November 3, 1997, and "To Stop the Money Panic: An Interview with Jeffrey Sachs," *Asiaweek*, February 13, 1998.

6. In 1990, foreign direct investment ($ millions) was 24,130; in 1997, it was 170,258, and in 1998, 170,942; portfolio investment in 1990 ($ millions) was 3,935, rising to 79,128 in 1997, and 55,225 in 1998. Bank and trade related investment was 14,541 in 1990, 54,507 in 1997, and 41,534 in 1998. Total private capital flows (in $ millions) 42,606 in 1990, 303,894 in 1997, and 267,700 in 1998.

7. On factors involved in financial and banking crises, see, e.g., D. Beim and C. Calomiris, *Emerging Financial Markets* (New York: McGraw-Hill/Irwin, 2001), chapter 7; A. Demirguc-Kunt and E. Detragiache, *The Determinants of Banking Crises: Evidence from Developing and Developed Countries*, IMF Staff Papers, vol. 45, no. 1 (March 1998); G. Caprio and D. Klingebiel, "Episodes of Systemic and Borderline Financial Crises," *World Bank*, October 1999; and World Bank Staff, "Global Economic Prospects and the Developing Countries 1998/99: Beyond Financial Crisis," The World Bank, February 1999.

8. M. Camdessus, "Capital Account Liberalization and the Role of the Fund," remarks at the IMF Seminar on Capital Account Liberalization, Washington, DC, March 9, 1998.

9. The American slowdown of 2000–2001 too has been traced to excessive market exuberance, an overinvestment in Internet and Telecom brought on in part by soaring stock prices. Marked fluctuations in the economy can arise even in the absence of mismanagement of financial institutions and monetary policy.

10. The debate surrounding Korea was part of a broader debate about capital market liberalization and the bailouts that follow when things go wrong, as they inevitably do—a debate that was held within the IMF and the U.S. government almost completely behind closed doors. It occurred repeatedly, for instance, as we prepared for regional trade agreements and for G-7 meetings. On the one occasion (the Mexican 1995 crisis) when Treasury brought the issue of bailouts to Congress and Congress rejected the proposal, Treasury went back to its usual closed quarters, figured out a way of proceeding with the bailout without congressional approval, and strong-armed other governments to participate (in a manner that engendered large hostility in many European quarters—the full ramifications of the strong-arm tactics of the U.S. Treasury have played out slowly over the ensuing years, as U.S. positions in a variety of contexts have subtly been opposed, e.g., the choice of the head of the IMF). The issues are complicated, but the U.S. Treasury almost seemed to revel in its ability to outsmart Congress.

11. In IMF, *Annual Report of the Executive Board for the Financial Year Ended April 30, 1998* (Washington, DC), p. 25, some IMF directors doubted the need for strict fiscal policies during the Asian crisis because these countries did not experience fiscal imbalance. Interestingly, the IMF in its similar report for 2000 recognized (p. 14) that an expansionary fiscal policy is behind the recovery from the crisis of Korea, Malaysia, and Thailand. See also T. Lane, A. Ghosh, J. Hamann, S. Phillips, M. Schulze-Ghattas, and T. Tsikata, "IMF-Supported Programs in Indonesia, Korea, and Thailand: A Preliminary Assessment," Occasional Paper 178, International Monetary Fund, January 1999.

12. Stanley Fischer, "Comment & Analysis: IMF—The Right Stuff. Bailouts in Asia Are Designed to Restore Confidence and Bolster the Financial System," *Financial Times*, December 16, 1997.

13. Over the years, I have never heard a coherent defense of the IMF's strategy of raising interest rates in countries with highly leveraged firms from any IMF staffers. The only good defense I did hear was from Chase Securities chief economist John Lipsky, who focused explicitly on imperfections of capital markets. He observed that domestic businessmen typically kept large amounts of money abroad but borrowed domestically. The high interest rates on the domestic loans would "force" them to bring back some of their foreign funds in order to pay off the loans and avoid paying such rates. This hypothesis has not yet been evaluated. Certainly for several of the crisis countries, net capital flow moved in the opposite direction. Many business people assumed that they simply could not be "forced" to pay the high interest rates and that there would have to be renegotiation. In effect, the high interest rates were not credible.

14. The Ministry of Finance official in charge, Eisuke Sakakibara, has subsequently written his own interpretation of the events in E. Sakakibara, "The End of Market Fundamentalism," Speech delivered at Foreign Correspondents Club, Tokyo, January 22, 1999.

15. For further details, see E. Kaplan and D. Rodrik, "Did the Malaysian Capital Controls Work?," op. cit.

16. During this crisis period, foreign direct investment to Malaysia showed a pattern similar to other countries affected by the crisis and in the region. Nonetheless, the evidence is still too preliminary to draw solid conclusions. A deeper econometric study (and more data) is required in order to disentangle the effect of capital controls on foreign direct investment from other factors that affect foreign direct investment.

CHAPTER 5

1. Much of this and the next two chapters is based on work reported more extensively elsewhere. See the following papers: J. E. Stiglitz, "Whither Reform? Ten Years of the Transition" (Annual World Bank Conference on Development Economics, 1999), in Boris Pleskovic and Joseph E. Stiglitz, eds., The World Bank (Washington, DC, 2000), pp 27–56; J. E. Stiglitz, *Quis Custodiet Ipsos Custodes? (Who Is to Guard the Guards Themselves?)* in *Governance, Equality, and Global Markets: The Annual Bank Conference on Development Economics, Europe,* J. E. Stiglitz and Pierre-Alain Muet, eds., World Bank (Washington, DC, 2001), pp. 22–54. In addition, see D. Ellerman and J. E. Stiglitz, "New Bridges Across the Chasm: Macro- and Micro-Strategies for Russia and other Transitional Economies," *Zagreb International Review of Economics and Business* 3(1) (2000), pp 41–72, and A. Hussain, N. Stern, and J. E. Stiglitz, "Chinese Reforms from a Comparative Perspective," in Peter J. Hammond and Gareth D. Myles, eds., *Incentives, Organization, and Public Economics. Papers in Honour of Sir James Mirrlees* (Oxford and New York: Oxford University Press, 2000), pp. 243, 277.

For excellent journalistic accounts of the transition in Russia, see Chrystia Freeland, *Sale of the Century* (New York: Crown, 2000; R. Brady, *Kapitalizm: Russia's Struggle to Free Its Economy* (New Haven: Yale University Press, 1999); and John Lloyd, "Who Lost Russia?," *New York Times Magazine,* August 15, 1999.

A number of political scientists have offered analyses broadly agreeing with the interpretations provided here. See, in particular, A. Cohen, *Russia's Meltdown: Anatomy of the IMF Failure,* Heritage Foundation Backgrounders No. 1228, October 23, 1998; S. F. Cohen, *Failed Crusade* (New York: W. W. Norton, 2000); P. Reddaway, and D. Glinski, *The Tragedy of Russia's Reforms: Market Bolshevism Against Democracy* (Washington, DC: United States Institute of Peace, 2001); Michael McFaul, *Russia's Unfinished Revolution: Political Change from Gorbachev to Putin* (Ithaca, N.Y.: Cornell University Press, 2001); Archie Brown and Liliia Fedorovna Shevtskova, eds., *Gorbachev, Yeltsin and Putin: Political Leadership in Russia's Transition* (Washington, DC: Carnegie Endowment for International Peace, 2000); and Jerry F. Hough and Michael H. Armacost, *The Logic of Economic Reform in Russia* (Washington, DC: Brookings Institution, 2001).

Not surprisingly, a number of reformers have provided accounts that differ markedly from those presented here, though such interpretations were more frequent in the earlier, more hopeful days of the transition, some with titles that seem to jar with subsequent events. See, e.g., Anders Aslund, *How Russia Became a Market Economy* (Washington, DC: Brookings Institution, 1995) or Richard Layard and John Parker, *The Coming Russian Boom: A Guide to New Markets and Politics* (New York: The Free Press, 1996). For more critical perspectives, see Lawrence R. Klein and Marshall Pomer, eds. (with a foreword by Joseph E. Stiglitz), *The New Russia: Transition Gone Awry* (Palo Alto, Calif.: Stanford University Press, 2001).

2. J. R. Wedel, "Aid to Russia," *Foreign Policy* 3 (25), Interhemispheric Resource Center and Institute Policy Studies, September 1998.

3. For further reading, see P. Murrell, "Can Neo-Classical Economics Underpin the Economic Reform of the Centrally Planned Economies?" *Journal of Economic Perspectives* 5(4) (1991), pp 59–76.

4. See International Monetary Fund, "IMF Approves Augmentation of Russia Extended Arrangement and Credit Under CCFF, Activates GAB," Press release no. 98/31, Washington DC, July 20, 1998.

5. There is an argument that the IMF really did not ignore this. In fact, some believe that the Fund was trying to close the devaluation option by making the cost of devaluation so high that the country would not do it. If this was indeed the argument, the IMF miscalculated badly.

6. There was, of course, more to the Russian government's announcement of August 17, but these were among the central features for our purposes. In addition, the Russian government established temporary controls of capital such as a prohibition on nonresidents investing in short-term ruble assets and a ninety-day moratorium on foreign exchange credit and insurance payments. The Russian government also announced its support to a payment pool set up by the largest Russian banks in order to maintain the payment stability and sent legislation for timely payments to government employees and for the rehabilitation of banks. For details, see the Web site www.bisnis.doc.gov/bisnis/country/980818ru.htm, which provides the original texts of the two public announcements on August 17, 1998.

7. On Tuesday, August 17, 1998, on the Moscow Interbank Currency Exchange the ruble against the dollar fell 1.9% compared to its level at August 16, but by end of the week (Friday, August 21) the depreciation was 11.0% (compared again to the August 16 level). However, at August

17, 1998, on the unofficial interbank trading market, the ruble had declined 26% by day's end.

8. See Chrystia Freeland, op. cit.; Richard Layard and John Parker, op. cit.; and Anders Aslund, op. cit.

9. For the implications and costs that barter imposes on the Russian economy, see C. G. Gaddy and B. W. Ickes, "Russia's Virtual Economy," *Foreign Affairs* 77 (September–October 1998).

10. The transition has not appeared to benefit the poor. For example, the lowest quintile of the population had a share of income equal to 8.6% in Russia (in 1998), 8.8 % in Ukraine (in 1999), 6.7 % in Kazakhstan (in 1996) (World Bank, *World Development Indicator 2001*).

11. Using a standard measure of inequality (the Ginii coefficient), by 1998 Russia had achieved a level of inequality twice that of Japan, 50% greater than UK and other European countries, a level comparable to Venezuela and Panama. Meanwhile, those countries that had undertaken gradualist policies, Poland and Hungary, had been able to keep their level of inequality low—Hungary's was even lower than Japan's and Poland's lower than the UK's.

12. See Stiglitz, "Quis Custodiet Ipsos Custodes?" op. cit.

13. For instance: If one liberalizes capital markets before an attractive investment climate is created at home—as the IMF recommended—one is inviting capital flight. If one privatizes firms before an efficient capital market is created at home, in a way that puts ownership and/or control in the hands of those who are nearing retirement, there is no incentive for long-term wealth creation; there are incentives for asset stripping. If one privatizes before creating a regulatory and legal structure for enduring competition, there are incentives to create monopolies, and there are *political* incentives to prevent the creation of an effective competition regime. If one privatizes in a federal system, but leaves state and local authorities free to impose taxes and regulations at will, one has not eliminated the power, and incentives, of public authorities to extract rents; in a sense, one has not really privatized at all.

14. For the Coase theorem itself, see R. H. Coase, "The Problem of Social Cost," *Journal of Law and Economics* 3 (1960), pp. 1–44. This theorem holds only where there are no transactions costs, and no imperfections of information. Coase himself recognized the force of these limitations. Moreover, it is never possible fully to specify property rights, and this was especially true for the economies in transition. Even in advanced industrialized countries, property rights are circumscribed by concerns for the environment, worker rights, zoning, and so forth. Although the

law may try to be as clear on these matters as possible, disputes frequently arise, and have to be settled through legal processes. Fortunately,
given the "rule of law," there is general confidence that this is done in a
fair and equitable manner. But not so in Russia.

CHAPTER 6

1. Though this was the *supposed* defense, as we noted earlier, even this
defense was questionable. The oligarchs did not use the funds to finance
Yeltsin's reelection. But they did give him the organizational basis (and
the TV support) he needed.
2. The transition countries currently governed by former Communist
parties or leaders are: Albania, Azerbaijan, Belarus, Croatia, Kazakhstan,
Lithuania, Moldova, Poland, Romania, Russia, Slovenia, Tajikistan, Turk-
menistan, and Uzbekistan.
3. I was put in an extremely uncomfortable position during my visit to
Russia in later 1993, in a meeting with Yegor Gaidar, the first deputy
prime minister who was in charge of economics. He knew his economics; and he knew that Russia was not dumping—by any stretch of how
that word is used in economics. What was I to say?
4. For details, see M. Du Bois and E. Norton, "Foiled Competition:
Don't Call It a Cartel, But World Aluminum Has Forged a New Order,"
Wall Street Journal, June 9, 1994. This article noted the close relation
between O'Neill and Bowman Cutter, at that time Clinton's deputy
director of the National Economic Council, as instrumental in order to
"cook" the deal. The sweetener for the Russians was an equity investment worth $250 million, guaranteed by the OPIC. The American
aluminum barons did everything to take care of the appearances in
order to avoid antitrust prosecution, and the American government
included three antitrust lawyers to draft the agreement, which, according to this article, was carefully vaguely worded in order to satisfy the
Justice Department.

In 1995, this cartel started to fall apart with the increase in world
demand for aluminum and the difficulties of enforcing the cartel
agreement with the Russian producers—see S. Givens, "Stealing an
Idea from Aluminum," *The Dismal Scientist*, July 24, 2001. In addition, Alcoa and other American aluminum producers were sued for
conspiring to restrain trade; but the case was dismissed in courts—see J.
Davidow, "Rules for the Antitrust/Trade Interface," Miller & Chevalier,

September 29, 1999, at www.ablondifoster.com/library/article.asp?
pubid=143643792001&groupid=12. For an editorial expressing an
opinion similar to that here, see *Journal of Commerce*, February 22,
1994.

The story does not end there: in April 2000, news emerged about
how a private monopoly was successfully formed to control 75–80% of
the Russian yearly production, creating the second largest aluminum
company in the world (after Alcoa). See "Russian Aluminum Czars
Joining Forces," *The Sydney Morning Herald*, April 19, 2000, and A.
Meier and Y. Zarakhovich, "Promises, Promises," *Time Europe* 155(20),
May 22, 2000. See also, R. Behar, "Capitalism in a Cold Climate," *Fortune* (June 2000).

CHAPTER 7

1. In the *New York Times*, Kolodko wrote: "But there was another, equally
   important facet of our success. Poland did not look to the international
   financial community for approval. Instead, we wanted Polish citizens to
   go along with these reforms. So salaries and pensions were paid and
   adjusted for inflation. There were unemployment benefits. We respected
   our own society, while doing tough negotiating with international
   investors and financial institutions." George W. Kolodko, "Russia Should
   Put Its People First," *New York Times*, July 7, 1998.
2. *Poland* also showed that one could maintain state ownership of the assets
   and not only prevent asset stripping but actually increase productivity.
   In the West, the largest gains in productivity are associated not with privatization, but with corporatization, i.e., imposing hard budget constraints and commercial practices on enterprises while they still remain
   state-owned. See J. Vickers and G. Yarrow, *Privatization: An Economic
   Analysis* (Cambridge, MA: MIT Press, 1988), chapter 2, and J. Vickers
   and G. Yarrow, "Economic Perspectives on Privatization." *Journal of
   Economic Perspectives* 5(2) (Spring 1991), pp. 111–32.
3. China's net private capital inflows were $8 billion in 1990. By 1999,
   China's capital inflows had soared to $41 billion, more than ten times
   the amount of money attracted by Russia in that same year (World
   Bank, *World Development Indicators 2001*).
4. See, e.g. World Bank, *World Development Report 1996: From Plan to Market* (London and New York: Oxford University Press, June 1996).

5. The best defense that the radical reformers in Russia have of their failure is this: we do not know the *counterfactual*, what might otherwise have been. The options available in these other countries were simply not available. By the time the radical reformers had taken over, a centrally guided reform like the one in China was no longer possible, because central power in Russia had collapsed. The takeover of the enterprises by the *nomenklatura*, the existing managers, which occurred in many cases anyway, *was* the alternative. On the contrary, I would argue that a recognition of these problems made it even more important not to conduct the privatization and liberalization strategy in the way that it was done. The breakup of central power should have made it easier, and more important, to break up the large national enterprises, especially in natural resources, into competing parts, leading to greater diffusion of economic power. It made it more imperative to ensure that a working tax system was in place before the sources of revenue generation were given away. China's reforms involved enormous devolution of economic decision making. The alternative strategies in the end might not have worked, but it is hard to believe that matters could have turned out worse.

CHAPTER 8

1. See S. Fischer, "On the Need for an International Lender of Last Resort," *Journal of Economic Perspectives* 13 (1999), pp. 85–104. Fischer, like many others advocating the lender of last resort view, makes an analogy between the role of a central bank within a country and the role of the Fund among countries. But the analogy is deceptive. A lender of last resort is required domestically because of the first-come-first-served basis of deposits, which contribute to the possibility of runs—see D. Diamond and P. Dibvig, "Bank Runs, Deposit Insurance, and Liquidity," *Journal of Political Economy* 91 (1983), pp. 401–19. And even then, it does not suffice to avoid runs, as the experience in the United States demonstrates forcefully. Only when accompanied by strong banking regulation and deposit insurance does a lender of last resort suffice to fend off runs. And no one—not even the most ardent supporters of the IMF—has advocated that it provides anything analogous to deposit insurance. Moreover, the rigidity with which the Fund has implemented many policies makes many countries wary of ceding to it much regulatory authority (even if the appropriate domain of reg-

ulatory authority could be defined, and even if issues of national sovereignty did not become paramount). It is worth noting that U.S. regulatory authorities have often argued that *well-designed* policies of forbearance are a critical part of macroeconomic management, while the IMF has typically argued against such forbearance. Elsewhere, I have argued that in doing so, the IMF has often failed to take account of the basic fallacy of composition: in the presence of systemic problems, the absence of forbearance may be self-defeating as each bank, unable to raise additional capital, calls in its loans, leading to more widespread defaults, and furthering the economic downturn.

2. What I call a "super-Chapter 11." For details, see M. Miller and J. E. Stiglitz, "Bankruptcy Protection Against Macroeconomic Shocks: The Case for a 'Super Chapter 11,' " World Bank Conference on Capital Flows, Financial Crises, and Policies, April 15, 1999.

3. While it is hard to blame the crisis on lack of transparency, lack of transparency did have its cost. Once the crisis had occurred, the lack of information meant that creditors withdrew their funds from all borrowers regardless of quality. Creditors simply did not have the information with which to distinguish between good and bad borrowers.

CHAPTER 9

1. The term *corporate governance* refers to the laws that determine the rights of shareholders, including minority shareholders. With weak corporate governance, management may effectively steal from shareholders, and majority shareholders from minority shareholders.

2. World Bank studies, including those coauthored by my predecessor as chief economist at the World Bank, Michael Bruno, formerly head of Israel's Central Bank, helped provide the empirical validation of this perspective. See Michael Bruno and W. Easterly, "Inflation Crises and Long-run Growth," *Journal of Monetary Economics* 41 (February 1998), pp. 3–26.

3. Economists have analyzed what are the attributes of such goods; they are goods for which the marginal costs of supplying the goods to an additional individual are small or zero, and for which the costs of excluding them from the benefits are large.

4. Economists have analyzed deeply why such markets may not exist, e.g., as a result of problems of information imperfections (information asymmetries), called *adverse selection* and *moral hazard*.

5. It was ironic that the calls for transparency were coming from the IMF, long criticized for its own lack of openness, and the U.S. Treasury, the most secretive agency of the U.S. government (where I saw that even the White House often had trouble extracting information about what they were up to).

6. The perception in some quarters is that those inside the country can decide on such issues as when the school year will begin and end.

7. The IMF's position of institutional infallibility makes these changes in position particularly difficult. In this case, senior people could seemingly claim, trying to keep a straight face, that they had been warning of the risks associated with capital market liberalization for a long time. The assertion is at best disingenuous (and itself undermines the credibility of the institution). If they were aware of these risks, it makes their policy stances even more unforgivable. But to those who were subjected to their pressure, these concerns were at most minor caveats, matters to think about later; what they were told was to proceed, and to proceed rapidly, with liberalization.

8. As we noted in chapter 8, the multiple objectives—and the reluctance to discuss openly the tacit change in the mandate to reflect the interests of the financial community—led to many instances of intellectual incoherence; this in turn made coming up with coherent reforms more difficult.

9. As its name indicates, a contingent credit line provides credit automatically in certain contingencies, those associated with a crisis.

10. There were more profound problems. While a contingent credit line could make sure that some new funds were made available in the presence of a crisis, it could not prevent other short-term loans from not being rolled over; and the amount of exposure that the banks would be willing to take would presumably take into account the new loans that would be made under the contingent credit line facility. Thus there was a concern that the net supply of funds available in the event of a crisis might not be affected that much.

11. These provisions allow a creditor to demand payment under certain circumstances—generally precisely the circumstances in which other creditors are pulling back their money.

12. In Europe, a great deal of attention has focused on one particular tax proposal, the so-called Tobin Tax—on cross-border financial transactions. See, for instance, H. Williamson, "Köhler Says IMF Will Look Again at Tobin Tax," *Financial Times*, September 10, 2001. There is now a

large body of literature analyzing the tax theoretically and empirically. For an account of this literature, see the Web site www.ceedweb.org/iirp/biblio.htm. Interestingly, even the former treasury secretary wrote an article that could be interpreted as supporting the principles underlying the tax—L. H. Summers and V. P. Summers, "When Financial Markets Work Too Well: A Cautious Case for a Securities Transactions Tax," *Journal of Financial Services Research* 3 (1989), pp. 261–86. But there remain significant implementation problems, especially in a world in which the tax is not imposed universally and in which derivatives and other complicated financial instruments have become prevalent. See also J. E. Stiglitz, "Using Tax Policy to Curb Speculative Short-Term Trading," *Journal of Financial Services Research* 3(2/3) (December 1989), pp. 101–15. For the original proposal, see J. Tobin, "A Proposal for International Monetary Reform," *Eastern Economic Journal* 4 (1978), pp. 153–59, and B. Eichengreen, J. Tobin, and C. Wyplosz, "Two Cases for Sand in the Wheels of International Finance," *Economic Journal* 105 (May 1995), pp. 162–72. In addition, see the collection of essays in M. ul Haq, I. Kaul, and I. Grunberg, eds., *The Tobin Tax: Coping with Financial Volatility* (London and New York: Oxford University Press, 1996).

13. This reform is receiving increasing attention. The Canadian government, partly as an outgrowth of its chairing the G-8 and the G-22 in 2001–2002, is holding a major conference focusing on such changes. The IMF's discussion of bankruptcies and standstills is seen by some as a preemptive move, in anticipation of initiatives by Canada and others.

14. As we saw, opening up a country to foreign banks may not lead to more lending, especially to small and medium-sized domestic enterprises. Countries need to impose requirements, similar to those in America's Community Reinvestment Act, to ensure that as they open their markets up, their small businesses are not starved of capital.

15. The debt crisis hit Argentina in 1981, Chile and Mexico in 1982, and Brazil in 1983. Output growth remained very slow throughout the remainder of the decade.

16. The reassessment (as we have noted) actually began earlier, under pressure from the Japanese, and was reflected in the Bank's publication in 1993 of the landmark study, *The East Asian Miracle: Economic Growth and Public Policy.* The changes in thinking were reflected in the annual reports on development, called the World Development Report. For instance, the 1997 report reexamined the role of the state; the 1998 report focused on knowledge (including the importance of technology) and information (including the imperfections of markets associated

with imperfect information); the 1999 and 2001 reports emphasized the role of institutions, not just policies; and the 2000 report took a much broader perspective on poverty.

17. Not surprisingly, the Bank still has not taken as seriously as it should the theoretical and empirical critiques of trade liberalization, such as that provided by F. Rodríguez and D. Rodrik, "Trade Policy and Economic Growth: A Skeptic's Guide to the Cross-National Evidence," Ben Bernanke and Kenneth S. Rogoff, eds., in *Macroeconomics Annual 2000* (Cambridge, MA: MIT Press for NBER, 2001). Whatever the intellectual merits of that position, it runs counter to the "official" position of the United States and other G-7 governments that trade is good.

18. There are many dimensions to this transformation—including the acceptance of change (recognizing that things do not have be done in the way they have been done for generations), of the basic tenets of science and the scientific way of thinking, of the willingness to accept the risks that are necessary for entrepreneurship. I am convinced that such changes, under the right circumstances, can occur in a relatively short span of time. For a more extensive articulation of this view of "development as transformation," see J. E. Stiglitz, "Towards a New Paradigm for Development: Strategies, Policies and Processes," 9th Raul Prebisch Lecture delivered at the Palais des Nations, Geneva, UNCTAD, October 19, 1998.

19. In several of the countries, debt service is more than a quarter of exports; in a couple, it is almost half.

20. Such debts are sometimes referred to as "odious debts."

21. An important exception is Jim Wolfensohn, who has pushed cultural initiatives at the World Bank.

22. Recently, developing countries have been increasingly pushed to comply with standards (e.g., of banking) that they have played little part in setting. Indeed, this is often heralded as one of the few "achievements" of the efforts to reform the global economic architecture. Whatever good they may do to improve global economic stability, the way they have been brought about has engendered enormous resentment in the developing world.

AFTERWORD
TO THE
PENGUIN EDITION

THE RECEPTION OF the first edition of this book was grati-fying. It showed not only that globalization had become the issue of our day but also that its ideas resonated with so many people. The widespread discontent with globalization goes well beyond the protest movements that have attracted the attention of the world in recent years. I am pleased to think that the book has contributed to the globalization debate, and may even have helped reshape it. No longer is it a question of whether globalization is good or bad: globalization is a powerful force that has brought enormous benefits to some. Because of the way it has been mismanaged, how-ever, millions have not enjoyed its benefits, and millions more have even been made worse off. This is now being recognized. The chal-lenge today is how to reform globalization, to make it work not just for the rich and the more advanced industrial countries, but also for the poor and the least developed countries.

In the months since the book was completed, the problems it identifies have mounted. The U.S. has raised its farm subsidies to new heights. Farm subsidies used to be criticized as a waste of money, a violation of free market principles, bad for the environment, and mainly going to rich corporate farmers rather than the poor small farmers that they were supposed to help. But to these complaints an even more cogent one has been added: by increasing the supply of the subsidized goods, the gains of rich corporate farms in America come largely at the expense of the poorest of the poor internationally. For example, subsidies to 25,000 American cotton farmers exceed the value of what they produce and so depress cotton prices that it is estimated that the millions of cotton farmers in Africa alone lose more than $350 million each year. For several of Africa's poorest countries, losses from this one crop alone exceed America's foreign aid budget for these countries.

Or take America's steel tariffs, allegedly imposed as safeguards against the onslaught of imported steel. America's steel industry has had problems for years; I encountered them when I was at the Council of Economic Advisors. The old steel behemoths had trouble restructuring. After the East Asia crisis decreased consumption and lowered wages and exchange rates, it was easy for East Asia's highly efficient firms to undercut America's firms. And, even if foreign firms are not *technically* more efficient, with sufficiently large wage cuts and low enough exchange rates, they can outcompete. Such is the case, for instance, in the former Soviet republic of Moldova, a country I recently visited, which has seen its income plummet 70 percent since it began its transition to a market economy (a particularly dramatic example of the failures described in chapter 6), and which in 2002 spent three quarters of its budget on interest and debt repayments.

The U.S. responded to these competitive threats by imposing tariffs on foreign steel. In the case of Moldova, the tariff was over 350 percent! If every time these struggling economies find a little niche in which they can make some headway, prohibitive tariffs are slapped upon them, what are they to think of the rules of the market game? It should be clear: these firms were not engaged in unfair trade practices. It was simply that American firms were, for instance, far less efficient than the East Asian firms, and failed to take the measures required to make them competitive. America freely lectures the developing countries on how they have to "face the pain," but is loath to do so itself. No wonder that charges of hypocrisy have grown. If the United States, the richest country in the world, with high employment, an unemployment insurance system, and a broader safety net, says that it must resort to protective measures to safeguard its workers, how much more compelling are the arguments for such measures in developing countries, with high unemployment and no safety nets.

The book emphasizes the many dimensions of globalization—globalization of ideas, of knowledge, of civil society. Globalization has meant that what is said in one place becomes known quickly around the world and policies in one country can have enormous implications for another. If there is dissonance between the speeches of U.S. government officials when they try to persuade the developing countries to sign up for a new round of trade negotiations and what those same officials say to Congress as they try to persuade that body too to give it more power, then that becomes known. Which statement are the developing nations to believe?

The good news is that there is increasing recognition of the problems of globalization, not just in the developing countries, which have long confronted them, but in the developed countries too. Today, many even within the financial community recognize that something is wrong with the system; many have themselves been hurt by the huge volatility. These financiers have in many cases responded positively to the ideas in the book; some, like George Soros, have put forward reform proposals of their own, and the G-7 has been lucky to have several finance ministers who have a genuine commitment to redressing the imbalances.

The problems in America's banking and corporate system—the Enron, Arthur Andersen, Merrill Lynch, and other scandals—have, of course, brought home the dangers of unfettered and unregulated markets. At the time I wrote the book, capitalism, American style, seemed triumphant. Countries were told by America's treasury secretaries to imitate our system of corporate governance and accounting. Now, those nations are not so sure that this was exactly the model to be followed. America's response to the scandals, a recognition of the need for improved regulation, was right, but it stands in marked contrast to the mantra of deregulation that the U.S. Treasury and the IMF preach abroad.

The book was fortunate enough to have been quickly translated into many languages (more than 25) and to receive a large number of reviews. I was pleased that, for the most part, even reviewers who were more positively disposed to the IMF or trade liberalization did little to challenge the criticisms I had raised concerning capital market liberalization, the intellectual inconsistencies underlying IMF policies, or the hypocrisy in trade policy. One of my concerns was that, for too long, discussions of these important matters had gone on behind closed doors, without the public scrutiny that they deserved, on the grounds that the matters required such technical competence that there was little reason to even attempt to bring them to the public sphere. I disagreed and wanted to stir up debate. I was amused by the contrasting readings: some complimented me on my sense of balance, others criticized me for my lack of balance. Some naturally raised the question of whether I was out to "settle scores," others complimented me for avoiding score-settling. Of course, having fought so many battles so hard, winning some and losing others, I felt intensely about the issues, as I said in the preface. But this is not a "kiss and tell book." It is a book about ideas, about economics and politics, dramas in which, of course, real people are actors. Identifying the individuals involved makes the events discussed more real. But if these particular individuals had not been there, others would have been pursuing much the same policies: there are underlying forces at work, and that is what the book is about. I tried to avoid making individuals the focus of the discussion, for that would distract from the arguments, and with one exception I believe I succeeded.

There was one instance in which I failed. One of my main criticisms of the IMF is that, in certain central ways, though it is a *public* institution, it does not conform to what we have come to expect of public institutions. In Western democracies, for instance, there is a basic right-to-know, reflected, for example, in America's freedom of information act. There is no such basic right at the international economic institutions. In America and most other western democracies, there is a concern about "revolving doors"—individuals moving too quickly from public institutions to well paid private ones closely connected with their public service. "Revolving doors" are a concern not only because they might give rise to conflicts of interest, but because the mere appearance of the possibility of such conflicts can undermine confidence in public institutions. A general might give a contract out to a contractor, in the hope—or even worse, with the understanding—that when he reaches the mandatory retirement age, the contractor will reward him by hiring him. If those who run the department of energy come from and return to the oil companies, there is the worry that they will be setting energy policy not in the interests of the country, but in the interests of the oil companies with which they have long term connections. That is why there are strong restrictions on such revolving doors even though governments are aware that there is a large cost—some good individuals who might otherwise enter government are deterred from doing so—and even when there are not formal restrictions, there is widespread sensitivity to these concerns. At the IMF, however, the movement between that institution and the private financial institutions, whose interests they are often criticized as serving, is not uncommon. While this movement is predictable—the Fund wants to draw upon those with expertise in finance, and the financial community wants to draw upon those with the global experience that time at the Fund provides—it is also problematic, especially because that institution is widely seen, above all in developing countries, not only as reflecting the perspectives of the financial community, but as acting in their interests, concerns which this book argues have more than a little validity. I noted one particular instance, the regrettable consequence of which was a public discussion of whether I was impugning the integrity of that individual. That was not my intention and I am deeply sorry for it. It also unfortunately detracted attention from the central *policy* issue.

Most disappointing but least surprising was the response from the IMF. I had not expected the officials there to like the book, but I thought it might provoke them into a debate on the many issues that I raised. After promising to engage in a discussion on the substantive issues at a launch of the book at the World Bank on June 28, 2002—a discussion I had tried to generate, unsuccessfully, in my years working there—representatives of the fund decided to engage in an *ad hominem* attack, to the embarrassment not only of the economists at the World Bank who had come to see real engagement, but also to IMF staffers who attended. The IMF attack gave those who were there a chance to see firsthand the IMF's arrogance and disdain for people who disagree with its perspectives. The IMF's unwillingness to engage in meaningful discussions is something many people in developing countries have seen. For those involved in making the arrangements for the forum—in which the Fund had repeatedly given assurances that it was to be a discussion of substance—it provided another instance of that institution's duplicity. So did its approach to the press: after asking that the discussion be off the record (I believe that such meetings should be on the record, but in the hope that it might facilitate greater openness, I deferred to their conditions), the minute the session was over, the IMF faxed and e-mailed the remarks of their chief economist, Kenneth Rogoff, to the press. They chose to include neither my remarks, those of the World Bank's chief economist, nor those of the commentators who followed. Rogoff's remarks were described by the IMF as an "open letter," which was itself a sham: the letter was certainly never received by me and almost surely was never sent to me. The IMF were trying to shoot the messenger and then call a press conference to announce what they had done.

There were several upsides to the IMF "ambush." First, it showed the general public what they are often like to deal with. Rather than engaging in an open discussion of the issues, they misled participants about their intentions and then tried to convert the discussion into a one sided *ad hominem* attack mixing innuendo and mischaracterization. There could be no better illustration of the points I had made in the book about the Fund's high handedness.

I received messages of support from around the world and sales of this book increased after the "ambush." Even though much of the press coverage centered on the fact that I had been attacked rather than on a discussion of the issues, the IMF helped me achieve what I had wanted: to draw attention to the issues of globalization and the problems of the international economic institutions.

The events of the past year have brought home to me more forcefully than ever that we are interdependent—that globalization is a fact of life. With interdependence comes a need for collective action, for people around the world to work together to solve the problems that we face together, whether they be global risks to health, the environment, economic or political stability. But democratic global-ization means that these decisions must be made with the full par-ticipation of all the peoples of the world. Our system of global governance without global government can only work if there is an acceptance of multilateralism. Unfortunately, the past year has seen an increase in unilateralism by the government of the world's richest and most powerful country. If globalization is to work, this too must change.

New York, January 2003

INDEX

Forthcoming in Allen Lane

The Roaring Nineties: The Seeds of Disaster
JOSEPH STIGLITZ

The 1990s promised prosperity for the world: a new era of unprecedented economic growth, with capitalism American-style reigning supreme. So why did it all go wrong?

As Chairman of Clinton's Council of Economic Advisors and Chief Economist at the World Bank, Joseph Stiglitz was uniquely placed to watch first-hand as the nineties unfolded. This definitive, shocking insider's account reveals the truth about that extraordinary decade of boom-and-bust.

The Roaring Nineties claims that much of what we understand about the decade's prosperity is in fact wrong – that it was the US's mistaken economic policies of the time that paved the way for worldwide recession. Yes, jobs were created, technology prospered, productivity rose, inflation fell and new markets opened up everywhere. But at the same time the seeds were sown for the economic problems we face today. Accounting standards slipped. Deregulation was taken further than it should have been. Politicians pandered to corporate greed. Investments were short-sighted. Unfair trade agreements ended up hurting the countries they were trying to help. Everything, in fact, fed the bubble that burst so decisively in 2000 amid crashing markets and corporate scandals.

This revealing book rewrites the history of the 1990s, taking the arguments of *Globalization and Its Discontents* and bringing them to the world stage, to show how a misplaced faith in free market ideology created problems that could cost us *all* dearly. But more than that, it lays out a blueprint for the future: for the role of the state and the European Social Democrats. The nineties, Stiglitz concludes, were a misguided attempt to achieve growth on the cheap – and we must learn from our mistakes or pay the price for years to come.

The Shadow of the Sun: My African Life
RYSZARD KAPUŚCIŃSKI

'Written with love and longing, as sharp and life-enhancing as the sun that rises on an African morning' *Sunday Times*

The Shadow of the Sun has been acclaimed as the best modern work on Africa and as a dazzling literary masterpiece.

'For more than forty years, Ryszard Kapuściński has been the definitive voice on all things African . . . Almost every page in this book comes alive with his quick brilliance . . . He brings the world to us as nobody else' Ian Jack, *Observer*

'One of the finest books I have ever read about Africa . . . Kapuściński has been visiting Africa as a journalist since 1957 . . . he has avoided "official routes, important personages and high-level politics" . . . it is here, in the margins, that Kapuściński has achieved something no other commentator I know of has done' Justin Cartwright, *Daily Mail*

'Vintage Kapuściński . . . a spectacular cast of leaders-in-waiting, road-block bullies, gunmen, witches, peasants, villains and heroes of almost every persuasion, in Ghana, Nigeria, Uganda, Tanzania, Ethiopia . . . His is the first wide-ranging, elegant, aristocratic intelligence since Conrad's to bear on Africa in all its perplexity' Jeremy Harding, *Evening Standard*

'What makes Kapuściński unique among war correspondents is the novelistic approach he adopts. He has V. S. Naipaul's gift for characterization and Isaac Babel's openness to life-threatening experience . . . *The Shadow of the Sun* is an indispensable book for anyone interested in great humanitarian writing about an indefinable continent' Russell Celyn Jones, *The Times*

'A wonderful read' Malcolm Reid, *Time Out*

dot.con: The Real Story of Why the Internet Bubble Burst
JOHN CASSIDY

'Bound to become a classic in its own right . . . Anyone with a smidgen of curiosity about the craziness of the past few years will thrill to this mini-saga' *Mail on Sunday*

'A marvellous book' *Wall Street Journal*

How could we all have been taken in by dotcom mania? Why did so many people believe the hype? And is anyone to blame?

It was the most gripping boom-and-bust drama of our time: a story of hysteria and harebrained schemes, of ridiculously over-inflated prices (and egos), of fortunes won and lost overnight.

In *dot.con* journalist John Cassidy, a consistently sceptical voice during this heady period, reveals what happened. That it wasn't just about a stock market bubble: *everyone* was along for the ride – from politicians to pundits, from a media willing to puff hopeless companies to the ordinary punter enticed by the prospect of instant wealth. And it was about how we saw ourselves, and refused to learn the lessons of history, as the twenty-first century dawned . . .

'For those who thought we knew it all already, it's the book we wish we had written' *Observer*

'An admirably lucid and comprehensive account of these feverish years' *Guardian*

'I can't recommend it more strongly' John Kenneth Galbraith, author of *The Great Crash 1929*

'Shrewd and entertaining . . . thoroughly persuasive' *Economist*

'The definitive history of the dot.com boom' *Sun*

Weird Ideas That Work: 11.5 Ways to Promote, Manage and Sustain Innovation
ROBERT SUTTON

'After reading it the only thing that will look really weird is much of current management theory' John Seely Brown, co-author of *The Social Life of Information* and director of Xerox PARC from 1990 to 2000

There is a growing concern – even obsession – with innovation in the workplace. But what does it take to build an innovative company? Managers say that creativity is vital to their business, without having much of an idea of what it is. Robert Sutton begins by demystifying creativity at work and then shows how companies manage and mismanage the innovative potential of their staff. His conclusions, drawn from close study of dozens of successful companies and rigorous academic research, will come as a shock to anyone who thinks you can 'just add creativity' to a business and watch the profits roll in.

There are massive rewards for original thinking, but an innovative company is – and has to be – a pretty weird place. Convinced that their ideas will work, creative people deceive their managers and disobey direct orders. They are sneaky, vindictive and misguided to the point of lunacy. They try ridiculous things and dismiss the advice of experts. Not only are true creatives messy and noisy, they're almost always wrong.

And that's if you're doing it right.

*

Think of some ridiculous or impractical things to do and act on them

Hire slow learners (of the Organizational Code)

Forget the past, especially your company's successes

Encourage people to ignore and defy superiors and peers

The Iron Wall: Israel and the Arab World
AVI SHLAIM

'*The Iron Wall* is strikingly fair-minded, scholarly, cogently reasoned and makes enthralling reading' Philip Ziegler, *Daily Telegraph*

'Anyone wanting to understand the modern Middle East should start by reading this elegantly written and scrupulously researched book' Trevor Royle, *Sunday Herald*

In the 1920s, hard-line Zionists developed the doctrine of the Iron Wall: negotiations with the Arabs must always be from a position of military strength. This doctrine, argues Avi Shlaim, became central to Israeli policy; dissenters were marginalized and many opportunities lost. Drawing on a great deal of new material and interviews with many key participants, Shlaim places Israel's political and military actions under an uncompromising lens. The result is a fresh and informed account of one of the world's most intractable conflicts of modern times.

'A milestone in modern scholarship of the Middle East' Edward Said

'Shlaim's usual appreciation for complexities and contradictions and his keen sketches of the principal Israeli actors make this very readable book one of the best and most illuminating accounts of Arab–Israeli relations in years' Yaron Ezrahi, *Foreign Affairs*

'Fascinating . . . Shlaim presents compelling evidence for a revaluation of traditional Israeli history' Ethan Bronner, *The New York Times Book Review*

'Brilliant and meticulously argued . . . it should be essential reading for all those interested in the modern history and international relations of the Middle East' Paul Wilkinson, *Scotland on Sunday*

The Secret State: Whitehall and the Cold War
PETER HENNESSY

'Riveting . . . an often terrifying account' *Observer*

'The insider's insider, if ever there was one' Anthony Howard, *New Statesman*

'Hennessy has discovered a few things about the "Secret State" which even British Prime Ministers during the Cold War did not know . . . Riveting, path-breaking and wonderfully readable' Christopher Andrew, *The Times*

As Cold War Britain came under the terrifying shadow of nuclear destruction, secret government plans were underway to ensure the survival of a chosen few . . .

Peter Hennessy's sensational book draws on recently declassified intelligence and war-planning documents, and interviews with key officials to reveal a chilling behind-the-scenes picture of the corridors of power when the world teetered on the brink of disaster. Who would have gone underground with the Prime Minister in the event of an attack? Where is this secret bunker? Under what circumstances would we retaliate? Where were the Soviet's UK targets thought to be? Whose finger was – and is – on the button? And what kind of world would have been left when the had dust settled and 'breakdown' had occurred . . . ?

'Effective and vivid . . . One of the fascinations of this book is the bureaucratic aridity to which Whitehall reduced concepts of bloodcurdling awfulness' Philip Ziegler, *Daily Telegraph*

'Excellent . . . rich and illuminating . . . with fears that a rogue nation might now have the capacity and the desire to attack Britain, Prof Hennessy has unwittingly produced a work that, sadly, may be of more than purely historic or academic interest' Simon Heffer, *Country Life*

Fast Food Nation:
What the All-American Meal is Doing to the World
ERIC SCHLOSSER

'A shocking exposé . . . *Fast Food Nation* could make a difference to the
way we eat. For ever' *Evening Standard*

'*Fast Food Nation* has lifted the polystyrene lid on the global fast food
industry . . . and sparked a storm' *Observer*

Do you *really* know what you're eating when you tuck into that juicy
burger?

Britain eats more fast food than any other country in Europe. It looks good,
tastes good, and it's cheap. But the real cost never appears on the menu.

Eric Schlosser's explosive bestseller, by turns funny and terrifying, tells the
story of our love affair with fast food. He visits the lab that re-creates the
smell of strawberries; examines the safety records of abattoirs; reveals why
the fries taste so good and what really lurks between the sesame buns – and
shows how fast food is transforming not only our diets but our world.

'Has wiped that smirk off the Happy Meal . . . Thanks to this man, you'll
never eat a burger again' *Evening Standard*

'Startling . . . Junk food, we learn, is just that . . . left this reader vowing
never to set foot in one of these outlets again' *Daily Mail*

'This book tells you more than you really want to know when you're
chomping that hamburger . . . Have a nice day? Listen – you should live
so long' *The Times*